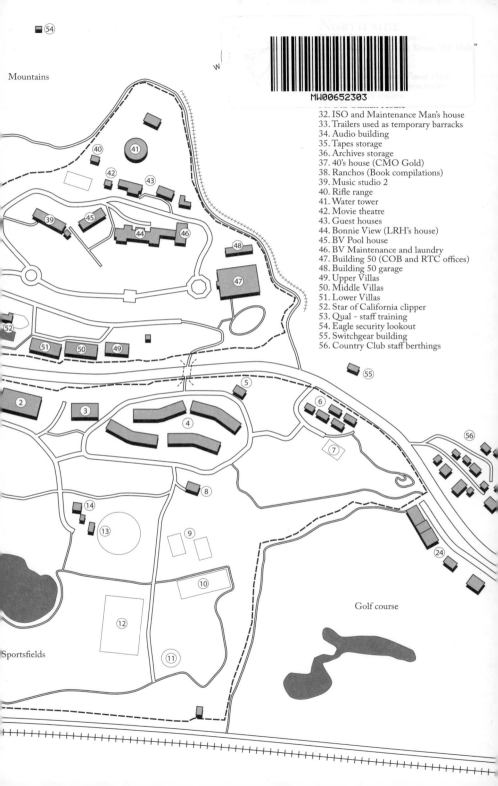

Mountains

32. ISO and Maintenance Man's house
33. Trailers used as temporary barracks
34. Audio building
35. Tapes storage
36. Archives storage
37. 40's house (CMO Gold)
38. Ranchos (Book compilations)
39. Music studio 2
40. Rifle range
41. Water tower
42. Movie theatre
43. Guest houses
44. Bonnie View (LRH's house)
45. BV Pool house
46. BV Maintenance and laundry
47. Building 50 (COB and RTC offices)
48. Building 50 garage
49. Upper Villas
50. Middle Villas
51. Lower Villas
52. Star of California clipper
53. Qual - staff training
54. Eagle security lookout
55. Switchgear building
56. Country Club staff berthings

Golf course

Sportsfields

BLOWN for GOOD

[signature]

Claire Headley

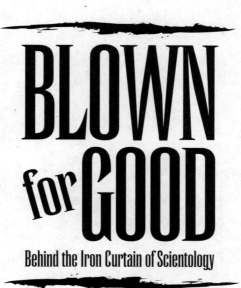

BLOWN for GOOD

Behind the Iron Curtain of Scientology

Marc Morgan Headley

BFG Books

Blown for Good, Inc.

www.blownforgood.com

BFG Books are published by

Blown for Good, Inc.
827 Hollywood Way Suite 213
Burbank, CA 91505

First published in 2009 by BFG Books, Inc.

Additional copies of this book can be ordered at www.blownforgood.com

LIBRARY OF CONGRESS CATALOGING-IN-PUBLICATION DATA
Publisher's Cataloging-in-Publication *(Provided by Quality Books, Inc.)*
Headley, Marc Morgan.
    Blown for good : behind the iron curtain of Scientology / Marc Morgan Headley.
    p. cm.
    Includes bibliographical references and index.
    LCCN 2009931081
    ISBN-13: 978-0-9825022-0-4
    ISBN-10: 0-9825022-0-6
    1. Scientology—Controversial literature. 2. Golden Era Productions—Employees.
    I. Title.
    BP605.S2H43 2010 299'.936
    QBI09-600123   2009931081

ISBN 978-0-9825022-0-4

Cover art, design and layout by Rectoverso Graphic Design.
www.rectoversodesign.com

Contents

Acknowledgements

I want to thank all those who have spoken out about what happened to them behind the iron curtain of Scientology. Reading these accounts reaffirmed my suspicion that these were not isolated incidences or circumstances that had only happened to me.

I wish to thank all those that host internet message boards and sites that provide a place for people to voice their thoughts and tell their individual stories. These have a value that cannot be overestimated. For someone who got out and found these, it helped me to regain a perspective, find out the truth behind an entire body of lies, and helped me come to terms with having spent half my life living based on false information.

They also provided me a voice with which to speak out. I have gotten hundreds of emails and letters from people, thanking me for exposing what goes on behind the scenes at the highest echelon of Scientology, and attributing to my postings their own decisions to do as I did and break free of the chains holding them prisoner.

Foreword

BY MARK "MARTY" RATHBUN

After reading the first several chapters of *Blown for Good*, I made a mental note to write the author an email. I was going to suggest he have someone else write an alternate Foreword because he might not like what I have to say. While Marc Headley and I were stationed at the same international headquarters property of the Scientology's elite Sea Organization for nearly fifteen years, his views of some of Scientology founder Hubbard's writings and my views differed greatly. I never had time to write or send the note because I could not put the manuscript down. I was gripped by Marc's personal story.

I came to find that while Marc's opinions about occurrences we both experienced varied from mine, there was every reason they should. After all, Marc did not get into Scientology on his own volition. As a child his mother willed it upon him. I got in after two years of college entirely by my own choice. Marc was forced by circumstances to join the Sea Organization. I had willingly signed on in order to fulfill a purpose. Naturally the way we read material and viewed matters would disagree. Nonetheless, when it came to relating facts – without regard to view or opinion – Marc's recollection and accuracy were remarkable.

Recognizing that Marc and I had utterly divergent reference points from which to view largely the same culture and experience, Marc's account became that much more fascinating to me. I began to wonder, how many people had I interacted with over twenty-seven years within the Church whose back story aligned more with Marc's than mine? On reflection, I decided probably more members of the Sea Organization (some eighty-five hundred strong when I left in 2004) who constitute the management of Scientology internationally had a frame of reference closer to Marc's than mine. After all, over the past thirty years Scientology's numbers of new members had been dwindling. The Sea Organization had increasingly relied on recruiting the teenaged kids of long-term Scientologists in order to keep its ranks filled.

A great deal of that majority were people whose lives I affected for better or worse from on high in the church's leading ecclesiastical body, Religious Technology Center. As I read how progressively insane the dictates from my controlling organization became as they literally rolled down the hill at international headquarters in the foothills of the San Jacinto mountains in Southern California, and how negatively they affected people on the receiving end, a deep sense of remorse enveloped me. Sure, I had sought out people I had known that I had visited injustices upon individually, apologized and made things right. But Marc's book recreated a culture I knew of and influenced, but did not live of. As I read of the pain Marc went through I remembered dozens of others similarly situated whom I knew during my Scientology experience but whose lives and feelings I was never afforded an opportunity to understand.

Marc alludes to others who will be telling their accounts from within the upper echelons of Scientology and how this will forward reform and healing. Such a scenario reflects Hubbard's prescribed system of management. Hubbard called for a remote management body to draw upon a multitude of reports from various points within an organization being managed, then coolly evaluating the facts to get the most complete and accurate view of what it is really like on the ground. Only then could an organizational problem afar be sanely and effectively handled. The system was called the Multiple Viewpoint System of Management.

Hubbard eschewed the notion that someone in an ivory tower – no matter how intelligent - can receive one report and then arbitrarily dictate what is to be done several thousand miles away. What Hubbard condemns is precisely what Marc describes as current Supreme Leader Miscavige's day to day operating basis. His description of Miscavige's obsession with handling everything himself, while preventing thousands of others from handling anything is not only very accurate, it is also what Hubbard described as the fastest way to destroy an organization. Add to the mix Marc's factual description of Miscavige as "evil and enjoy[ing] watching other people suffer", and you have the perfect recipe for disaster.

Ironically, Marc supplies the first comprehensive and largely accurate report on the monster Miscavige has created which may mark the beginning of the only thing that can save the subject from the avarice of Miscavige. The multiple viewpoint system applied from without. The Lord knows, and as Marc makes clear, it can never be applied from within. And ironic that this report comes from the very person Miscavige has been spending hundreds of thousands of dollars to destroy for the past few years.

Marc's account of the trials and tribulations one goes through in leaving it all behind captures the agony and ecstasy one inevitably experiences in following through with abiding by his or her conscience. It is not an easy barrier to break through. Before Marc's book the only artistic expression that came close to expressing that passion for me was U2's Walk On: *and I know it aches, and your heart it breaks, but you can only take so much, Walk on...* Marc has now provided a narrative that allows the reader to experience that treacherous ride for his or her self.

Finally, Marc deserves props for speaking out during a period when few with quality, inside information did. I know what he faced. I helped to create it. Hopefully this book will help to civilize it.

Author's Note

At the age of 16, I started working for Scientology in Los Angeles. Soon I was promoted up the ranks and within one year I was placed at Golden Era Productions, located at the International Headquarters (Int Base) in Hemet, California, where I would spend the next fifteen years. Fifteen years within the confines of Scientology would eventually result in my isolation and total disconnection from my friends and family for the rest of my life.

When I eventually left in 2005, it took me over a year to speak out about my experiences as a Scientology staff member, the abuse and the inner workings of the Sea Organization.

After writing several of my accounts on different internet sites, I was flooded with hundreds of requests to put them all in a book. Everything that I have written in this book are my own experiences and my opinion of what happened to me. I have detailed the working conditions and labor practices of my former employers.

Many words and terms used throughout the book are foreign to most outsiders. While I have tried to define these within the text, there is also a glossary in the back, which defines all of them. It could be said that if two Scientologists were talking to each other about Scientology it would almost seem they were speaking a different language, I have done my best to translate the language of Scientology.

My experience as a member and an employee of Scientology's Sea Organization have been chronicled to expose the inner workings of the institution and to shed some light on the internal abuse, discrimination and mistreatment within the organization.

While I am not a lawyer and not familiar with the ins and outs of the laws, it is my intention to publish these experiences in the hopes that others will read this and become aware of institutions like Scientology and in turn, avoid falling prey to *any* organization that might attempt to perpetrate similar abuses against them or someone they love in the future.

Why and how did I let this happen? In this book, I attempt to lay the groundwork enough so that you can see that, like language, culture and other environmental factors, some of this stuff is programmed in at an early age. It just happened that way, and I try to explain the key points where I thought this was happening.

I also have a hard time trying to compare my experience to something else that exists. The closest comparison I have been able to find has been the Iron Curtain. The people who were behind the Iron Curtain might have been considered "free" by their leaders. They also probably did what they were told and lived their lives as best they knew how under those conditions. They were not allowed to leave and if they attempted to it was dangerous and, in many cases, fatal.

Since I left in 2005, I have had hundreds of nightmares about being recaptured. After writing this book I have fewer and less frequent nightmares. Whether this is a direct result of me writing down and reliving several years of experiences is anybody's guess. Either way, I feel that this book has been a therapeutic process for me and helped me to heal my mental and emotional wounds as well as understand what happened.

Thanks.

Marc Headley - 2009

Blown for Good

Walking in My Shoes

They are driving right alongside me in the black Nissan Pathfinder. The roads are slick from the rain and I am in no position to do any sort of maneuvering with my bags on the motorbike. I round the turn past the golf course heading into town. For a split second I contemplate going off road down into the riverbed but with the rain, there is a good chance that it might contain water, and it is just too risky with the security guards right on my tail.

After we get over the bridge, Danny and Matt yell out through the window of the SUV that I need to pull over to the side of the road or they are going to make me pull over. My helmet visor is now starting to fog up. I am trying to keep my attention on the road. "I just need to get into town and I will be fine," I keep telling myself. The truck is right next to me, and they are yelling out the window for me to pull over. I can't look over, it's too dangerous to take my eyes off the road and I need to pretend they aren't there. That is when I realize that the truck is drifting further and further towards the shoulder. They are going to run me off the road! I cannot believe this is happening! There is nowhere for me to go. They are keeping up with me, no problem. I have not factored in the rain. If only it hadn't rained! It rains about ten times a year in Southern California, and the day I decide to blow is one of those days! The truck continues to drift over; I am now out of space. The shoulder is not drivable, even for my dual sport Yamaha TW 200. My attempt to blow is going to end right here with a bang. I have been gone for a whole minute and this is it. What a lousy attempt I am making to leave.

As I run out of road, it is only a matter of seconds before I hit the ground and the bike goes skidding. My two bags of clothes are sliding along in newly wet dirt that is becoming muddier as each drop hits the ground. One of the bags is a small suitcase. Secured to the bike with a single bungee cord, it will never stay on in a full-blown crash. The other is a large duffle bag on my lap, held there only by gravity, which is no longer on my side.

Somehow I manage a stuntman type fall off the bike in anticipation of the crash. I had crashed my bike a few times before over the years and never really gotten badly hurt. Wearing a helmet, I know that I can expect only a few broken limbs should the worst happen. I think it was the adrenaline that really saved me. When you are locked up for 15 years and there is no way out, when you finally decide you are going to break out, the rush you get is indescribable. I was now being run off the road by the security truck, needless to say my fight or flight response was working double duty.

As quickly as I hit the dirt on the side of the road I get back up yelling at Danny. I do not even think about being hurt or that I have rolled on the ground a bit. I just pop up and start freaking out.

"What are you trying to do? Kill me?"

Without an ounce of emotion, Danny says, "You need to come back, Marc. Get in the truck!"

I do not reply.

I survey the scene and see where my bags have landed. I walk over to where the suitcase is and pick it up. No major damage. As I turn around, I catch Danny moving towards my bike. He takes the key out of the ignition! This is going from bad to worse in milliseconds.

"Give me the key back, Danny! Give me my key back right now, Danny, or I am going to go ballistic!"

Danny starts to get back in the Pathfinder. I know he will never give it back. Unless…

I make my way into the middle of the highway and start waving my hands at passing cars for help. Danny throws that key back to me faster than you can say, "This is going to get us in some big trouble!" I catch the key. Both Danny and Matt stand there as if I had just pushed a button that put them in "standby" mode. I am amazed at how waving one's arms at passing cars triggers their total inaction – instantly. We are outside of their little playground and their rules mean nothing out here. They are helpless.

I am back in play. Back to the plan. What was the plan? Well I am going to get into town. That is the first part of the plan. Actually, that is pretty much the whole plan. The rest of the plan will depend on how the first part of the plan plays out. Not going so well right now. As I stand the bike back up, I notice that the clutch lever has snapped off in the crash. Great news. Even better, the carburetor is leaking gas and is surely flooded or at least not fully operational. Just what I need, a broken bike to slow down my carefully planned escape. Oh yeah, it's still raining too. Did I mention that one of the rear view mirrors has snapped off as well? I get the bags back on the bike. Danny and Matt climb back in the truck as if to continue our little game of follow the leader. The bike has an electric starter. I pray that it fires up. It does. Now to get it into first gear. Without a clutch lever, I have to get the bike rolling and bump it into gear so as not to stall it out. My first attempt is a joke. I am so anxious to get out of there; I jump the gun and shift too soon. My second attempt works and I quickly move to second gear. A lot of good that does me. Whatever happened in the crash has completely destroyed the bike's carburetor. I am at full throttle and get it up to only 5-10 miles per hour. The black Pathfinder creeps along behind me. I am starting to wonder how I can possibly ditch these guys at 5 miles per hour?

I am also thinking, "Did these guys just almost kill me?" What the hell was that all about? I just got run off the road by a truck and here they are behind me again. At least we are slowly getting closer to town and there are more cars around. Hopefully that will thwart any more crazy attempts to get me back to the Base.

As we are driving down State Street towards Hemet, in the rain, at 5 mph, the Pathfinder suddenly pulls a U-turn and speeds off in the opposite direction faster than you can say "Danger - Will Robinson!" Odd. Why would they take off like that? Don't know - don't care.

I am completely baffled, but whatever. They are leaving and I am leaving. Now I can get into town, get my bike working and get the hell out of here.

Before I am accustomed to no longer having the Pathfinder on my tail, I see a police car jamming up the road in the direction of the Gold Base. No faster than I see him, he has already passed me and as I watch in my one remaining rearview mirror I see him pull a U-turn and up go the lights and siren. This isn't my day! I am now getting pulled over! This sucks.

First, I get run off the road, next pulled over. If this guy gives me a ticket for the broken mirror, I am going to lose it!

Since I am going a whopping 5 miles per hour, it is no big deal for me to pull over. If I were going any slower, I would be walking.

I take off my helmet, it is still raining although not as much as a few minutes ago. I see the cop sitting in the car getting his stuff together. He has to get his notepad, run my plates, all the normal stuff while I sit wondering how bad this is going to be.

He gets out of the car and comes towards me. I turn off the bike and put the kickstand down.

I hang the helmet on the one good mirror.

"Good morning, Officer," I say like everybody says when they get pulled over by a cop and it's morning time.

"Good morning. Can I see your license?" he asks, in stereotypical cop lingo.

I dig it out of my wallet and hand it over. I got a driver's license in 1991. Every few years, I get a letter from the DMV and I renew it by mail. The picture is 14 years old and barely resembles me, but nonetheless, it is me.

He takes the license and goes back to his squad car. I don't have anything on my record. No moving violations or accidents, nothing. I think I might have had a speeding ticket years ago, but besides that I was clean. No arrests. No felonies. I was at Golden Era Productions for 15 years, so I was, by all accounts, a model citizen according to police records. If you even get pulled over for speeding, you can't drive anymore, so I was pretty clean on the driving record.

He is back in less than a minute.

"So, where are you headed?" he asks.

"Just into town," I reply, wondering where the hell this is going.

"Are you okay?" he asks.

"Yeah, I'm fine," all the while thinking that I am the furthest thing from it right now.

"You've got a bit of mud on your pants," he says, sounding like someone who would consider that other than "fine."

"Yeah, damn rain. I must have brushed up against something muddy this morning." Brilliant, I am the most retarded person in the world with this dialog. "Is he buying this?" I think to myself.

"Well, we got a 911 call that there was an altercation on the road a bit back with two vehicles, and one of them fits your vehicle's description," he says to me.

Someone saw them run me off the road! Now what do I tell him? I am not trying to mess up anyone's day or cause any trouble; I am just trying to get the hell out of Dodge. If I make any kind of stink with the cops, I will surely get declared a suppressive by Scientology and they will make my life miserable.

"Oh, yeah, a few of the people that I work with were trying to get me to stay. I am going to visit my dad for a few weeks and they just needed to get some numbers from me where I could be reached."

"That is why you have the bags?" he deduces.

"Yeah, yeah, that's right," I sigh.

"So you are fine?" he asks, knowing full well there is more to this than I am letting on.

"Oh, yeah, I'm good. Just heading into town and I will be fine."

He gives me back my license and is about to walk away when up rolls Muriel, the Public Relations Officer at Golden Era Productions. She rolls up right next to both of us on the side of the road in the Port Captain Office Honda.

"What's the matter with Marc?" she asks the officer through her passenger window as she continues to roll it down.

"You know this gentleman, ma'am?" he asks back.

"Oh, yeah, he works at Golden Era Productions," Muriel says, connecting the dots to his puzzle in one single sentence. The PR person irrevocably messes up the PR. Wouldn't you know it. Here I am, keeping this totally out of the realm of "Bad PR" for Golden Era Productions, and in one short sentence, Muriel sinks that ship without even coming to a complete stop in her vehicle!

"Nothing is wrong, ma'am, just a routine traffic stop. Move along," he says to her as he motions her to get back on the road. I can see his whole demeanor change right then as he processes this new information.

He watches as she drives off, turns to me and says in the matter of fact "no more crap" voice, "Where you trying to get to, dude?"

"U-Haul in town," I reply, knowing that he thinks something is up and I might as well just do what I need to do to get out of here.

"Another squad car is on the way; we will escort you and make sure you get there okay."

"Cool," I say as I go for my helmet. I put it on as if we are done with the conversation part of the traffic stop, assuming that I am not going to get a ticket. Correct in that assumption, he heads back to the shelter of his car. A light sprinkle is still falling, and as soon as I put the helmet back on, the visor fogs right back up. I lift the visor just in time to see the second car coming down the road towards us.

He pulls up behind the first car and they both get out and talk for a second.

They get back into their cars and the first cop rolls in front of me while the second one pulls up behind me. I start up the bike, bump it into gear and we are off.

I think, is this good? It could be good. It could be really bad. Are the guys at the base going to flip out when they find out from Muriel that the cops are escorting me into town?

So much for a quick, quiet escape. I had never heard of anyone using the local police to get away. Seems like that works rather well.

It is January 5th, 2005. It is now about noon. My life has just restarted. It is at this exact moment I realize I am blown for good.

Lie To Me

My parents moved to Los Angeles in the winter of 1979.

We had been living in Kansas City, Missouri. My father was working at the Kansas City Municipal Bus company as a mechanic. My mother was working at a restaurant. I was 6 years old and in first grade. My sister, Stephanie, had just turned 5.

One of my father's college band buddies, Steve Smuck, had moved out to Los Angeles and was trying to get the band back together so that they could make it "big" in LA.

So we packed up all our stuff into a large moving truck and made the drive. We had a VW Beetle that we towed behind the truck. I remember the trip like it was yesterday. My uncle, who was also my dad's good friend, made the trip with us. My younger sister and I would switch off riding in his car while the other would ride in the truck cab with mom and dad.

There was a stretch in the Colorado Rockies where we were separated and I really thought I would never see my parents again. After several hours of being separated, Uncle Chris decided to park at a gas station rest stop and let them catch up with us. Sure enough, a few hours later they came around the bend and we were reunited! I remember the feeling. It was one of those moments when the elation is immeasurable, but the exact feeling, the view of the truck coming down the road; everything is burned into your memory forever.

When we arrived in LA, it was culture shock for us. Here we were, a small family from Kansas City, and the cost of everything in LA was at least double what we were used to paying back home. We had spent pretty much all of our money on gas for the truck on the way over. We were broke. I was only 6 years old, but I knew it.

When we were living in Kansas City, we had a house. We did not own it, but we lived in a house. We had a front yard, a back yard, we even had a garden. We would play in the street with other kids on the block. It was a good time.

When we got to Los Angeles, we stayed with my dad's friend Steve and his girlfriend at a house they were renting off of Franklin Avenue in Hollywood. My sister and I slept in the living room on the couch. "This is temporary until we get our own house," our parents told us.

Christmas came and reality set in that we were no longer in Kansas City. I was used to getting cool stuff for Christmas. This Christmas would taint my view of Christmas for years to come. I got a baseball glove and a pile of unsalted peanuts (in shell) wrapped in a brown bandana. I did not play baseball nor did I particularly enjoy the game. My favorite color was blue, while the color I hated most was brown, and I had never worn a bandana, nor planned to. After opening these super presents, I was kind of like okay; now let's hope I get some good ones to balance these out, because otherwise I might have to move back to Kansas City on my own. There were no other presents—that was it! No more.

Even though this is the first Christmas that I can recall, I knew that this Christmas did not measure up to past ones. I could have gotten a broomstick and a dustpan the year before. At least it had been logged as a good Christmas in my mind. So this is really the first memory that I associated with our newfound city. Los Angeles sucks! With the little information I had obtained, I was able to determine this at a very young age.

A short while later, we moved to a house in Echo Park, a "good deal" my parents had found. My sister and I were pretty excited. Our own house again! The excitement was short lived. We moved and it was a nightmare.

The house itself was pretty decent in terms of size. It had at least three stories and was on a hill. But the front door had no knob. It had a padlock that you had to unlock to get in and then you had to take the lock and move it to the inside to lock the door. This seemed odd to me, not like most doors I had seen up until this point.

There were a lot of things in the house that were odd. Plumbing, carpets, closets, smells, sinks, all had oddness about them. It was like someone had lived there before us, but not really.

The hill we lived on was more like the local neighborhood dump. There was literally 50 dump trucks' worth of trash over a small dirt hill adjacent to our house. I would occasionally see people bring their garbage down the street and just toss it onto the hill.

Apparently no one had lived in our house for a long while. Officially, that is. The house was apparently overrun by transients and squatters. They certainly had not been doing a lot of household repairs or complaining about the garbage being dumped on the hill next door.

My parents did, however, attempt to make it as nice as possible while we lived there, which was only for a few weeks. They were getting a divorce. I don't really think I understood what this meant at the time, but I knew that it would mean that my mom and dad would be living in different places. That seemed okay to me and not that big a deal.

My dad ended up moving to an apartment on Tamarind Street back in Hollywood. It was across the street from a huge castle. I thought this was pretty cool. My mom ended up living with a new friend of hers on Carlos Ave, right next to Hollywood Blvd. In fact if you looked out the window at the back of the house, you could see Hollywood Blvd!

The arrangement was that my sister and I would stay with my mom for most of the week and spend the weekend with my dad. We liked going to our dad's place because he had cable TV. My mom did not like TV and did not have one. My dad would also take us out to eat at restaurants while mom had been converted to a "health food nut." She rarely had edible food in the house during the week, so that weekly restaurant run was a lifesaver.

My mom had a new boyfriend every few months. A lot of times she would end up moving in with her boyfriends and that meant we would have to move too. My dad, however, lived in three places the entire time he was in LA. I once made a list of all of the places we lived in the first ten years in LA and figured out that I had moved an average of twice a year for 10 years!

At first, I went to public school right off Franklin Ave in Hollywood, Cheremoya Avenue School. I went there because it was free and near where we lived. I was fine with the school. I was learning things and got into the occasional fight, so it was just your normal everyday school.

After the second year of school my mom wanted me to go to a private school in Los Feliz. It was called Apple School. My dad's friend Steve was into this organization called Scientology and they had a school in Los Feliz. I remember going there and seeing they had football fields, grass and all sorts of cool stuff, so I was okay with going to school there.

The way the schooling was done was different than what I was used to. Each person was allowed to do his or her own thing and you would not have to do what the rest of the class was doing, but could instead study on your own. We had these things called checksheets, and when you did a step on the course, you had to check it off. I had to do a special course on how to study that was created by L. Ron Hubbard. It was called the *Basic Study Manual*. We had to look up lots of words in dictionaries and make little clay people to demonstrate what we were learning.

I had made some good friends at my new school. John Peeler lived right up the street from me in Hollywood and we were good friends. Since it was Hollywood, a lot of kids were child actors or children of famous people. Another friend who lived next door to the school was a movie star. His name was Barrett Oliver. He was on a bunch of TV shows like *The Incredible Hulk* and *Knight Rider*. *Knight Rider* was my favorite show, so I thought he was pretty cool.

One day after being at the school for a year or so, my mom told me that I was going to go to a different school. Supposedly, the people that ran the school did not want to have it be a Scientology school anymore and because of this I HAD to go to a different school. I liked the school and could have cared less about the Scientology part of it. My mom said that we did not have a choice. If Scientology said the school was bad, then we had to leave and go to a different school. If I did not leave the school, my mom would get kicked out of Scientology.

This was my first taste of how Scientology would change my life and how no matter what I did, I had no say in the matter. What could I do anyway? I was just a kid. No one really cared what I wanted. I just did what I was told and went along with the new school idea.

I ended up going back to public school. The only good thing was I did not have to make any more clay people and was not having to look up words in dictionaries. I did miss my friends but ended up making new ones.

Whenever I would live with my dad, I would hang out at the apartment building where he lived. There were a lot of cool kids there and some of them had famous parents. One girl that I liked and used to hang out with, Brandy, her dad was an actor. He was in some movie with Clint Eastwood – Geoffrey Lewis was his name. Sometimes Brandy's sister, Juliette, used to come and hang out as well. Their mom, Glennis, lived in the apartment building, so I would see them a lot when they came to stay with her. Their step dad, Craig, worked for my dad at a roofing company, so we all knew each other. Brandy had a little sister, Dree, who I used to babysit when she was about 2 years old.

One of the people I talked to a lot was the mother of an actor. Her name was Elaine, and her son was a guy named Michael D. Roberts. He was in the movie *Space Pirates* and he had been on a bunch of other TV shows. His mom, Elaine, was cool. She would give me advice about stuff and was like a grandmother to me.

There was this huge castle across the street from my apartment building called The Manor. It was owned by Scientology and I had a few friends who lived there, too. One guy, Sky Dayton, lived there and we went to his apartment all the time to make candles. Another friend was Channing whose dad was some big composer guy named David Campbell. I never really saw his dad, but Channing's brother, Beck, was around sometimes and seemed to be real cool. They used to shoot movies at the Manor all the time, it was Hollywood after all. They shot a movie there with Eddie Murphy and Nick Nolte called *48 Hours*. They actually shot this movie on the 7th floor and in the lobby. It was quite exciting as they shot tons of bullets into the reception desk and the hallways on the 7th floor. They also shot a movie with Billy Crystal and Danny DeVito called *Throw Momma from the Train*.

A few months went by and my mom told me that a new school was opening up and most of my friends from Apple School would be going there. I had to take a bunch of tests, and if I passed, I could go to this new school. Mom took me to this place on Wilshire Blvd called Applied Scholastics. I did the tests and it was looking good. Applied Scholastics was filled with Scientology books and stuff and I could tell that the guy giving me the tests was a Scientologist because he used all the lingo. He told me this new school was going to be a very "upstat" school and if "my ethics were in" I would be able to attend. Total Scientology lingo. "Upstat" meant *up statistics*, which means you produced more than you did the week before. For kids, "upstat" meant being good, not throwing tantrums or upsetting your parents too badly. "Downstat" was bad and if you were downstat, you did not get any ice cream or treats. No one wants to be downstat, now do they?

I remember thinking that going back to a Scientology school could be a drag. I had gotten used to not having to do all of the Scientology study stuff and now I would most certainly have to do it again if I got into the new school. Well, all my old friends would be there, so maybe it was worth it.

Months went by and the new school finally opened. It was called the Delphi School and it was awful. All the things we had to do at Apple School were nothing compared to this new place. EVERYTHING we did was Scientology-based. Every subject we did was written by Scientologists and had checksheets. We had to do another course on how to use Scientology Study Technology: The Learning Book Course. After we finished a course we had to do an exam and hold what looked like soup cans and be asked questions on a Scientology E-Meter. We started school at 8:30 A.M. and went until 5:30 P.M. every day. We even had to clean the school classrooms and do work for the school as part of our schooling.

All the teachers were Scientologists, and some, it seemed, had been in Scientology forever. The school's headmaster, Henning Heldt, was a certifiable prick. I remember him talking and everything out of his mouth was "Out-Ethics," "Misunderstood Words," "Off-Purpose," "Overts," "Withholds". It was as though this guy did not know any words besides Scientology ones. I never liked him and it felt like his job was to make sure the students were miserable.

Most of the other teachers were not much different. It was weird, because most of them seemed to know each other real well, but they hadn't worked at a school before and had not been teachers. They were hardcore Scientologists.

Delphi also had an "org board" just like at any other Scientology organization. The school had a lot of the same post titles you would find on a Scientology Organizing Board. It was on a huge blue Formica chart with tons of Dymo tape labels giving the post titles and names of the people that held them. I had seen the exact same type of boards at the local Scientology orgs in Los Angeles.

In 1985, my parents could no longer afford to send both my sister and I to Delphi. One of us had to go back to public school. Guess who the lucky one was? Me, of course!

By this time, my mom was living with a boyfriend in a house out by the beach in Venice. We had to drive 90 minutes each morning to get to Delphi by 8:30 and I was not going to be missing that!

I would be attending the local public school in our district in Venice. Turns out that we lived right on the district border and if we had lived one block further north, I would have ended up at a better school. Well, that wasn't the case, so I ended up going to Westminster Avenue Elementary School. I had to walk through a pretty bad section of town to go to school and back, but other than that it all seemed to be pretty cool.

On my first day I was not well received. The school was HUGE. The last public school I went to was dwarfed by this place. There were at least 1500 students. As I remember it, I was the ONLY Caucasian kid in my class. There was actually one other girl who was Caucasian, but she was physically handicapped. I was not particularly bothered by this fact, but some of my classmates were. I only went to the school for a few months, but for those few months, I was in a lot of fights that I surprisingly didn't win.

After a few months, I was done. I decided that I would no longer be going to school. I had grown physically while attending this school, mostly due to the need to survive! I did not want to spend every day looking over my shoulder. For a few weeks, I would leave in the morning just as I always did, but instead of going to school, I would go to the beach. This worked until the school contacted my mom.

When she confronted me on it, I told her about the fights and told her that I would not go, period. I told her that once we had enough money for both my sister and I to go to Delphi, I would attend school again. She was optimistic that this would be only a few months away, so she agreed.

My routine was pretty good. I went to the beach every morning, and spent the entire day at the beach, on the boardwalk, Muscle Beach or about town. I then headed back to the house to do some chores. I had it easy. I was hanging out with street performers, lifeguards, local surfers, people who had money but no jobs, people who had jobs but no money, you name it. I rode my bike everywhere and just hung out with people. It was a wild mix of people and cultures. During that year I learned more than my entire previous years of school. I also learned how to fend for myself and was not afraid of other people at all.

At last, after a yearlong vacation from school and anything structured, my parents had enough money to put me back into Delphi. When I first went back it was a bit of a shock because I had really been on the streets for the past year, and now I was going back to the sheltered white bread kids who had not been exposed to life yet and were still worried about who liked who and what the current favorite band was on KIIS FM.

I almost got expelled my first week back. I was getting into a lot of fights and this time, I was not losing. These kids were weak and non-violent. I was accustomed to an environment where, if you did some trash talking, you had to back it up with physical fighting. These kids did the trash talking but as soon as you punched them out, they ran off to the teachers! After adjusting to the rules, and realizing that I had nothing to prove to these people, I was able to blend in and get back in the groove.

I had a few friends that I liked at the school. Vonnie Ribisi was cool. Also, I liked his sister, Marissa, a lot. She was actually my very first girlfriend. If we did more than kiss a few times, I considered that really lucky. I hung out at their house a lot and since Vonnie and I were friends, I also got to see his sister a lot. My sister also hung out with Marissa and Vonnie's other sister, Gina, a bit. I went out with Marissa for about three months. We broke up on Valentine's day; I was unhappy with not doing much more than holding hands and needed to move on.

I also had to play the Scientology game because now, if you were not progressing with your Scientology studies in addition to your school studies, you were considered "off-purpose" and would get in trouble with your parents. Most kids attending Delphi lived in the LA area, so going to the local Scientology center at night to study was doable. Luckily, we lived way out in Venice and did not get home until 8:00 P.M. so I had no worries in this department and never did any courses or further Scientology studies.

Then my mom broke up with her boyfriend and we moved back to Hollywood. I no longer had an excuse not to study after school at the big blue buildings, "The Complex," in Hollywood.

In 1988, I did the Student Hat. I was 15 years old. I thought this would be a piece of cake as I had already done two other courses on how to study the Scientology way. This course, though, was way more than I thought it would be. In addition to reading all of the L Ron Hubbard teachings on how to study, I also had to listen to 15 hours of L Ron Hubbard's public lectures given in the 1960s. What's more, I was quizzed daily on what I had studied and asked definitions of words and to explain concepts. This was not much different than what was done at Delphi, but most of the stuff we were studying there had some practical application and was useful everyday stuff that made some sense. Now I had to really bend my mind to see how the stuff Hubbard was talking about had anything to do with what I was studying. Sometimes he just appeared to be rambling and, because someone was recording it, you got stuck with it. Also, if you did not pass your quizzes and routinely flunked exams, you would get in trouble. It was not like school; these people were pissed at you for not taking this stuff seriously.

My friend and I decided to go to the movies one night instead of to course, and the next time we showed up for course, we were told that we were going to go to Ethics. Ethics was where you got your punishment assignment for doing something wrong from a Scientology viewpoint. The Ethics Officer told us that we had to do a "Danger Condition" and get back to course.

"Conditions" are about a dozen different formulas L. Ron Hubbard wrote up, and someone applies the steps of the formulas to their life to change how they are doing. The worse you are doing, the lower the condition you have to apply. But in reality, they are mostly used to punish people. Usually, when you are in the higher conditions, people are not around chasing you up for conditions write-ups. You had to write up what you did for each step of the condition and get it checked by someone to make sure that it was okay. As soon as you are in trouble the first thing you get asked is "What condition do you think you are in?" or "You are assigned a condition of Confusion!" Conditions are also used as an incentive. For example: "You can't have time off until you are out of your Doubt Condition!" They were used as a threat, such as "If you don't get this work done, you are assigned a Liability Condition!"

I never liked this because it was usually up to the person approving or assigning conditions to decide what condition formula you did. It was completely arbitrary and widely abused by one and all. Hubbard originally developed the conditions for staff and they grew into an entire subject, which became much broader and open to negative interpretation.

After several months on course, I completed the Student Hat and passed the final exam. After completing this course, the first thing I had to do was go see a guy at the organization whose job was to sign me up for my next course. I was ready for a break and not planning to do any more courses right away. Since my mom paid for the course and I had no money, I did not sign up.

After a few months my best friend, Jesse and I went on to do the E-Meter Course. This seemed easy enough and would get our parents off our backs for a few months about doing more courses.

The E-Meter Course was a course on the manual for the E-Meter and some exercises that taught you how to operate the thing. In Scientology, the E-meter is a tool pretty similar to a lie detector. It is used in all counseling and is said to detect areas that need to be addressed. It is also used by ethics officers to find people with withholds (crimes) and who have done things they don't want found out about. So the E-meter is central to many activities in Scientology and it was considered important to learn how to use it. After we completed this, we stopped going to course.

Over the next few months, I spent more and more time with Jesse. I stayed at his house a few times a week and since we went to the same school, it worked out great for me. My mom was starting to preach the Scientology stuff all the time. She had moved in with her latest boyfriend and he was a dedicated Scientologist. To make matters worse, he lived one block away from the huge Scientology complex right off Sunset. Living this close to Scientology was too close for comfort.

My mom's boyfriend, Dan, was on his Operating Thetan (OT) levels and went to the Complex daily. Operating Thetan levels are the upper and confidential levels of Scientology. You don't ever find out what is on them until you do them. It turns out that Dan's software company did a lot of computer database programming for Scientology and he was very dependent on them for his weekly income, so he did whatever they wanted. I did not like Dan at first. Until then, I had never seen an apartment as messy and disgusting as his. There was literally crap everywhere. He not only had the one apartment for his living quarters, but two more right next door and across the hall where he had his businesses.

In these "offices" it was wall-to-wall computers and filing cabinets. Now before you think "under the desk computers", let me tell you what kind of computers these were. They were VAX/VMS systems. They had large tape drives and were about as big as refrigerators. He had about twenty of these things, along with tape drives, stacks of tapes and cables. Add to that a never ending snake of wires going every which direction and double stacked filing cabinets piled high with papers, trash and junk and you had Dan's offices.

His living quarters were not much different. Clothes, trash and odd furniture items piled with random junk all over the place. It was a one-bedroom apartment and we would be moving in immediately. The idea was that my sister and I would have our bedroom in the dining/living room, which was about eight square feet. My mom was going to get us a bunk bed so we could have some space for a dresser. Oh, did I mention that this would still also be the living room and we would have a table there for eating?

My mom somehow thought that this was living in the lap of luxury. She brought up how this place was better than the apartment we were living in a few months back. We previously had a bachelor apartment that was one room with a small bathroom. Anything would be an upgrade from that! Dan's apartment was not my idea of home.

At least I had Jesse's place where I could crash. Jesse had just moved into a HUGE house in Tujunga. It was minutes from where we went to school and Jesse had his own room. Jesse had two sisters, one who was about eight years old and the other who was a baby. Jesse's mom was pretty cool. She and my mom knew each other, but were not really close friends. The only thing they had in common was the Scientology stuff.

Jesse's dad was very similar to my dad in that he was not really pushing Scientology and just wanted to live life and have some fun. His dad had bought jet skis, water rafting equipment, bikes, guns, etc. My dad regularly took us to the movies, restaurants and the beach and was generally cool with whatever we did. Jesse's dad seemed more interested in fitness and vitamins than Scientology.

One day I was talking to Jesse about going to live with my dad. This meant that I would have to quit school because my dad lived about 2 hours away and the tuition was too high. I could not stand living with my mom anymore and between her and her new boyfriend, I was being pushed to the edge. Jesse said that maybe I could stay with his family and was going to talk to his parents about it.

Turns out that I could not have picked a better time. Jesse's mom was planning to move to Clearwater, Florida, with the baby so that she could work full time on getting up the "Bridge" — the Scientology metaphor for spiritual progress. Clearwater is where the Flag Land Base was. This was the biggest organization in all Scientology, and if you were in Scientology and you were going to Flag, it might as well have been Disneyland for Scientologists. They even had a slogan: "The Friendliest Place on Earth - Flag." The only thing better than Flag was the *Freewinds*. The *Freewinds* was a cruise ship owned by Scientology that sailed around the Caribbean delivering services to the highest level Scientologists.

Jesse's dad thought that if I moved in with them, it would work out well for all involved. Here's the other good part, Jesse's little sister Diana, was going to stay behind in LA and Jesse's dad was going to hire a full time babysitter for her. He promised not to disappoint us.

I told my mom that I was going to live with Jesse. There was not anything she could do about it and I am sure in her mind, it would be easier since I could not stand living with her and her boyfriend and I openly displayed and voiced my views on a regular basis.

Moving in with Jesse took about five minutes. I had moved so many times to so many places that I had cut all my belongings down to clothing items. I had no crap to cart around. After ten or so moves, I tended to lose track or cut loose on the items one normally accumulates over time.

Since I was already at Jesse's house a few nights a week, living there permanently was not a big change. We rode to school in the morning on our bikes or got a ride from another friend who lived a few blocks away. Oh yeah, the babysitter got hired. She was right out of a frickin' centerfold, I swear. She was of foreign descent, I think Brazilian. Maybe not, but I could easily imagine her on a beach in Rio... Anyway, she was nice. She cleaned and cooked for us and kept Jesse's sister out of our hair. But most of all she was easy on the eyes and no matter what she said got a smile out of us.

One Wednesday night, when we came home, there were a bunch of cars in the driveway we had not seen before. We walked in the door and Jesse's dad was in the living room with a bunch of people from Scientology. We could tell — we knew them from the Advanced Org Los Angeles (AOLA). One of them was from the local Flag Office, one from the local *Freewinds* office and one from IAS. The IAS is the International Association of Scientologists. Mostly, they go around getting rich Scientologists to donate money to support legal battles. This was not a good scene. It is one thing if they are hitting you up for money at their offices. They were in the damn house! The only way you get these people to leave is to give them money, and lots of it. Apparently, there was never enough money to "Clear the Planet," the

Scientology battle cry for saving mankind, as fast as needed. The sad thing was that Jesse's dad had the money. He had just sold off a company and had a boatload of cash he was sitting on. They probably knew that, which is why they were here. And it was Wednesday! Anyone in Scientology knows that you never go see a Registrar on Wednesdays or Thursday mornings!

In Scientology, the official end of the work week is at 2:00 P.M. on Thursday. All of the statistics from everybody working in the organization are added up and tallied and whoever got less done than the week before is "downstat" and everybody else is "upstat" – meaning their statistic is higher than it was the previous week. The staff with up statistics get rewarded and the staff with down statistics get penalized. They are particular about enforcing the penalty part and not so much about the rewards. Registrars, or "Reges" as they are referred to, are the number one priority within the organization. The registrars are the staff members who get people to pay the organization money. If the registrars don't make money, nobody gets paid. When you are only making $35 a week, getting paid is a huge deal. The registrars have a tremendous amount of pressure applied to them in order to make the money they need. The ones with Jesse's dad were big time registrars. These guys don't walk away without at least a few hundred thousand dollars raised between them.

The next morning we got up and, luckily, their shakedown did not last all night long. They were gone. Jesse's dad was gone. Hopefully, they did not clean him out.

When we got home from school, Jesse's dad told us he had some news. "We are all going to go to Flag and the *Freewinds* over the summer!" he told us.

So they cleaned him out! From the Flag Registrar he bought his whole damn Bridge services for him AND his wife up to Operating Thetan (OT) Level VIII, which is as high as you can currently go in the Scientology world. From the *Freewinds* registrar, he bought a bunch of courses for himself, Jesse and me as well as accommodations for a few weeks. And from the International Association of Scientologists, he gave 40K and became a Patron! I estimated he dropped a cool 600K for all that, if not more.

Somehow, I am now going to Clearwater, Florida and the *Freewinds*. The ship part I could enjoy, but Flag would be a drag no matter which way you sliced it.

To sell us on the Flag idea, Jesse's dad already had a plan: we were going to bring the jet skis and make a road trip to Florida. We would go jet skiing at all the lakes on the way from LA to Clearwater. That would work.

The summer came and we made the trip. We ended up going jet skiing a lot and took a very scenic route to Clearwater. When we arrived it was just as we thought it would be, it was awful.

Flag is called "Flag" because when L. Ron Hubbard founded the Sea Organization in the 1960's, he did so at sea. There were several ships that eventually made up the flotilla of vessels that the Sea Org operated from. The ship in which Hubbard worked was known as the Flag ship and he was referred to as the Commodore of the fleet. When the Sea Organization moved ashore in the 1970's, they moved their operations to Clearwater and never changed the name. The Flag ship Apollo operations transferred to the Flag Land Base, otherwise referred to as FLB or just Flag.

In 1988, Flag was staffed by hundreds of Sea Org members. They had several buildings and all were filled with Sea Org members dressed in navy like uniforms. They even went so far as to have rank insignia and Sea Org officers wore shoulder boards and gold braid lanyards.

Jesse and I signed up for the Pro TRs Course. This was the Professional Training Routines Course. On the first part of the course, you read a ton of background information on how Scientology came to be, what it is and how it was still around. Then you have to listen to some more 1960s lectures with LRH rambling on about stuff that has nothing to do with the price of rice in China, much less Florida in the late 1980s. We had a pretty cushy schedule and hoped to drag out the course so we could mess around most of the time and get back to LA after summer. We were scheduled to be on course in the morning until lunch and then until 3:30 in the afternoon. From 3:30 until the end of the night, we went to the beach or went swimming in the pool at the Fort Harrison Hotel.

This was working out just fine until one of our supervisors spotted us in the pool at the Fort Harrison Hotel one night. The next day she pulled us aside and told us that we were being dilettantes and that we were off-purpose. We were 15 years old! She told us that it was unacceptable that we were on such a light schedule when we were just doing nothing but what we wanted the rest of the time. This was considered "chasing butterflies," something that L. Ron Hubbard mentioned in the most important Scientology policy, entitled Keeping Scientology Working. I remember thinking at the time that she probably wished she could go swimming in the pool but Sea Org members were not allowed. I also thought that going off and having someone take pictures of us literally chasing butterflies and then showing them to her would probably not help the situation.

We were in a tight spot and did not want to make any trouble and get into a bunch of ethics trouble, so we said that we would go on course for more time. Instead of ending at 3:30 P.M., we now ended at 5:30 P.M. Two more hours. Wow. We figured that if we went to course a little bit more during the day, we would finish the course faster and have more DAYS off to screw around! It was a good deal. We finished the course and screwed off for a good week or two before the trip to the *Freewinds*.

I remember seeing the Course Supervisor at the Sandcastle one day when we were jet skiing in the bay next to the building. I waved at her, knowing that she probably had her blood boiling while believing that the planet, or the entire universe, was busy being flushed down the toilet. In hindsight, a jet ski would have been highly valuable if the world was, in fact, being flushed away. I would have surely outlasted the bulk of the people clinging to soup cans attached to E-Meters or books written by Hubbard.

We went to the *Freewinds*; I did this tiny course that shows you where everything is on the ship and how to get into a lifeboat should the thing sink. I was announced at the "Graduation" that week and had to say something about the course. Everybody does the course. No one wants to do it, but it is a requirement. Sort of like everything in Scientology, you have no choice. And then after you do something you don't really have a choice in doing, you get to tell everybody how much you loved it. If you don't come out the end of a course in Scientology with flying colors, you get in big ethics trouble and most often have to pay more money to find out why you are unhappy and then possibly pay even more money to do other remedies that are believed will make you happy again. I went along and said, "I was now happy to know where everything on the ship was." Everybody clapped and the next guy said something about the course he finished. Yippee!

I then did another course – The Route to Infinity Course. Jesse and I liked the "get through the course fast and then mess around" method. We decided to go from morning until the end of the night and do the course fast. This course consisted of a bunch of LRH lectures from the 1950s. Jesse and I whizzed through the course in three days and partied for the rest of the cruise. We drove around the islands all day on mopeds, jet skied, and scuba dived or just did nothing and hung out on the ship. One night we got in trouble for watching the movie *Robo Cop* on one of the lounge decks that had a TV. We had rented it on the local island and brought it aboard. The Sea Org girl who wanted it turned off said that it was too "enturbulating" for the other passengers and we had to stop playing it. In Scientology, being enturbulated is the worst thing you can experience. It is like being upset and having your "personal space" or "universe" encroached upon. So, we turned the movie off. She left. We turned it back on. All the other "enturbulated" passengers somehow made it to the end without drowning themselves at sea. In fact, I do remember them being a bit angry when the Sea Org girl made it seem like they were not going to find out if Robo Cop was going to take down the bad guys or if he was going to meet up with his wife and kid. They did brighten up when we popped the tape back in, though.

Besides having a better set of sea legs and some fun island trips, we were ready to leave the *Freewinds*. We had been there two weeks and it was time to go.

We got back to Flag and realized that we still had one more course that we had to do, The Method One Course. The stated purpose of this course is recovery of your education – hard to do when you haven't even graduated high school yet. You look up definitions of any words you have ever run into that you didn't know the meaning of. We decided to do this course since it was the last course we needed to do in order to become Fast Flow. In Scientology, every time you read something, you have to get an exam from another student who has already read the thing you just read. This person quizzes you about what you read and asks you key questions to test your understanding of the materials. If you do not answer any one question correctly, you have to go re-read the document and get another checkout from that person. Then at the end of the course you have to take an exam, if you do not pass the exam with a score over 85%, you have to go back and re-do the entire course from the beginning. Well if you do the Student Hat and Method One, you become Fast Flow, which means you do NOT have to get any checkouts or take any exams at the end of the course. It means you are smarter than the rest of the people in the course room and when you read something, you understand it and don't need to sit there for hours trying to figure out what the hell Hubbard is talking about. The only way you get in trouble with Fast Flow is if a supervisor thinks you do not understand, he can quiz you on the spot and if you flunk for any reason he can revoke your Fast Flow status.

There is even another level above Fast Flow, which is called Super Literate. To become Super Literate you have to look up in a dictionary every single word that L. Ron Hubbard uses on the Student Hat Course, which includes the typed transcripts of all the lectures Hubbard gave on the subject of study. This is called the Primary Rundown (PRD). And then you do Method One. I think the only difference between the two statuses is that if you are SuperLit or Super Literate, you cannot be challenged whether you understand something or not, they just have to take your word for it that you understand and go from there.

We went full time on this Method One course and spent a month with our heads buried in dictionaries. We did see some folks on the Primary Rundown and they had been on the course for eight months and they were only half way through! We were glad that we were only going to be Fast Flow.

We finished the Method One Course and had a lot of time to mess around. We went to some parties, went jet skiing a lot and were having a great time our last few weeks in Clearwater.

Just when we thought everything was going great, things started happening.

One of the teachers at Delphi was named Adam Hancock. He was our soccer coach, and he was the one watching the LA house while we were in Florida. Evidently he had been down into the basement and borrowed one of Jesse's dad's guns for an acting class he had been attending. He was going to do the Mel Gibson scene from *Lethal Weapon* where he shoots himself in the head using a gun with no bullets in it. Well, this would have been fine except for the fact that Adam had put a loaded clip into the gun and then taken it out. One bullet stayed in the chamber and he shot himself for real in the acting class. We got the call from our teacher, Eve Darling. She knew Adam from the Delphi School in Oregon, from which they both graduated. She was devastated. We were devastated. He shot himself with one of our guns! He lived but was on life support and was most likely going to be a paraplegic if he in fact survived. Adam was like a brother. We grew up together and he was our teacher for a long time. We had been to his house, met his wife and hung out. He was a really good guy.

After this, things took on a serious tone. Both our girlfriends had come out to Florida around this time. We were spending a lot of time with them and they lived at the Sandcastle so we were around Flag a lot more. One day Jesse met with some Sea Org members and I thought that they were probably trying to recruit him. Being at Delphi and being around LA, we got used to Sea Org recruiters. They were always trying to get the young kids into the Sea Org. In fact most of the LA organizations had kids as young as 12 working in them. Sea Org members were everywhere at Flag, though. The whole place was run by the Sea Org; so much so, they probably numbered in the hundreds, at least. There were a lot of them.

Jesse did not come back that night. I saw him the next morning at the Sandcastle. "I am joining the Sea Org," he told me.

"What the hell?" I said. "What about all the stuff we were going to do?"

"Ali joined too!" he said.

Ali was his girlfriend. She was best friends with my girlfriend, Star. We all went to Delphi in LA and we had been dating these girls off and on for months. It was not like we were anything more than girlfriend and boyfriend or had done any more than held hands and fooled around a bit. It sure was not the kind of relationship that you follow into a billion year contract!

"Oh, so this is about getting some action now?" I asked. I couldn't believe it.

"What about Star? Did she join too? I can tell you right now that I ain't joining even if Star did. That is crazy talk, I can't believe you joined!"

"Well I did. I'm going to pack up my stuff today and start tomorrow. I start right away," he said decidedly.

"So, wait a minute. You didn't even join up for LA? You are going to stay here? That is lame. Florida sucks, dude! How the hell could you join, but to then join up for the Sea Org down here? Oh man, they must have told you some crazy stuff for you to do that." I was pissed. I walked off to go find Star and find out her version of this crazy story.

I found Star in her room crying. She asked me if I heard.

"Yeah, what the hell?"

Apparently, Ali and Jesse ended up meeting with the recruiters. Ali got signed up first and then helped them team up on Jesse. That is what they did. They got one friend in and then they used that friend to get the rest of the friends in. I had seen it happen so many times before. Jesse and I usually just blew them off. In LA they would come up to us and we would just say, "LSD." You can't be in the Sea Org if you have taken LSD, so if you said, "LSD" that was the end of the conversation before it even started. We used to tell them we had large debts, too many kids, a brother that worked at the LA Times, whatever we could think of that would give us a good laugh and blow them off instantly.

"What are you going to do?" Star asked me.

"Well, I sure as hell aint joining the Sea Org in Florida!" I answered back, hoping that she was in the same frame of mind.

"Yeah, but where are you gonna live? If Jesse stays here, where are you gonna go?"

Dumbfounded, I realized she was right. "Damn, I hadn't thought of that!"

Where the hell am I gonna go? Good damn question. I am screwed. I have to go back and live with my mom. This is turning out to be a really crappy day. Maybe I can watch the house when I get back! Maybe there is a way to work this out. There has to be a way. What the hell is Jesse's family going to think? Jesse is going to be in the Sea Org and I am going to be there for what reason? I am just a fifth wheel at this point, no use in keeping me around at all.

When I got back to the apartment where I was staying with Jesse and his family, Jesse's dad asked if I had heard the news. Oh yeah, I had. He then asked what my plan was. He was really cool about it. I just said that I was still trying to figure that out. He said that he was going to sell his house in Los Angeles. Great. There goes 99% of my plan.

I had to call my dad. I ended up going back to LA, staying with my mom and hoping things worked out for the best.

No sooner than I arrived back, I realized that this would never work. My sister was working for my mom's boyfriend's company doing data entry. They wanted me to work for him as well. As long as I could make some extra bucks, I was cool with working. Then they explained to me how the "making some money" part works. The data entry they want me to do is of all of the sales leads that they have gathered up at conventions, sales meetings and so forth. They have hundreds of these cards with people's information on them that they wanted us to enter into the computer systems for the sales team. If the sales team called one of these people and made a sale, only then do we get a commission. I told my mom and her boyfriend that I was born on the weekend, but not last weekend! Screw that! I could work for them for one hundred hours entering this junk into the computer and maybe, if I am lucky, three months from now, you are going to cut me a check for 15 bucks?

"What about your exchange with us?" my mom asks.

Oh, great. Here we go. As soon as she asked the question, she headed for the bookshelf and pulled out one of many large green volumes by LRH that has every single policy letter on exchange and anything else I had no interest in hearing about at the moment. She started going on about exchange and the fact that I needed to give back to her boyfriend in exchange for him letting me stay in his apartment. In Scientology, the subject of exchange covers the fact that nobody gets anything free. There is a balance that has to occur in all parts of your life. Just as you have to pay when you buy something at the store, same applies to everything in your life. If my mother's boyfriend provided a place for me to live, I had to work for him instead of paying rent. As I had been being supported by her all my life, I owed her for the last 15 years of rent and food.

I need to find a place to live, I thought to myself while giving my mom a blank stare as she recited L. Ron Hubbard straight from the pages of one of the large green books from the shelf.

It took me about a week to work something up, but I made a deal with one of my friends at Delphi. Her sister was away at the Delphi campus in Oregon and they had an empty room in their house where I could stay. I was free! I could get out of here and start living on my own.

I told my mom that I was not interested in her exchange system as the apartment they were providing sucked and was a wreck so I was trading up to something better and she would not have to provide anything for me. So between us, we decided that it would be best if I moved out.

I moved in with Lorin and her family. Lorin was this exceptionally tall, slender girl who had freckles and was really funny. Her mom and step-dad both worked for Scientology in some capacity but did not preach the Scientology gospel. Living with them was pretty simple.

One day on the way back from school, Lorin's mom dropped the bomb on me. "Jim (Lorin's step dad) and I are selling our house! We are going to get an apartment in Glendale and use the money from the house to pay off our debts so we can join the Sea Org. We are joining the Sea Org."

Everyone looked at me all happy expecting that I was going to be overjoyed to find that yet another temporary residence of mine was being pulled out from under me for some reason related to the damn Sea Org!

Are these guys trying to mess with me? I thought. This is insane. First Jesse, now Lorin's parents.

"Wow, that's great!" I exclaim, wondering how the hell I was going to get out of this pickle.

That night I had to decide how I was going to sort this out. Going back to my mom's was not an option. My dad lived too far away for me to stay in school. I did not know of anyone else that had an extra place for me to stay. Suddenly it came to me. There was a guy at the school who worked for half the day at the school, and the other half of the day he did his studies. The school not only paid for his education, but he got some cash as well. They called it a work/study program. It was for the less affluent students that had parents that could not afford to pay for tuition. If I did that program, I could use the money I made from the school to pay rent and survive while still going to school. The next day I went over this idea with the school administrators. They liked the idea. The school staff even suggested that I rent a room from one of the other teachers at the school that had an extra room and that would solve my living arrangements!

My supervisor (teacher), Eve Darling, was who I worked for at the beginning. Eve was cool. She had been my teacher since I first started at Delphi. I did assistant type functions for her and filed student tests and paperwork. Eve was more like one of the older kids than our Supervisor. She had graduated from Delphi Oregon, and after that she worked at Delphi LA as a Course Supervisor.

It all worked out rather nicely. I moved into a house right up the road from where Lorin lived, in Tujunga. I became the lower school students' soccer coach, paper-filing guy and eventually took over staff training at the school. I studied my school materials in the morning and all afternoon I worked. I loved it. Also, shortly after I started working at Delphi, my dad ended up moving back to Nebraska. So I was really on my own at this point. I was making money, supporting myself and relied on nobody but myself. I was 15 years old and officially living on my own. I did not have a lot of money, but at the same time I did not have that many expenses. I ate a lot of Ramen noodles and ham sandwiches.

This lasted for several months before it happened. The Sea Org recruiters came to the Delphi campus. They were interviewing all the staff, but not students. There had been some stink about recruiters stealing students from the school and the school, even though it was very low on the Scientology hierarchy chart, still had balls enough to keep them from talking to students on the school campus. Also these recruiters had come from ABLE, so the school was forced to let them do what they wanted. ABLE stands for Association for Better Living and Education and was over Applied Scholastics which was itself over Delphi and to whom they paid licensing fees for using the L. Ron Hubbard materials. Since I was still a "student," I would be off limits.

Two people from ABLE were interviewing staff one at a time. They were there for days. Every day, they cycled through staff members and some people wanted to join, but did not qualify for some reason or other. The recruiters gave these unqualified people "Project Prepares", which were essentially a list of actions that if done made them eligible for the Sea Org. After they had been there for a few days, I realized that my current landlord, Linda, had previously mentioned that she was unqualified for the Sea Org and had thought about joining before. Sure enough, when I got home that night, she was all excited. I knew it was coming. It was like the force that I could never get away from. I was going to have to warn people that if they let me live with them, that they would automatically be joining the Sea Org within the next few months. Sure enough, the words came out of her mouth.

"I have a new "Project Prepare." I will be able to join the Sea Org in a couple of months!" Linda exclaimed happily.

"That's great!" I said, thinking that I could one day sell my "living services" to Sea Org Recruiters all around the world. I could be on a contract and just live with people they wanted to get in. They would support me and in turn, I would send people to them every few months. It would be the same as what I was already doing, but I would get compensated for it. I thought that this was a great idea although it did not solve the issue at hand. I was back to having no place to live. I could always find another place to shack up, but then I might need a car, it might be further away. Not that many staff lived close to the school. I was at my wits' end. I had moved every few months and it was beginning to take its toll on me. I was broke already. My list of friends was getting smaller and smaller as I lost the ability and funds to go out and have fun like everyone else. I was 15 years old. The only things I should have been thinking about was how I was going to clear up my acne and get laid. And here I was trying to figure out how to make next month's rent, eat and then maybe, if I was lucky and still had some money left, somehow get laid.

The next day when I got done with my morning study session, my boss told me that the recruiters were waiting to see me.

My boss was Rona Bowles. She seemed very nice. I liked her a lot. She seemed to be doing well for herself. Her husband was Tim Bowles. He was a partner at this local law firm Bowles & Moxon. They did all sorts of cases for Scientology and they had money. The other partner at the firm, Ken Moxon was married and his wife worked at Delphi too, Carla Moxon. Their daughter, Stacey, and their son went to Delphi, too.

"I thought I was off limits to them!" I told Rona.

"Just go talk to them for a few minutes," she said.

I went. They were using an empty office at the school that had a VCR and TV in it and were showing videos to people. I walked in and said that I only had a few minutes. It was a woman and her husband, Martha and Boris Levitsky. They were different than other recruiters I had run into. They were not like the Sea Org recruiters at all. They did not wear Sea Org uniforms. They were on a "Project" from ABLE. They told me that the Association for Better Living and Education was different than other Sea Org units. As our meeting progressed, I got more and more interested in what they were talking about. I had seen Sea Org members for years and hated that they had no money, no time to themselves and lived with fifty other people in filthy rooms that were overcrowded. I wanted nothing to do with that. ABLE staff got minimum wage, they did not live with other Sea Org members at the Complex. They lived in normal apartments nearby. They also did not work in "Orgs", they worked in schools and Narconon Drug Rehabilitation Centers and other places just like I was working at Delphi. They also said that ABLE staff did not have to wear Sea Org uniforms like other LA Sea Org members. They showed me a video of Narconon Chilocco. It was this huge Indian Reservation in the middle of Oklahoma. They said that if I wanted to, I could work at Chilocco. I would have my room and board taken care of, I would get paid a few hundred bucks per week and I could do whatever I liked and would still be helping people.

Also, because I was almost 16, I could stop going to school legally and would no longer have to worry about that.

I seriously considered doing this. No more school. No more housing issues and I would still make some cash. I would not have to do all the Sea Org stuff I hated and I could go off and be at Narconon Chilocco and help people get off drugs. Doing this would solve so many problems at once. The recruiters made it seem like the solution to all of the problems that I had. If I was getting paid minimum wage and having my expenses paid for, I could save up and get some good work experience. I had been "living on my own" for a few months at best. I decided that I would join. I was going to Chilocco!

Work Hard

had a day or two to pack up my stuff, sort out my paperwork and make arrangements I needed to make before starting the EPF. The Estates Project Force.

I had a few boxes of clothes and some records and a stereo system. I packed all that stuff up and Martha and Boris hauled it all over to the Association for Better Living and Education in Hollywood.

I was taken around to meet the staff. Everyone there seemed all happy, everyone was in suits and ties, there was one guy who said he went to Delphi Oregon and that I was doing the right thing. The building looked to be just recently renovated. I myself had never even heard of the building, the Association for Better Living and Education or any of this a week prior.

So I signed some papers and then I was off to do the Estates Project Force (EPF). I signed a contract that said I was going to be in the Sea Org for the next billion years, literally. Like there is some kind of enforcement arm of the Sea Org that is going to track me down in the next life?

The Estates Project Force is essentially one's introduction into the Sea Organization. You learn the theory behind the Sea Org, the basic operational procedures, the do's and don'ts and concurrent to that you do heavy manual labor. The stated idea behind the heavy manual labor part of it is that a Sea Org member is supposed to be able to do any task assigned, no matter how menial and despite the fact that normal people would never want to do it. If you make it through the program successfully, you become an official Sea Org member.

A girl named Veronika Kegel was my new buddy and she was the one I would report to until I finished the EPF. I signed the paperwork, including the billion year contract and she informed me that I was going back over to the Complex.

"Wait a minute! What do I need to go to the Complex for?" I asked.

"Well, that is where the EPF gets done," Veronika explains to me.

"Wow, that really sucks, this place is nice, I should just do it here," I said.

"That's probably why it is NOT done here!" she happily replies as we headed off to the elevators.

Up until this time, I had always regarded the Complex as the filthiest place I had ever seen. This was after growing up and living next to Hollywood Boulevard for several years. Hollywood Blvd in the 1980's was crap. In the 80's you were lucky if *your* walk-of-fame star did not have crap or puke on it when the sun came up. It was dirty. Well the Complex somehow had logged itself lower than Hollywood Blvd in my mind.

The Estates Project Force was a tightly and heavily supervised activity. I was introduced to the EPF In-Charge. This "I/C" was the person over the whole operation. He had a guy that worked for him that was the Deputy In-Charge. There were several different Units within the Estates Project Force. Each Unit had their own I/C's and each person on the EPF reported up to their individual I/C who then reported up to the next guy and so on. I thought I was going to do some courses, I did not know there needed to be such a strict organizational structure to do some simple courses.

Turns out that most of the structure was for the work that was to be done outside of the course room. The EPF were given crappy jobs that no one else wanted to do. MEST work is what they called it. MEST stood for Matter, Energy, Space and Time. Any type of work that occurred outside of your head was MEST work. Sea Org members had to be cause over MEST in order to get the planet cleared. So the EPF was half MEST work and half study. Studying was over for the day when I arrived, so I got to learn about what MEST work I would be doing.

We were to run everywhere we went. We sort of double-timed while in a group. We were not to be seen or heard hanging around or goofing off for any reason whatsoever. We were not to speak unless spoken to and we were told to do our work and study until we were done and then we would get assigned to our post if we passed the Fitness Board at the end of the Estates Project Force.

Cleaning dumpsters, taking out trash, doing dishes, hauling stuff, mopping floors, you know, stuff most people would have someone else do if they had the option. Well the EPF was the option for the local Sea Org staff that worked at the Complex. We would do all their dirty work and be happy doing it.

Since study time was over, I got to start with the work portion of the EPF. I was assigned to a unit that was working in the galley. The galley was the part of the Complex that I logged as the filthiest place on earth. The galley, or kitchen as everyone else on land normally called it, stank, and regardless of when I went in there over the next 15 years, it always smelled like rotten ass. So of course, that is where I got to do my EPF.

We had the job of doing the dishes after the hundreds of crew members came through and ate any one of the four meals that were served there each day. After all the dishes were done, we would get the next meal set up and have everything in place before the rush of people came back in. If you were lucky, you would get dishes or clean-up; the one job you did not want to get in the galley was "potland." Potland was an overflowing mountain of dirty pots that never diminished no matter how many people were assigned to clean them. The pots usually had nasty smelly things stuck to them, and they did not clean easily.

Now, I had never worked in food service before, but I knew that some things being done were not up to five-star qualities. One of the girls in the same unit as me, Heather Ashworth, was about eight years old. She was rather tiny, too small to stand next to the sink and wash pots—so she was in the sink washing the pots! Standing *in* the water with a scrub brush in hand cleaning the pots. I had never seen anything like it.

Never once did I see a single hair net, gloves or any kind of smock. Everyone had their standard issue blue shorts and t-shirts with their worn out black combat boots.

After spending the rest of the night in the galley, it was time for bed. As explained to me by my In-Charge, Bill, the EPF got to go to bed early so that study could be done in the morning, before a long day's work. So we would be able to secure at 10:00 P.M. and be up at 6:30! I was like - what the hell are you talking about - early?

"Well almost everybody secures at 11:00 P.M. but we get to go early so we can get eight hours sleep to be studentable," Bill said cheerily, as though we just won some kind of lottery.

"This is where the men's showers for this floor are," Bill pointed out as we walked by a set of swinging wood doors that looked as if they had been wet for 30 years.

Holy shit! I am in the army! Communal frickin' showers for the entire floor!

We came to the room where the Estates Project Force males were housed. No sooner than we walked in the door, several EPFers were already racing towards the showers. Turns out that if you didn't get in and shower quickly, you would not get one. The rest of the hundreds of crew members that worked at the Complex got off post shortly after we did and the showers, bathrooms, hallways would overflow with people. It was the last place you wanted to be, walking around half naked as the "new guy." Valuable information to have, I thought, picturing myself walking half naked through all these serious Sea Org member types.

Before I could even crack a smile at the picture in my mind, I was taken to the room where I would be sleeping. It was about 25 feet long by 20 feet wide. It had at least 30 beds in it. Most were stacked at least two or three high. There were no dressers. There were only people's bags and some personal items next to the bed on the floor or wedged into the bottom springs in the bed above. Yes - springs. These bunk beds must have been 30 years old. There were no mattresses here; these were steel frames with metal squeaky springs and three inch pads with the thinnest sheets and barely thicker blankets. No air conditioners, no heaters. A few oscillating fans that blew in air from outside so that there would be just enough oxygen to support life until morning. Of course, I was the new guy so I got the top bunk on a triple stacker. As much as I was interested in getting more familiar with the room and my new bed, I had to get a shower. I had at least two meals worth of greasy food water soaked into my hands and arms, and no matter how much I washed them off in the kitchen, the smell just stayed with me. I grabbed a towel and my toiletries and headed towards the door.

"Where are you going?" Bill asked.

As the words reached my ears, I thought that either I am the smartest person here or this guy is the dumbest. Could not get enough of those dishes, figured I'd go down and dry a few more for morning, I thought, but answered, "To the showers." Knowing that the latter would not get half as much of a laugh from the other EPFers, but I did not know these folks and wanted to play it cool.

"Not without sandals, you're not!" Bill answered back.

"Huh?" I replied, questioning both him and the conversation that was taking place.

"Per the Flag orders from L. Ron Hubbard, you can't take a shower without your sandals. You need to bring them with you in order to be able to take a shower." Bill was putting his own set on as he was reciting this.

"No one told me about any sandals, I don't have any and I need to take a shower," I state, as if that will be enough to get a shower around this place.

"Well, you should get down to the canteen and get yourself some," Bill said as he casually left the room towards the showers.

Getting down to the ground floor and back was a good 15 minutes with the slow ass elevators. I didn't even know where the damn canteen was anyway! I grabbed my towel and headed towards the showers. I will take my chances with the whole sandals rule. I go through the swinging doors and wouldn't you know it, right on the wall of the shower room was a white sheet of paper that has the sandal rule from L. Ron Hubbard printed out in big letters in quotes! I glanced over at the few showering EPFers, each of them were wearing sandals. You have to be kidding me!

As I was leaving, Bill came out from the wall of crappers and headed towards the showers while pointing to his watch with the "better hurry" look.

What a douche, I thought to myself, imagining how he would look with a new pair of sandals shoved in his mouth.

I got down to the ground floor by the painfully slow elevators that seemed to stop at every floor even though most of the time no one was there.

I got out and asked a girl in the hall about the canteen, "It's downstairs, next to the galley," she said.

I was there all damn day and nobody told me about this, but now when I had this tiny window of time to get a badly needed shower, I had to go out and buy some sandals. This is brilliant. I finally made it to the canteen. I looked around. The place was packed with people. There were so many people buying candy bars, soda, gum and cigarettes, that it was almost silly. As I looked around, that was all the place had: junk food and cigarettes. No damn sandals!

I went to the guy at the counter and asked him where I could get some sandals in my panicky new guy voice. "George's General Store," he answered while selling someone a pack of Camel non-filters and not even looking at me.

I knew where that was, and I thought they might even have some sandals there! George's General Store was a tiny building across the street from the Complex that was like a mini market for Scientologists. It had everything from vitamins to dictionaries. And oddly enough, sandals too. It was half the size of the canteen and had twice as many people inside. Half these people were buying junk food and the other half were like me, buying random items that you would not normally find in a mini market.

After I paid for an overpriced and rather plain pair of flip flop sandals, I made my way back across the street to the Complex with a towel still in tow and my new sandals. The elevator had about 50 people waiting for it. The rest of the Complex staff were now off duty and going up to their rooms! I headed towards the stairs and up five flights to the floor the EPF dorm was on. As I left the stairwell and headed towards the showers, I realized that no showers were going to be had. There was a line of at least ten guys queued up outside the showers! There were guys waiting inside, too!

I caught my breath and went back to the room. No shower tonight. Maybe if I got up early enough, I could get one in the morning.

I dumped my towel by my bag and grabbed my toothbrush, I headed toward the bathroom and realized that the bathroom in the dorm was just a sink and that's it. There was no toilet in the room anywhere. There were three guys waiting to brush their teeth and two brushing at the same time, huddled around the sink.

This was a signpost moment. I should have picked that up. I did not. Somehow, I rationalized all of this and thought that, once I was done with the Estates Project Force, I would be back in an apartment instead of living in barracks.

I brushed my teeth alone and went to bed. It took me a few minutes to get used to a sea of sporadic squeaks throughout the room, but as I laid there exhausted, I dreamt of what a hot shower would feel like in the morning.

That next morning would be one of the worst I had ever had, followed by several thousand more that rivaled it. At 6 A.M., people were milling around the room. I was dimly aware of these people, but still sleeping.

Bill shook me and I was instantly awake. He was dressed, as were most of the others in the room. "You have to eat breakfast," he said, as he walked out the door, "to be studentable."

Again, I had the picture of him eating my sandals for breakfast as I realized I had just missed my chance for a shower! This sucks.

I grabbed some of the tasteless eggs and a piece of burnt wheat toast. Breakfast of champions around here, I thought. The entire Estates Project

Force had to meet in the Vehicle Repair Unit after every meal. This was the large area right outside the EPF In-Charge office where the broken down Sea Org vehicles were parked. A bus and a few cars were parked there with their hoods open. They looked as though they hadn't been worked on for weeks, maybe even months.

Each Estates Project Force unit lined up and reported each person as present or accounted for. After every person was verified as present or their whereabouts as known, we were briefed on who was supposed to complete the EPF that week, as well as a briefing on who and what punishments were received by those who were not performing as expected.

The EPF In-Charge seemed like a really cool laid-back guy. He was a regular-sized black fellow, probably in his late 20s, maybe early 30s. He had his uniform perfect every time I saw him and was pretty straight to the point. You could tell he had a sense of humor and smiled often. I thought to myself that this guy seemed to be happy here.

Before we went off to study, we had to do some Chinese school. Two EPFers went in front of the group with a large printout of an L. Ron Hubbard quote printed on it in huge text. The EPF In-Charge recited it and we had to parrot it back to him. He read it over and over and we repeated it back. After 15 minutes of recital, we were done.

Some of us were sent off to study while others had a different schedule, working while we studied and then studying while we worked.

When I got to the Estates Project Force course room the Supervisor met me. He gave me a list of the courses I was supposed to do. It read:

Product Zero:
1. Basic Study Manual or Student Hat
2. Basic Cleaning Course
3. Intro To Scientology Ethics Course
4. Welcome to the Sea Org Tapes
5. Basic Sea Org Member Hat Course
6. Keys To Competence Course

This was great news. I smiled as I read it. I would be out of here in no time. I told the Supervisor that I was ready to start the Tapes because I had already done the first two courses listed. I did them as a public Scientologist. The Course Supervisor was also pleased since this meant I would already be well into the courses and he could get a completion faster.

I estimated that 75% of the people in the EPF course room were kids younger than me. The other 25% ranged in age from their late teens to 40 years old. There was a huge board on the wall that showed each person and their progress on the list of courses they had to complete. The majority of people in the room appeared to be on the first few courses. I could see that I was going to be getting through this line-up faster than they were used to. I mentioned to the Supervisor that I was Fast Flow. He asked me where I did my courses to become Fast Flow. I told him I did them at Flag the year before. Having done anything at Flag was better than doing them anywhere else. "No checkouts for you then!" he said happily, "You should be able to get through these courses rather quickly."

I listened to two entire tapes that day. The entire course consisted of five lectures total, so I figured I would be done with my first course within the next two days. The tapes were not like the study tapes I had listened to on the Student Hat course. Hubbard seemed to let his hair down a bit more, but he was still all over the place in terms of subjects covered.

On the first tape LRH talked about how it is harder to live at sea and, if you can live at sea, then you are better than the average landlubber. In the second tape he went over all the types of crews there are in the Sea Org, different types of drills that get done in the Sea Org and how to do them.

After study, we had lunch back in the galley. Someone told me that it was actually called Lebanon Hall. Turns out the entire building used to be a hospital and was called Cedars of Lebanon. Named after the trees that were used in King Solomon's Temple in Jerusalem in the Bible.

I was a bit sore from the work the day before, but took it a bit easier and made it through okay. At the end of the day, I got into the showers as soon as we got back and was able to get back to my dorm before the crowds hit.

The next day I got through two more taped lectures. The first was on why the Sea Org was so successful, which I thought was funny since the lecture was given 20 years earlier and the Sea Org had only a few thousand members worldwide. He talked about how Sea Org members handled things that came up and how they were smarter than the average bear. He also talked about how he and some of his former shipmates were stoned out of their minds on 135-proof rum in the ice-cold Alaskan Sea. I think the point of that story was how a Sea Org member needs to cope with his surroundings! The next lecture was all about how Sea Org members make things go right no matter what the circumstances. He also talks about how the Sea Org was an elite organization and that it was built upon an old pattern of past elite organizations.

I got through another day of dish washing without incident. At the end of the day I had to go get some boxes from another part of the Complex and bring them to the EPF In-Charge before I could secure for the night.

When I arrived at the EPF I/C's office, I knocked and was asked to come in.

I was amazed at the office itself. Everything in the Vehicle Repair Unit area, which was where his office was located, was covered in dirt. However the interior of his office was well decorated with nice furniture and tons of sea-related items such as wood tillers, small model boats, etc. There were at least three or four deep blue plush couches and very nice wood coffee tables. The carpet was a bit worn but matched the overall design and motif of the room.

The EPF In-Charge was sitting at his giant wood desk with his feet perched on top of it. He was smoking a cigarette and reading a magazine. He put it down as I walked in, I could have sworn it was some kind of Playboy or Penthouse. He looked like the polar opposite of what I had seen so far. Here was the guy that was in charge of the whole operation and he had not a worry in the world. He motioned for me to place the box on the desk and as I did he said that I was "dismissed."

As I left I couldn't help but realize that I hadn't seen the EPF I/C very often since I had arrived and he probably had been in the office the entire time.

The next day I completed the last lecture. It was all about how the world is one big public relations spin and anyone who wants to rule the world needs to know public relations. In the Sea Org there was a post called the Public Relations Officer and Hubbard said over and over, "it is a P-R-O world" and "P-R-O is king!" While I listened to the tape, I thought of the EPF In-Charge talking to his seniors about how hard he was working at getting people through the program. Then I realized he was probably in his office right this second, hard at work on this month's centerfold.

I started my next course, which was a compilation of short issues written by Hubbard in the 60s and 70s about how to do things the "Sea Org" way. It included the most mundane things such as how long to spend in the shower and always to wear sandals! There was an entire issue about the type of uniforms that would be worn by who and when, etc.

After lunch, we had our normal muster with the entire EPF. Some person from the local Central Training Organization had come to tell us about a revision being made to the Estates Project Force courses. She told us that the different levels of training were being revised and *The Keys to Competence Course* was no longer a requirement to complete the Estates Project Force. That meant that anybody on the EPF that was in the middle of that course could finish the EPF right now!

Of the 50 people on the EPF, there were about five on that course. Those five people were happy to be getting out of there. Me, I only had to finish the Basic Sea Org Member Course and I, too, would be able to get out of there.

That night while cleaning in the galley, out of nowhere, about 50 people came running through and started scrubbing the floors with toothbrushes! It was like something out of an Alfred Hitchcock movie. Like a flock of black birds had swooped in and landed on the floor of the galley. They were all dressed in black t-shirts, black shorts and black socks with black boots. They looked similar to EPFers, but these people looked horrible. While EPFers mostly had a "newbie" look to them and were unhardened, these people had a withered look to them. None of the women had any make-up on. Most of the men had leather looking faces and thick hands with fingers that looked as though they had been doing construction work for decades. When they came in, a cloud of foul body odor came with them. It was almost enough to make me gag. It reeked worse than the galley itself.

"Looks like someone screwed up bad!" one of my co-workers leaned over and told me as we watched the crowd scrub the grout on their hands and knees.

"How can you tell?" I asked him—he said it as if it was some sort of ritual that the Rehabilitation Project Force frequently did, scrubbing floors with toothbrushes.

He then proceeded to give me the lowdown on the Rehabilitation Project Force, or RPF. "Well, normally," he explained, "the RPF do heavy construction or jobs that go on longer than the EPF could handle. They do drywall, electrical, plumbing, you name it. They also do the really super nasty jobs like clean out the trash compactors or manure the lawns. If someone really screwed up on the RPF, then the whole group of them get punished and are forced to do things like scrub tiles with toothbrushes."

It was not getting the tiles any cleaner, but it was a pain in the ass and humiliating. It was a lesson not to let anyone screw up. It was also a message to all Sea Org members who were not on the Rehabilitation Project Force: "Don't end up on the RPF!"

He then went on to tell me how they didn't get a day off. They had to sleep in designated RPF barracks. They could be on the RPF for years or for decades in some cases. They had to run everywhere they went and if they screwed up really bad, they would be sent to the RPF's RPF. That was a separate RPF within the Rehabilitation Project Force. The penalties and punishments were worse than they were within the normal RPF and one had to get through a certain number of steps of punishment to get out of the RPF's RPF and be on the normal RPF again. I vowed right then, I would never do the Rehabilitation Project Force no matter what happened to me.

It was my fifth day on the Estates Project Force, and I was done. It was a Wednesday and when we were done studying for the day, I only had a few hours left and I could finish my course. So instead of risking that I would not complete by Thursday at 2:00 P.M., they told me to keep studying and get done today. Once I was done with the courses I would no longer be doing manual labor anyway.

Most of the other people were very surprised to see someone finish so quickly. A few other EPFers had been there for weeks or even months. I had, to my credit, already done a bulk of the required courses before I got there, so that certainly did not hurt. Lucky for me, the few courses I had already done in Scientology were on the list for the EPF.

I was supposed to get a Fitness Board in order to start working at the Association for Better Living and Education International. A group of people would review my test scores, my study record and my performance while on the Estates Project Force and decide if I was fit to join the Sea Org. Veronika Kegel at ABLE International came and met me at the Complex. She was there to pick me up and get me over to ABLE Int. I was done with the Estates Project Force and getting out of there!

The Landscape is Changing

I arrived at the Association for Better Living and Education. The first thing that Veronika told me was that I would start by answering the phones. I was confused. I asked her where I was being posted. She said that once my Fitness Board was approved and I was found fit for the Sea Org, my post would be assigned. But for now, I would sit at reception, answer the phones when they rang and direct incoming calls accordingly.

Before I began, I needed to go down the street and get a tie, some nice slacks and a dress shirt. Unlike the rest of the Sea Org staff, ABLE Int staff wore Uniform "K" – or "civvies" as they called them – civilian clothes.

She showed me how to use the phone system and gave me a short list of 15 staff that worked at ABLE Int.

Most of the calls were for the Registrars, Dick Story and Tom Woodruff. People were constantly coming and going for these two guys. They were either talking to someone on the phone or someone was sitting in front of them at their desks. They were asking people to donate money for Narconon, Criminon, Applied Scholastics or the Way to Happiness. Veronika explained to me that they needed to make at least $300,000 per week to meet their quota.

Everyone else seemed to sit at their computers all day and type and that was it. The Executive Director of ABLE was a white South African lady who claimed to have been in the Sea Org since she was 16 years old. She must have been in her late 30s so she had been in awhile. Her name was Rena Weinberg. She had just been brought over from South Africa where she had been the head of an Applied Scholastics group over there. Her husband was over The Way to Happiness fundraising area.

Veronika kept checking in on me and giving me extra things to do. It did not take me long to figure out that everything I was now doing were functions she had done herself before I had shown up. I was answering the phones, writing letters, filing, taking out the trash, cleaning the reception, you name it, it was my job and it all had to be done each day.

Veronika also let me in on the fact that at ABLE they never used full words, EVERYTHING was abbreviated:

Applied Scholastics = APS
The Way to Happiness = TWTH
Narconon was said "Narconon" but spelled "NN"
Criminon was said "Criminon" but spelled "CN"
Social Betterment Corporations = SBCs
Hollywood Guaranty Building = HGB
Western United States = WUS
Promotional materials = promo
Eastern United States = EUS
Trained and Processed (lists of all types of Scientologists) = T&P
Statistics = Stats
Gross Income = GI
Letters Out = LO
Letters In = LI
Bulk Mail = BMO
Veronika was the Supercargo or S/C
The Executive Director was the ED
Flag Banking Officer = FBO
The Treasury Secretary was the Treas Sec
The Dissemination Secretary was the Dissem Sec
Cycle of Action or Start - Change – Stop = "a cycle"

The list went on forever.

I could not believe how abbreviated everything was. Later that day, Veronika told me something that would illustrate this to the core.

She said, "The ED ordered that I go over to PAC and see the Dissem Secs from ASHO and AO and get the WUS and EUS T&P BMO lists that we use each week for our SBC promo. I should be back here at the HGB by dinner. If the FBO or Treas Sec ask where I went, can you tell them that I am on a GI cycle for the stats."

That translates into, "The Executive Director ordered that I go to the complex to pick up some mailing lists for our promotion, I will be back by dinner. If anyone asks for me, that's where I will be."

Days went by and finally I got my Fitness Board approved. It was a piece of paper that said I was fit for the Sea Org. It was actually a letdown when I saw it. I was expecting a big meeting where I'd be questioned in front of a board of people. It was nothing like that at all. In fact, after I read it, I got the impression that it was just rubber stamped and printed. I never met any of the people who approved it or even heard of them for that matter.

Veronika told me that based on my test scores; I would be posted in HCO at ABLE Int. I would be doing the same things I was already doing. There were no people posted in the entire division of HCO at ABLE. HCO was the Hubbard Communications Office. This was the area responsible for personnel, communications and ethics. Veronika's post was the Supercargo ABLE Int. She was over the first four divisions of ABLE, the Executive Division, Hubbard Communications Office Division, the Dissemination Division and the Treasury Division. There were three or four people in the Executive Division, two people in Dissem, nobody in Treasury and no one in HCO. Veronika was the HAS HFA, or Held From Above. Anytime someone on the org board had to do jobs underneath them, this was called HFA. Veronika was wearing all of the posts in HCO HFA.

So now that I was temporarily posted in the Hubbard Communications Office, I was the HCO Area Secretary, the division head over HCO. I was surely not going to Narconon Chilocco in Oklahoma to kick back on the Indian reservation anytime soon. I was also going to be responsible for all of the posts below me that were not filled. This was another signpost moment. I spotted it, but I had gone a bit too far down the rabbit hole at this point. If I left now, I would end up with a "Freeloader's Bill", an invoice for the cost of the courses I had completed so far, and would face disciplinary actions or justice actions for leaving the Sea Org.

My posting was approved and HCO Area Secretary it was. As far as I knew, I was the youngest division head in the building. It was more depressing than it was impressive. I was going to have to do all of the functions of the entire division on my own. I could not complain about people since that was one of my departments! The Executive Director, Rena Weinberg, told me that I had to get more people! She briefed me on how Martha and Boris (the two people that recruited me) were supposed to get another 10 people into ABLE before they could do their new project and that this would help, but that I needed to get some new people on my own.

There was also the matter of the statistics. I had a number of these that I had to report each week. Every single Scientology organization in the world had to report their statistics each week. It was sort of a ritual. The week ended at precisely 2:00 P.M. on Thursday. Anything that happened up until that point in the week was counted and reported up. All of these statistics from all around the world were being funneled to a great big think tank that would analyze the statistics and give direction on how to get them back up from going down or further up. No matter who was or wasn't reviewing them, I had to make sure that I kept track of all of the stats I was responsible for or heavy penalties would be assessed.

Among these statistics were Bulk Mail Out, Letters Out and Letters In as well as Admin Personnel / Tech Personnel. My life would revolve around these stats. For bulk mail out, I would get mailing lists from the Complex and then get the lists to the bulk mail house company who'd receive the promo from commercial printers and then mail out all these glossy fliers.

For letters out, I would have to sit at reception and type hundreds of form letters to lists of people that had donated money to ABLE Int and ask them to donate more money.

For new recruits, I would also write letters to all of the people that had filled out any personnel surveys or info questionnaires that ABLE Int had.

Bulk mail out and letters seemed easy enough to get out each week. I just had to make sure that I did a bit more each week. Week after week, no new staff showed up. Martha and Boris had gotten a bunch of people to the Estates Project Force, but none were graduating and making it to ABLE Int.

I was also in charge of Chinese School at the three daily meetings, or musters. Each day all of the crew had to line up by division in front of the org board of ABLE Int and learn every section of the board verbatim. We had to learn all of the posts, divisions and valuable final products for all areas of ABLE Int. We did this for 15 minutes each day or until the Executive Director, Rena Weinberg, said that we were done.

ABLE Int's Valuable Final Product was "*Subvert the subverters by creating an overwhelming popularity for LRH's social betterment technology and cause a total revolution in the fields of drug rehabilitation, education, criminal reform and morality."*

I was not sure how my writing form letters every day was "subverting any subverters" but I did them anyway. After weeks and weeks of getting no new recruits, I had to try something different. I had been assigned lowered conditions several times and was going to be given a Committee of Evidence if I did not get some recruits into ABLE. Lowered Conditions were a set of policies by LRH that dictated steps that one had to do based on Conditions of Existence. There were higher states such as "AFFLUENCE" and "POWER" and then there were the ones used as punishment within the Sea Org such as "LIABILITY". If you were assigned lowered conditions over and over again and did not respond with increased statistics or "upstats" then you would get a Committee of Evidence, or Comm Ev. This was an ad hoc group of other staff members who acted as a military tribunal and meted out justice to fellow staff members who weren't performing up to par. A Comm Ev could assign you hours and hours of amends or even worse, assign you to the Rehabilitation Project Force. I started going after people I knew. I called or wrote every kid I knew from Delphi. I wrote to all of the people in the files. I even called my sister in Oregon. Stephanie was going to Delphi up there. That was the boarding school version of what we had in LA. She was there for the summer. After a few hours on the phone with her I succeeded, she was going to come to LA and meet with me! I might get someone.

My sister took about three hours to join once she met me in LA. I showed her the building I worked in, told her how much money I was making, conveniently left out the part about getting my butt kicked to get new people and told her how utterly awesome everything was. She joined. I had gotten someone in! It was a miracle. I had just turned 16, so that made her 15. When she got off the Estates Project Force I knew exactly where she could work, with me in the Hubbard Communications Office. I would make her the Cope Officer. The Cope Officer is the junior below the HCO Area Secretary. The Cope Officer is supposed to do just that, "cope," while the HAS gets more people to enlist as new Sea Org members.

My sister took a bit longer to get through the Estates Project Force. It turned out that the guy running the program, and who had gotten me through the Estates Project Force, was not only reading Playboy magazines in his office, he was sleeping with one of the younger female recruits in his office. They'd eventually blow the Sea Org together. After this there was a big shakedown on the Estates Project Force and a few more people were sent to the decks or to the Rehabilitation Project Force for not reporting any of the lewd behavior of their former boss. Steph completed the EPF a few weeks later and sure enough, she became the Cope Officer at ABLE Int. I could now spend all my time trying to get recruits and get more people into all areas of ABLE!

Two months and zero recruits later, I was up for a Comm Ev. I hadn't recruited anyone else, and Stephanie had been false reporting how many letters were being written. It was a disaster. I was going in front of a Committee of Evidence and there was no way around it.

I was a wreck. I was interviewed by a bunch of people on why I did not get any recruits into ABLE Int. I had no good answers as to why I was so bad at getting people into the Sea Org. The only thing I could come up with was the Sea Org was not a very glamorous place where people wanted to work. I also brought up that I was supposed to be in Narconon Chilocco and was not supposed to have been assigned to ABLE, that wasn't what was promised to me. They would have none of it.

The committee decided that I was improperly posted, in fact the posting was illegal and that while I was a useless recruiter, I never should have been put on the post in the first place. I was reassigned until properly posted. All I could think of was that I was NOT going to the Rehabilitation Project Force.

Now that my sister was my boss, so to speak, she had me writing her letters on a full time basis. Between writing letters for her, I was also working in the Treasury Division. I was filing and getting the accounts in order. The Flag Banking Officer was doing all the Treasury functions which was not her job, so anything I did was helping her.

The Flag Banking Officer was part of the finance network, which was internationally based at "Int". Int was a mysterious place that was where all orders and some people came from every once in a while. No one knew where "Int" was or how to get there, but it was where all of the head honchos in the Sea Org were posted. The Flag Banking Officer was going back to Int and someone else was supposed to take over for her. As part of this turnover, the new person on the post was not supposed to be doing any treasury functions, instead it would be done entirely by Treasury staff, which was comprised of only me. The Flag Banking Officer told me that I should tell everyone that I was going to be the Treasury Secretary and that was that. I wasn't sure about this, since my last Division head post did not turn out very well.

After a few weeks, the new finance person arrived on post and I was introduced to him as the Treasury Secretary. I went along with it and no one said anything different. No posting order, no red tape. I had just decided to help and it became my official post.

I did well with my new title. Besides being good with numbers, I really liked money! I did all the payroll, checks, and bills, kept all the files, did bank deposits, etc. I became extremely skilled on issues that had to do with business taxes and how filings for the IRS were done. It was 1989, I was 16 years old and doing taxes for an international company that made hundreds of thousands of dollars, probably millions actually. There was a huge project going on at the Complex, called the Audits Tax Force. The tax force was comprised of different treasury staff from organizations all over the place that were responsible for the tax filings for their organization. Everything within the tax project was reviewed by two staff members, Ellen Reynolds and Coby Knight. They worked in the Int Finance Office and were regarded as the gods of taxes in Scientology. There were rules we had to follow to make sure that all of the laws were being adhered to in terms of taxes being taken out of pay, and which staff members were under a certain age. There were hundreds of kids throughout the Sea Organization who were under-age and they had lists of all of them! I saw the list once and it was pages and pages long. I was told that those kids were worth more than they were being paid in a year just in terms of a tax write off! I was amazed at how much paperwork there was involved in dealing with taxes.

There was one point where it was debated that ABLE Int staff members should not be getting minimum wage because the other Sea Org units weren't paid even a fraction of minimum wage. They were paid $35 per week. For a few weeks, I was instructed to make out all of the payroll checks to the staff, and then have them sign the checks back over to the organization. This way, the money was paid out on the books, but the staff would "donate" it back to the institution. The first week I tried this was a nightmare. First, the staff weren't going along with the idea very well. The few who did endorse their checks told me that they would be reporting this to the Executive Director, Rena Weinberg. Then, when I got to the bank to deposit the few checks I had, the teller gave me a weird look and brought her supervisor over. He flat out refused to deposit the checks. He explained to me that you cannot have employees sign over checks back to the company. Big no-no. I ended up giving everybody back their checks and telling them it was a big mistake.

Later, when I went back to the Audits Tax Force, they told me that the minimum wage would continue at ABLE Int until something else was sorted out. There was too much scrutiny from the IRS to screw everything up on behalf of the Association for Better Living and Education's tiny payroll.

One day while sitting at my desk someone came up to my cubicle and said "Hey!"

It was Jesse Radstrom. He had been posted in Clearwater, Florida for the last year or so and I had not seen him once. He was in LA?

"Hey, man!" I said as I shook his hand. "What the hell are you doing here?"

"I'm here getting my clearances so I can go to Int," he said.

"Wow, some big shot we have here, folks!" I answered back.

We chatted for a few minutes and then he said that he had to go. We would meet on Hollywood Blvd and grab a bite of pizza for dinner.

We ended up going across the street from the Hollywood Guaranty Building. He told me about how he and Ali Mintz had been dating off and on but how she had left Clearwater and was already posted at Int. He was going to become staff in the Watchdog Committee, which was responsible for overseeing progress in several different areas of Scientology internationally.

He told me that he was in the process of getting security checked full time and once he was done, he would be posted at the International Base. Sec checking was when someone asked you a predetermined list of questions about things that were considered unethical, such as promiscuity, drug use, etc. and the person administering the check watched the E-Meter to see if it reacted to the questions. If you were "clean" and had nothing to hide, the needle on the E-Meter would "float" across the dial and the questioning was continued until the person had a floating needle on all the questions.

Anyone going to the international headquarters was asked pages and pages of questions during the security check to make sure that only the best people went up to the base. I had never had a security check before, but Jesse assured me he had received several security checks while in Clearwater. We wrapped up and went back over to the Hollywood Guaranty Building.

As we walked up Ivar Street to go through the staff entrance, a few people were walking from the parking lot across the street. One of the guys seemed to know Jesse and I hung back a bit while Jesse talked to this guy I had never seen before. He was rather short and had bars on his shirt, like military stripes, and all sorts of campaign badges signifying he was highly ranked. They talked about how Jesse had just arrived to LA and was expecting to be up at Int within the next few weeks. The high-ranking muckety-muck told Jesse that he would be expecting him and walked off with a few people in tow.

As we walked away, I asked Jesse who that guy was. He looked at me as if I was insane. He asked, "You don't know who that is? That was David Miscavige — COB RTC!"

Perplexed, I asked, knowing the reaction would probably be similar to the first question, "So, who is David Miscavige — COB RTC?"

"He is only the highest ranking Sea Org member in the whole world!" Jesse exclaimed while putting his hands above his head motioning how high this guy was. "Religious Technology Center is the highest org in all of Scientology, and he is Chairman of the Board!"

"And you know him how?" I asked, now that he told me he knew *the* guy to know in the Sea Org.

"He was in Clearwater a lot while I was there. I was in the Commodore's Messenger organization in Clearwater, and they take care of anything and everything for COB while he is there," Jesse told me as we rode the elevator to my floor. "Commodore Messenger Org Clearwater. That is where I was posted before I came here to get my clearances for the International Base. That is how I got recommended for Int. I think COB put in a good word for me."

"Well, I got to go man," I told him as I got out at my floor.

"I will see you around," Jesse said as the elevator doors closed.

I hadn't seen Jesse in at least a year, but he seemed like the same guy, just a little tamer than I remembered. And this Dave Miscavige, COB RTC character seems to be some sort of big shot, too. I wonder if the ABLE guys know about him.

At the dinner roll call, the crew was frantically running around. The Executive Director said to skip roll call and that she needed to get everybody into production right away!

"Chairman of the Board is in the building!" she said frantically as the staff showed up for the evening round up. "Get on post and get busy! Make sure your areas are clean and make sure that if COB walks in, you stand at attention!"

The staff members scattered in every direction. Wow. They did know who this COB guy was. For the next hour people were frantically stashing things in drawers and clearing off their desks, marking their stat graphs, clearing out the communication baskets and doing all of the things that were supposed to have been done throughout the week.

The Executive Director's assistant, Danielle, came over to get something from me and started giving plausible ways that Mr. Miscavige got in the building undetected. "I'll bet he has a special entrance," she said.

I answered back, matter of factly, "I think he just walked in the front entrance during dinner time. My friend and I were talking to him down on the street before he came in."

"What?" she said as she started running back to the Executive Director's office, "Sir, Sir, Marc spoke with COB on the street."

"Marc! Get in here!" Rena shouted from her office.

I had to tell them in detail what happened, who said what and when in excruciating detail.

"Do you realize if you have some sort of communication cycle with COB and we do not know about it, we can get in trouble? It puts us in an instant Danger Condition as we are being bypassed by COB. We have to know anytime this happens," Rena explained to me.

Wow, I had no idea Dave Miscavige was such a big deal. Up until today I had never even heard of him before.

"Did Ray Mithoff or Marc Yager say anything to you?" Rena asked.

"I have no idea who those people are," I answered back, perplexed.

Under COB were three Inspector Generals, for Tech, Ethics and Admin.

After Rena explained to me who held these posts, I realized these must have been two of the guys that were with Dave when he was down on the street. Inspector General for Tech, Ray Mithoff, and Inspector General for Admin, Marc Yager. The fact that they were both over six feet tall actually seemed to accentuate how short Dave Miscavige was.

Just as Rena was explaining the chain of command, that these guys worked directly under COB and were also the highest executives in all of Scientology, we heard someone in ABLE Int reception say "Good evening, Sir!" We jumped up and I ran off to my cubicle.

Rena and her assistant headed towards the reception area.

It was Inspector General for Admin, Marc Yager. Rena met him there and started showing him around the office. He seemed very interested in each area and opened desk drawers, looked through paper baskets on desks and even looked through trash baskets. When he came to my area, he asked me if I had any bills in my drawers that had not been entered into the computer. I did not and said so. He promptly went to the next area. As he walked away from my cubicle, I felt a great relief.

From everything I had heard, these types of inspections could change everything. This was pretty stressful. If these guys find something considered wrong, you could be in the Rehabilitation Project Force in a matter of minutes.

About 20 minutes later, the Inspector General for Admin had left our office and proceeded next door to do an inspection of WISE Int (World Institute of Scientology Enterprises).

Rumor spread that Marc Yager thought the place was filthy and that we needed to get the place cleaned up. But we could not clean yet, because COB could come in at any second and we had to be in production, not cleaning. We normally worked until 10:30 P.M. and took buses or got a ride with someone who had a car to the apartments down the street from the Complex. That would not be the case tonight. We stayed on "production" until midnight. At midnight we were mustered up and briefed on what had happened with the inspection. Marc Yager had found dust in the reception area behind one of the main doors. One of the registrars also had a dirty ashtray on his desk. That was it. Because of this, the place was deemed "filthy" and we had to stay tonight and get the entire place "white glove" clean.

After we thought we were done cleaning, we had to call someone from Commodore's Messenger Org International Extension Unit. When they got around to it, someone would come down and wipe random surfaces with a white cotton glove on one hand. If ANY dust was collected, or if the glove was soiled in any way, we would flunk and had to fix it along with any other spots that had not been thoroughly done and then request another inspection. If you flunked, you could count on at least another hour before you would be re-inspected. White Gloves could go on for hours until someone finally gave up and said to go home. One time we never left. We got a pass at 7:00 A.M. and there was not enough time to get home and back in time for morning muster, instead we slept a few minutes at our desks and went to breakfast. We eventually got to the point of requesting an inspection at 4:00 A.M.! Luckily, the CMO guys had all gone home already, so we got to leave at 5:00 A.M.

The next day, we slugged through our work for the day. Around dinner time, we found out a bunch of executives got in trouble for keeping their crews late the night before. Apparently more inspections were done today and some guy who had been up all night cleaning was sleeping at his desk when COB walked in. This was classic. If the place was dirty, it had to be cleaned. But we only had 15 minutes of cleaning time and no one really did it unless under great pressure. So whenever some executive flapped about the place being dirty, people were kept up all night to clean by their superiors. When someone was found sleeping the next day, the execs didn't catch any heat, just the seniors of the groggy staff. Either way, we were told every single person in the building was going to go home on time tonight. No disagreements from me on that one.

Later that week, Miscavige and the Inspector Generals went back to wherever they came from and things started going back to normal. I learned from talking with different staff members, the executives from Religious Technology Center were only around for a few hours. The resultant chaos would last a few weeks, but at least we were being ordered home every night on time. A few weeks later, Jesse would complete his clearances and disappear to the International Base.

The Policy of Truth

I finally settled into my routine at ABLE Int as the Treasury Secretary. I was relatively happy with the way things were working out. I was getting paid about $250 per week, I had very few expenses and no time to spend the money I was making. I had several thousand dollars saved up and I was able to buy myself a lot of new clothes and personal items when I needed them.

My sister was also doing well. She was still in the Hubbard Communications Office and her division had gotten at least one or two other staff. One was a Mexican girl who was made the Master at Arms, her name was Betty Gonzalez. She was responsible for checking up on all the staff and made sure they were doing what they were supposed to and when they were supposed to be doing it. I am not sure what Stephanie told this girl, but she seemed to have a little bit more time for me than most everyone else at ABLE. If I was EVER slacking off in any way, Betty would show up. I was certain that Betty had it in for me. I didn't make much effort to avoid her, but when she got on my case about something, I ignored her. She didn't like my attitude and made sure to make me aware of this.

One morning, our entire staff was briefed on a mission that had arrived from the International Base and that several staff members were going to be interviewed. A mission usually comprised of two or more Sea Org Members who were sent from a Sea Org base to resolve a situation on an urgent basis. ABLE had sent out a few missions to Narconons and some even to Applied Scholastics to resolve situations or local issues. Generally, when a mission showed up, it had been sent from a higher echelon and whatever the mission personnel ordered, that was what you did. Turns out there was a list of people they would be bringing back to the International Base.

As the day passed, someone told me they had seen the list and that my sister's name was on it! That was fine by me. I didn't know much about the mysterious base except that it seemed to be the place where the executives hung out. Other than that, if my sister got promoted, I was happy for her. I didn't expect I would be promoted any time soon since I had just been taken off my previous post of HCO Area Secretary and was arguably a wrench in the system in terms of the average obedient staffer.

One of the missionaires met with my sister, and, sure enough, she was on the list. She would be turning her post over to Betty, the Master at Arms, and going onto her clearances. Oh, goody, security checking. I wasn't going to miss that one bit. Good luck to Stephanie. Hopefully, she would make it through the security check. If you went onto clearance lines, you could assume it meant they had reviewed your personnel file and nothing in it was bad enough to disqualify you for a certain posting or being posted at the International Base. The further up the echelons of Scientology you go, the stricter the qualifications. When you made it to Int, you could eventually move higher to Religious Technology Center, which had the strictest qualifications of any organization in the world of Scientology. You had to have been a saint your entire life in order to qualify. A lot of people conveniently leave things out of their life history and personnel forms, such as when they stole something from a store, or got arrested for smoking pot, or anything that they did not want to reveal. These were the sort of things that came up in the sec checking on the E-Meter. If you had some deep dark secret that you never wanted to tell someone, it would come out after 50-200 hours of being interrogated on the E-Meter, which to most people would be the equivalent of being hooked up to a lie detector machine and interrogated for hours on end about your innermost thoughts and secrets.

Some people that were qualified "on paper" were routinely never sent as things came up in security checking that disqualified them. These people were usually posted somewhere in LA or sometimes at the Hollywood Guaranty Building. Sometimes if things came up that were considered severe, they would be kicked out of the Sea Org. The worst case I had heard of was a guy who worked at ABLE Int and previously at Narconon. Prior to working at Narconon, he was a student at Narconon, translation: he was a recovered drug addict. His secret wasn't safe and it came up, supposedly in a sec checking session, that he used to share needles with a girl that was now HIV+. After he got out of session he was rushed to a local testing facility and sure enough he was HIV+. He was escorted out of the building and the Sea Org within an hour. No one saw him again.

So Stephanie better not have left anything off of her life history forms! Not that she had been sharing needles with someone or could have done anything that potent, she was 15 years old and she had never gotten in any kind of trouble that I could remember.

Two of the missionaires came and saw me in my area. I assumed they were there to brief me about Stephanie going onto clearance lines. They introduced themselves and gave me a telex to read. Scientology still used TELEXES in 1990! Yes, they had a whole numbering system and they had to be formatted a certain way and there was actually a course on how to write them! Anyway, they gave me this telex which was a few paragraphs about how International Management was gearing up to do the biggest dissemination in the history of Scientology and a lot of people were needed to move to the headquarters to make this happen. Following the text was a list of 50 people who were named to take part in this dissemination. A few of the people I knew, but for the most part it was a list of people that I had never heard of before. I saw my sister's name and I was like okay, I gave them back the telex. They asked me how I felt about this and I said that I was happy for my sister and I wished her luck. They looked at each other a bit puzzled and told me to read the list again.

I didn't read the entire list after I reached my sister's name, I had already seen a ton of names that meant nothing to me. But there it was, clear as could be – my damn name! My name was on this list! I couldn't believe it. I thought that surely someone had screwed up, how the hell did my name end up on this list? I wasn't officially posted as it was. I had just been removed from a post and I was the local screw off at ABLE. Also, I was only 16 and had no experience doing anything. Why was my name on this list? Then I got to the bottom of the list and read the name of the person who had written the telex and compiled the list: Watchdog Committee Programs. That was my old friend from Delphi – Ali Mintz. She had put my sister and me on the list because she knew us. What a scam! How was I possibly going to get through a security check? Hopefully, I wouldn't end up on the Rehabilitation Project Force from whatever came up.

The missionaires could see from the look on my face that I had seen my name. This telex took on a whole different meaning now. I actually re-read the entire thing now that it affected me and was not just some random order that had come down from the glass ceiling. I was in a tricky spot. I can't refuse a promotion. It is sort of like admitting you have skeletons in the closet, or a myriad of other things, but it boils down to the fact that you are defying their code of ethics no matter what your reason is for refusing. Just then, I thought of the policy about someone having to be replaced before they could move to another post. This was my saving grace. It would take months for another person to be recruited to fill my post, and even then, they would have to do the entry program, and then I would have to turn everything over and the IRS tax stuff would have to be completed. So I hoped everything would go okay and that I would make it through this if I was ever replaced on my post. I grinned and thanked them for coming.

I asked them what they had planned for my replacement. Technically there was a bit of a loophole on that part, because I was never *officially* posted as the Treasury Secretary, I did not officially have to be replaced. I was essentially free to go!

I wrote up what I did each day and handed this over to the new Cope Officer, Betty. The look on Betty's face was priceless. I was being promoted and Betty, my watchdog, could not stand to see it happening.

Most of the people who worked on clearances were part of the Commodore's Messenger organization. They worked on the 11th floor and were younger girls and a few guys. They had an exact system of what someone needed to do to get through clearances and proceed on to the International Base. The problem was that not many people had been getting approved for the promotion and a lot of people were held up on the security check because their dirty laundry started to air out.

I couldn't imagine how I would get through my own sec checking when I had skipped school for a full year and was your average unruly child and caused my share of trouble.

The person in charge of the clearance unit was a girl named Claudia Olander. Claudia was from Europe but you could barely tell. She had been in the United States long enough to lose most of her accent, but she was Swiss. She had long dark hair and was slender. She was in her early twenties and I thought she was one of the hottest girls in the building. I had a hard time listening to her when she was talking to me as my mind would wander. Anyway, she was nice.

I spent the first day of my clearances doing tests and filling out "Life History" forms. They were exactly that. I had to write down my entire life up to this point. This included ANY sexual experiences I had had, with who and what dates they occurred. I had to list every friend I had, past and present, relatives names and where they lived, anything about my life had to be on the form.

My auditor—Scientology "counsellor"—was a woman named Pat Bromley. She was from the Senior Case Supervisor International Office. She was an older, slender, sort of cute blonde woman who seemed pretty happy whenever I saw her. She was someone who, even if you imagined them mad or upset, you could at the same time picture them giving you a cookie. She was seemingly incapable of anger. She was the perfect auditor for me. We started with the sec checking and she was asking me about all sorts of things that I was not expecting:

Was I a reporter for a newspaper? Was I a plant? Did I have ties to any pharmaceutical companies? Had I ever been hypnotized? Had I ever been electro shocked? Had I taken Angel Dust? Was I an undercover operative for a government agency? Had I ever publicly spoken badly about Scientology in a media article? Was I wanted by the Police? Did I have family that were employed by the government or did they have upper level security clearances? The questions went on for pages and pages. Every once in awhile she would stop and ask me if I was thinking about anything. I responded "No, just that I am not involved in any of these things you are asking me about." After the first batch of questions, she informed me that I did not need to answer each of them with a verbal response, and that the E-Meter would in fact give her my answer. So instead of saying "no" after every question she asked, I could just sit there and stare at her, the wall or the E-Meter itself. Cool. This will be a breeze.

My sec checking took three full days. It seemed like there were hundreds and hundreds of questions. After the first few hours during the first day, I zoned out and focused on not falling asleep. I thought to myself how unbelievable it was that it took people months to get through this, people must have had "yes" answers to the questions for it to take longer than a few days. Pat was happy, I was happy. As far as I could tell, we were done.

But after the initial list of questions, there was another list that was about the previous list! I was in shock. A list of questions about the list I was just asked about. This time another guy asked me this new list. His name was Bruce Hines, who also worked in the Senior Case Supervisor International Office. He seemed cool and the list wasn't as long. Had I lied about an answer? Had I thought about another answer when asked a question? Did I purposely influence the E-Meter to get out of answering a question? All I could think about while he was asking me questions is that I had not answered any questions! I had sat there thinking about nothing or how Pat was kind of hot and even though she was at least 15 years older than me, she seemed like she could be decent in the sack! And if I was not thinking about Pat, I was imagining going a few rounds with Claudia!

After Bruce was done he told me that the folder would go up and that the completed staff work for my promotion should be completed in the next few days.

I headed back up to the Clearance Unit and Claudia told me that my promotion proposal was going to Int tonight for review! It was Tuesday and I could potentially be approved and at the International Base by Thursday if we were lucky. The promotion proposal was a Completed Staff Work. If you want to do anything in the Sea Org, you have to have a Completed Staff Work approved in order to get authorization to work. If you wanted to go see your mom who was in town for a day, you had to get a CSW approved in order to do so.

Most of the people in the clearance unit were amazed that I had zipped through my entire sec check in under a week. Claudia had written so many CSWs for Clearances, she had already written the CSW and just plopped my name in the appropriate places. She asked me to help her pump up how awesome I was and how I should go to the International Base. After all was said and done, we managed to make my unimpressive history look like I was God's gift to the Sea Org.

The promotion proposal would now be sent to the headquarters and we would be informed if there were questions. Claudia told me there were always questions and these things could sometimes go back and forth for weeks before being either approved or disapproved.

The next day I hung out in the clearance office and helped Claudia with her work. I was bringing folders to people in the building and gathering up tests from people and doing busy work while we waited for the results.

It was after lunch when Claudia got a call from the International Base. They could not figure out how I qualified for promotion while only being in the Sea Org for nine months. There was a qualification that you had to have at least one year of experience in the Sea Org before moving up to the headquarters. Claudia told them that I had worked at Delphi for six months and that between that and ABLE, I was qualified. They bought it. They told her that my promotion proposal was going on to the last approval terminal and that we should hear back later that night.

At 8 P.M., Claudia came in to the office where I was grading someone's tests and told me that I was approved! Holy shit, that was fast! I am really going. This is really happening. She said that I was going to be taken to my apartment to get my stuff and that I was going to be taken to the base tonight. I could only imagine how long it would take to get there, given I had no clue where the International Base was.

The location of Int was strictly confidential, no one actually spoke about where it was or anything about it for that matter. If you knew where it was or had been there and told anyone about this, you, along with anyone you told, would instantly be assigned to the Rehabilitation Project Force! For this reason, I had never really thought about its location, but figured it to be somewhere north of Los Angeles. Everyone always referred to it as "up" so I assumed it was north, maybe Sacramento or San Francisco. I had seen a few pictures of "Gold", short for Golden Era Productions, and also known as the International Base, and everything was always so green. This, factored in with the "up," Int must have been somewhere very green.

A black gal named Renee Norton met me in the clearance unit. She stood out because there were only about 10 black people that I had ever seen in Scientology, so I remembered that I had seen this woman around. She had a few gold bars on her shoulder boards and everyone was always calling her "Sir'. In the Sea Org you call any senior officer "Sir" regardless of their sex. Renee told me that she was the Supercargo Golden Era Productions and that she would be driving me to my new home at Gold.

We went to the parking lot across from the Hollywood Guaranty Building. She led me to a run-down Red Nissan Hatchback that sat parked in the lot. "Wow, this thing is going to make it all the way up to Int?" I hoped so.

We stopped by my apartment near the complex and grabbed my clothes and a few of my things. She said that the rest of my belongings would be packed up and sent to me in the next few days.

We got on the road and headed to Gold.

Everything Counts

We got on the freeway and took the 101 to the 10! We're heading east. I wondered where the hell we are going. After a while I recognize the route as the same way I had been to Big Bear once or twice before. Was Gold in Big Bear?

After two hours, I suddenly woke up as we came up on a huge blue and yellow lighted sign that said Golden Era Productions in huge letters and had a crawling red digital readout below it. For a super secret place it did not seem so secret. If you drove by and did NOT see the sign, I would say that you were definitely visually impaired.

We pulled up to a guard booth that had a security guard in it. Renee said that she had "Marc Headley" with her. They look at a list in the booth and let us pass through.

Renee said that we had to go to Motor Pool and wash the car. Part of me is wondering what the hell she just said and the other part knows what she said and is wondering why the hell we are washing this heap at midnight?

We pulled into a parking spot near a huge garage and sure enough, she grabbed a hose. We made little effort to actually clean the car but went through the motions, the car *was* wet. She told me that I needed to meet with Ray McKay. He was going to be my buddy and tell me what to do. But right now, I needed to catch the bus to the barracks, or as we knew it, berthing. She gave me an apartment number and told me where the buses were leaving from, which would be my next ride.

I made my way towards where the buses would be and noticed a ton of other people heading in the same direction. I stuck out like a sore thumb. Everyone was dressed in all white Sea Org uniforms and I had on a button down long sleeve shirt and a pair of dress pants with black loafers. A few people asked me who the hell I was. I explained that I had just arrived and was looking to get to the buses.

"You're heading in the right direction. We're almost there," one guy said as we walked toward the buses. He told me that he knew who I was and that I was supposed to stay in his dorm. His name was Tom Pope. He told me that Jesse Radstrom was in the same dorm and that was how he knew me.

We got to the buses. Three old white school buses were lined up and had herds of people climbing onto each. He motioned to me that we needed to get on the last one.

"Does it matter which one we get on?" I asked.

"Yeah, they all go to different places," he said. "If you get on the wrong one, you won't end up at your berthing."

"How can you tell which one is which?" I said, noticing that there wasn't signage on any of the buses.

"Well, all the people getting on this bus live where we live, so this is our bus," he said as we jumped on the bus.

The bus looked even worse on the inside, it really was a school bus and the seats were very close together. It seated around forty people but there were at least sixty people jammed in. Tom and I were standing because most of the other people had bars and tags that said they were from Commodore's Messenger Organization International. Since I was a newbie, I figured that standing was probably my best bet and most of the guys standing up were from Golden Era Productions. At least 30 guys were standing in the aisle. I could see the other buses were just as packed. When I saw this, I remembered how the buses in LA were packed out the same way. Then I remembered a joke that we used to tell when we were kids before I ever joined the Sea Org.

It went something like this – "How many Sea Org members can you fit on a bus?"

"All of them!" Cue howls of laughter. I always thought that joke was hilarious since it was totally true. If a Sea Org bus pulled up, it did not matter how many Sea Org members were standing there, when it pulled away, they would all be gone. Sea Org buses were like magic portals that swallowed them up and it seemed that it could fit any number of them in any configuration no matter what size it was.

It was definitely the end of the day, and most of the people on the bus smelled like they had put in a full day's work. The bus was ripe and every window was opened.

As we were getting ready to pull out the gate off the property, a list was being passed back through the bus and each person had to write their name on the list and pass it along. A security guard also got onto the bus and walked through looking at each person. When he got to me, he asked if I was the new guy. I told him I was and he walked past.

"What's up with that?" I asked Tom.

"Everybody has to be accounted for. There is a record of every person that comes and goes from the base," he told me as the bus made its way to the gates.

All the gates were remotely operated from the main security booth Tom told me as we saw it open and the bus drive out.

"Where are we going?" I asked Tom as we turned left out of the gate.

"We are going to a place called Devonshire in Hemet. There are a bunch of apartments where a lot of base staff live," he said.

We drove down mostly one road for the entire 15 minutes on the way to the Devonshire. At one point during the drive, the most noxious smell filled the bus and I appeared to be the only person reacting to it. As I looked around the bus, my eyes met with Tom and he smiled and simply said, "Turkey farm."

"Where do the other buses go?" I asked Tom. I noticed a bus in front of us as we drove down the road.

"Well, there is Devonshire, the one we are on, then there is Kirby, Hillside or 'Hill Slide' as we call it, then you have the Religious Technology Center berthing. Then there are a bunch of places that are next to the Base where people live. Oh, and there is the Ranch, or Happy Valley, as it is sometimes called. And some people live on the base itself and don't ever leave. That covers where the buses go. Most of the bus drivers live at the places they drive to, so if you get on the wrong bus, you will have to walk to your proper berthing from wherever the bus stops. That is usually a good one-hour walk depending on which wrong bus you get on. You could talk the driver into dropping you off, but it will cost you. They are not going to do it for free. Just don't get on the wrong bus!" he explained to me, chuckling at the end.

We rolled up to Devonshire and the bus stopped in the middle of the parking lot. Everyone piled out and scattered like roaches. I walked with Tom to my new apartment.

We walked in and there were two guys already in the apartment, Paul and another guy. It was a two-bedroom place and there were four guys in each bedroom and two more guys who stayed in the living room. The place was not that great. It was almost identical to the place I had been at in LA, in terms of size and roommates. The outside grounds were a bit nicer, but any apartment you cram 10 guys into is going to suck about the same.

As I got acquainted with the guys already there, a few more walked in. Jesse was one of them.

We talked for a bit and then he showed me where I was supposed to sleep. It's 1:00 A.M. I really should have gotten to bed. I brushed my teeth and had a quick shower. When I got out of the bathroom, the place was dark and everybody was out cold.

I climbed into my bunk and as I lay there staring at the ceiling, I wondered to myself if I was going to last very long at this place.

At 7 A.M., Tom shook my bed and said, "Get up, dude. You don't have much time before the bus leaves."

I shaved and dressed quickly and we were out waiting for the bus at 7:40. Tom told me that it would come any minute.

Now that it was light outside, I could see the smelly turkey farm as we drove by. It was located on Sanderson Street. I could see that the entire area surrounding the Devonshire apartments was a mix between new tract houses and spread out farming community. Most houses had at least two or three cars or trucks parked in the yard and at least one looked like it had not been driven in years.

As we got near the base, the list was passed around; Tom wrote his and my names on the list and gave it to the people seated behind us.

We pulled into the base, the list was handed off to the guard in the booth and we pulled up along a pathway that led to a large building with people streaming in both entrances from the buses being unloaded.

"This is the dining hall – or Massacre Canyon Inn," Tom told me as we walked through the double doors that led into the huge hall.

The dining hall was huge. There were buffet style lines on both sides of the dining hall. Tom and I headed over to the "crew side." As we waited in line for eggs and toast, Tom explained to me that there were two sides of the dining hall. One was the crew side and the other was the officer side.

The officer side had a few stewards that served the executives. For the head honcho tables, there is a dedicated steward just for them.

"What do we have on the crew side?" I asked him looking around.

"We have ourselves, if you want something, go get it," he said.

On the officer side, everybody was sitting down eating, while on the crew side, most people were dashing around trying to get some food and crawling over each other as the "hot boxes" came out with trays of eggs and toast inside.

By the time we got to the table and set it up with plates and silverware and started eating, it was time to clean up and line up for roll call. I was not a big breakfast person anyway, so I was not that concerned with the 10 minute eating slot. I grabbed a few things off the table under direction from Tom and headed towards the trash bins and dish racks. The dining hall was a mix between a cattle drive and an assembly line. It was a science to unload the dishes into the trash, quickly file your dirty silverware into their respective bins, neatly stack your plates on the piles of dishes on the racks and then file your drinking glass back into the glass racks sitting there. Being the new guy, the line was jammed up behind me and I could sense the frustration of the people behind.

Tom was waiting at the other end smiling. "You'll get used to it," he said. "You know, you can also do two trips so you don't have your hands so full while going through."

Now he tells me.

When we got outside, Tom immediately lit up a cigarette. Camel non-filter. I myself had just started smoking a few months before and preferred Camel Lights. The Camel non-filters seemed to be the cigarette of choice around here. I noticed the night before that Jesse had also smoked those.

Tom told me to follow him to where we would have muster.

Muster is where everybody from any given Sea Organization is rounded up, lined up and accounted for. Every single person must attend all scheduled musters throughout the day. Usually there are at least four musters each day. Breakfast, Lunch, Dinner, and mid evening. Additional musters could be held at any point during the day and penalties for not attending musters were never fun.

"What's with your uniform?" Tom asked.

"I was at the Association for Better Living and Education. We wore civvies every day of the week. I was never issued any other uniform parts," I told him, noticing that no one else was wearing civvies and that I stuck out like a sore thumb again.

"This is Building 36," Tom told me as we arrived to the muster location. As we walked towards the huge building, Renee Norton, the Supercargo, came up and told me that she would tell me where to stand. Tom walked over with us and told me to just stand behind him. He said that he was in the Hubbard Communications Office as well and I could just stand in the same line. Until I got posted, I was an Expeditor and I would stand in line with him.

As 8:30 A.M. drew closer, more and more people showed up for the muster. I had never seen this many Sea Org members in one place at one time. There must have been at least 300 people lining up. The individual lines of 10 or 15 people went down the road at least 100 yards.

At 8:29:55, a tall guy with bars on came out of the big building and stood in front of the muster lines, there were about 5 or 6 other people standing there in a line on either side of him. As he came to a stop, somebody yelled "Aten-Hut!" and everybody stood at attention.

Each division was called out, and the person in front of the line for that division yelled out who was present or accounted for. This went on division after division. It seemed to go on forever. After the last Division was called out, the tall guy said, "At ease." And everybody put one foot apart and clasped their hands behind their backs. Damn these guys were really formal! At ABLE Int, we stood around in lines and muster took about one minute start to finish. We had been here for what seemed to be at least 10 minutes and that was just roll call!

The tall guy asked if there were any announcements. Renee, the Supercargo, raised her hand, stepped forward and motioned for me to come forward as well.

"We have a new arrival, Marc Headley. He is the first arrival from the mission that went down to the Hollywood Guaranty Building!" she said. Everybody clapped.

"Thanks," I said and went back in line, mortified that I had to go up in front of everybody.

"Well, since it is Thursday, we will make this quick. Dismissed!" the tall guy belted out before I even get back into line.

"This is Ray McKay," Renee said, introducing me to an older guy who had a bit of a haggard look on his face. "He is going to do your routing form with you and get you grooved in."

"Hi," I said as people scattered around us in all directions.

"What's with the uniform?" Ray asked me as we headed into the building.

I told him, and thought I would need to get a white uniform before I was asked that another 300 times.

"Yeah, we might want to see the Uniforms Officer right off, so she can get your sizes and see what we can get for you right away," Ray said.

We went into the reception area and everything was done up in bright yellow laminate. The desks, the walls, everything. The place looked like it was designed by someone who REALLY liked that late '80s laminate look.

As Ray was explaining to me what we were going to do on the New Arrival Routing Form, we walked down the hall to see the uniforms officer. As we knocked on the door, we could hear someone screaming loudly in the office next door. The door opened and it was the tall guy with officer bars from the muster.

He was at least six foot-something tall. His hair was slicked back perfectly and not one hair was out of place. His uniform shirt was perfect. There was not one crease in the wrong place. I could have sworn it had been ironed while he was wearing it because just putting the shirt on would have caused a wrinkle somewhere. There must have been a full can of starch on his sleeves alone.

"Hello, Sir," Ray McKay said instantly as the tall guy appeared.

"Both of you get in here now!" he barked at us. "This is Ray Reiser; he will show you what to do. When all the films are out, you can go back to your routing form."

"Yes, Sir," McKay and I said in unison as the tall guy walked out of the office.

Ray Reiser was a small, frazzled, slightly crooked thin man with salt and pepper hair. He was running around stacking boxes and trying to figure out what we were going to do. In the background, he had a funky contraption of several film projectors that were simultaneously playing films on a giant white screen on the wall. All around us there were stacks of film reels, boxes, rolls of sticky labels and shelves that had projectors, empty reels, trash and anything else you could think of crammed onto them. The room also had a peculiar smell to it. It was a mix of chemicals with a bit of a funky twist to it.

"Okay, these have all been checked," Reiser pointed out. "Match the film reel up with the right film binder and then put them into a cardboard box."

"Who is the tall guy?" I asked McKay.

"That is the Commanding Officer Gold, Wendell Reynolds," McKay said. "We would be smart to hang out here until 2:00 p.m. It would not be smart to piss him off on your first day."

Ray and I looked around and tried to make sense of what Reiser had told us. There were piles of junk all over the office and after 30 minutes or so, we figured out what we needed to do and started making a pile of the boxed up films. As we did this, Reiser sat watching the films on the wall and switched the audio between them that was playing out of the 4 foot tall speaker in the corner of the room.

When I did Scientology training at Flag, I had seen a few of these films made by Golden Era Productions. I had never imagined that some tiny guy in a room full of junk was the one cranking them out.

"Do you have more packing tape?" I yelled out to Reiser loud enough to overpower the din of noise coming from the projectors and the large speaker blaring in the corner.

"Yeah," he yelled back. "On the bottom shelf by the bubble wrap."

I made my way between the metal shelves and looked on the bottom shelf. It was surprisingly empty in comparison to the rest of the office. Behind a bunch of laid out bubble wrap, which also had a sleeping bag on it, I saw a few rolls of tape that were unused.

"There is a sleeping bag down there!" I told McKay as I came back over to our makeshift packing station.

"Yeah, I would guess that Reiser has been here for a few days at least," McKay answered back.

The packing station we had set up was on a table that had film rewinds on it. There were motorized poles that the film reels went on. Underneath there was a light table that was turned on. Just then I noticed an open bottle that had paper tape on it that said "MEK" on it. There was another one right next to it that said "PERC." They looked like the bottles you have in chemistry class that are blood colored and have the little black plastic top.

"What is PERC?" I asked McKay.

"Film cleaner," McKay answered.

"Perchloroethylene," Reiser said as he walked over. He had gotten up from his Rube Goldberg projector contraption and the blaring soundtracks had stopped for now. "I use it on the films that come in from the organizations. They are really dirty and this is the only stuff that you can use to clean the films."

"Whatever reels have sticky goo on them, I use the MEK to get that off. That's Methyl Ethyl Ketone. If you see any tape residue on the end of the film or leader, use the PERC to get that off," Reiser told us.

"It seems pretty potent," I said as I squinted at the smell.

"Yeah, the fact that there is no decent airflow in this office does not help the smell," Reiser added. He told us he was going to be right back. "I need to get something," he said and walked out the door.

Not 30 seconds later, we heard more screaming. It was the Commanding Officer again. Reiser came flying through the door with the CO Gold a half second behind him. Reiser reeked of cigarette smoke as did the Commanding Officer.

"This guy does not leave this room until all of these films are turned over to delivery!" the CO yelled to us, pointing at Ray Reiser.

"Yes, Sir," all three of us answer in unison as he walked out of the office.

As soon as he was gone, Reiser said that he picked the wrong stairwell spot to take a smoke break. The Commanding Officer was right above him and bitched him out the second he spotted him.

"It's the only way I can stay awake," Reiser said, taking another sip of his stale, cold coffee.

"How long have you been up for?" I asked Reiser.

"Not that long, since Tuesday," he mumbled, firing his projectors back up. "Well, I actually did get two hours sleep last night, So I guess I shouldn't complain."

"Why is he watching the films at the same time like that?" I asked McKay.

"He has to check the picture and sound quality to make sure they can go out to the organizations," McKay answers.

"Wow, and he can do that in his sleep?" I asked. Reiser was now slumped over and had nodded off in his chair in front of the projectors.

"Ray! Wake up!" McKay shouted. Reiser straightened up and went back to "watching" the films.

By 11:50 A.M. we had packed up all the films Reiser had checked. We were cleaning up and doing busy work while we waited for him to turn the next batch over to us. I could tell from the way McKay was looking at his watch that we were not going to eat, or there would be a debate on who would get to go and grab a quick bite. Right then, Reiser started swearing and throwing his arms in the air. His switcher box had broken and the audio was no longer playing over his speaker. That meant he couldn't check any more films until he fixed it.

McKay told Reiser that we were going to lunch and we would come back afterwards to help him with whatever else he needed.

Ray did not answer us. He was already on the phone yelling at someone about "downtime." I knew he was contemplating what the Commanding Officer would do to him. I did not want to be around for that.

"What is Reiser going to do?" I asked McKay as we walked towards the mess hall.

"He's gonna have to make it go right," McKay answered, knowing that Reiser was totally screwed.

Lunch went by very quickly and before I knew it we were back at Building 36. This time muster went quickly, since it was right before 2:00 P.M. Everybody wanted to get back to post with only an hour or so left in the week.

Muster was over and we walked back to Reiser's office. There were at least four people already there hovering around his projector station. There was a rather large fellow tinkering with the audio switcher box while the CO Gold and a few other people took turns yelling at Reiser.

A few minutes after we arrived and were pretending to be busy, the audio came back on.

"Well done, Bruce!" the CO Gold said, "Now stick around in case it breaks again. And you guys, get all these films packed up and out of here."

The CO left and the other people that were with him followed close behind.

Ray introduced us, "Marc, this is Bruce Ploetz. He is the technician for this line. Bruce, this is Marc Headley."

We exchanged "hellos" and Bruce went back to tinkering with another audio switcher that he had opened up.

"Is it always like this around here?" I asked McKay.

"It depends."

"No, usually worse," Bruce piped in.

Two o'clock rolled around and most of the films were already upstairs in the delivery area. Ray and I made our way back to the reception area to get going on my routing form.

I had to see nearly 20 different people on the routing form and McKay took me around to a bunch of them. Turned out that I had to do an Int Base Orientation Course, and a bunch of the people on the routing form I would see while doing the course, so we skipped over those for now. As we walked around, I couldn't help but notice that people were not friendly towards McKay. Each and every person seemed happy enough to meet me, but they talked down to McKay like he was a dog or something.

"What's your deal?" I asked Ray.

"I just got busted off post as General Manager," McKay said, seemingly in disagreement with what he was saying.

"What is the General Manager?" I asked, never having heard of this post on any previous organizing boards I was familiar with.

"The General Manager is over all of the production divisions of Gold," he said. "Cine, Audio and Manufacturing."

"What happened that you got taken off post?"

"A whole bunch of overt products were sent out from Manufacturing, and a Committee of Evidence recommended that I be removed," he answered.

"Is that why everybody is giving you the cold shoulder?" I asked.

"Yeah, probably." We headed back to reception.

Once there, I filled out some paperwork about where my cleaning station would be and tried to find out when I would be getting the rest of my clothes and belongings from Los Angeles.

We went to dinner and after muster went back to completing the last of the routing form steps.

By the end of the night, we had completed most of the routing form, with the exception of the items that I would do on course the next day.

McKay and I parted ways and I made my way over to the bus.

I was exhausted and I smelled like a mix of MEK and PERC that had worked its way into my hands. It was 11:00 P.M. and my first day was brutal. Between the crazy morning and walking all over the grounds, I was wiped out.

I passed out on the bus ride home and woke up as we arrived at Devonshire.

I walked into the room and passed out on the bed.

"Get up, Marc!" Tom was standing next to my bed. I looked at my watch. It was 1:00 A.M. "You're smelling up the whole apartment! You smell like gas or something!"

"It's chemical stuff from Ray Reiser's office," I said as I rolled over in the bed.

"I don't give a crap what it's from, open a window and wash that stuff off. You're going to gag us to death with that smell!"

By 2:00 A.M., I was out of the shower and had removed most of the smell from my hands.

By the time my head hit the pillow, I was back asleep.

Stories of Old

The next day I started the Base Security/Public Relations Course.

The course gave the history of the International Base and what the staff were supposed to tell anyone they ran into that was NOT from the base. This was called the "shore story."

There were a ton of rules of what could and couldn't be done. There were several issues in the pack that laid out the rules and explained what was acceptable at the Int Base:

- No one could know that the base was located in Hemet. No family, no friends, no other staff from other organizations within the Sea Org, no one.
- No one could know that International Management of Scientology was here. As far as anyone in Hemet or San Jacinto was concerned, all staff at the Int Base were involved with the production of the Audio Visual materials for Scientology internationally.
- When in town for any reason, any name tags had to be removed and placed in a pocket.
- All mail was to be sent through the internal mail system. No U.S. mailboxes in town were allowed to be used for any reason whatsoever.
- No outside calls were to be made from pay phones off the property.
- All personal mail was to be mailed in unsealed envelopes. When Security received the mail, they would read it, and if it was up to security standards, it would be sealed and sent.
- Someone from Security would monitor all phone calls in or out of the base. If you wanted to make a phone call, you had to do a routing from and write a Completed Staff Work to get okay to do so.
- If you wanted to drive a car, you had to do car school. Anyone who had not completed car school was not allowed to drive for any reason whatsoever.
- If you got in an accident or got a speeding ticket, you were "off the

road." To get "back on the road" you had to re-do the part of Car School you missed or re-do the entire course if this had occurred on more than one occasion.

- No documents of any kind were ever to leave the property. Nothing was to be taken home to berthing, under any circumstances. If you were caught with any kind of documents, you would instantly be assigned the lower condition of "Enemy."
- Nothing regarding one's post or pertaining to the base could be spoken about while off the premises.
- No local taxis could be used for transport.
- No staff member was allowed to use any public transportation for any reason whatsoever. The only transport that was to be used was transport provided or personal transport if car school had been completed and proper insurance and registration were in place.
- Anyone who left the base without authorization would be considered "blown", the equivalent of what the military would refer to as AWOL.
- Any breach of any of the security rules would result in a Treason Condition assignment or possibly assignment to the Rehabilitation Project Force depending on what you did.

After studying all the rules I was required to follow, I headed down to lunch. Becoming a bit paranoid by this point, I asked some of the guys at my table about these rules.

One of the guys laughed. He said that these rules were the new "relaxed" rules! "When I first came here, I was blindfolded and came in a van with blacked out windows. I was actually here for almost 4 months before I even knew where we were!"

Before I knew it everyone was piping in. "Six years ago when I first got here, if you drove to LA, you had to be trained on how to 'lose a tail.' It took three or four hours to make the 90 minute trip to LA with all of the detours one had to take to make sure there was no one following you!" one girl at the table stated.

"What about all the guns they used to have in the Main booth?" another girl asked as people started up about all the crazy stuff that went on.

"That's nothing. When I first got here, no one could even leave the property for any reason at all. There were only one or two people that were even allowed to go off the property. I was here for one full year before I went anywhere outside the gate!" said a big burly guy before getting up to clear his plate.

It was starting to sound like a Monty Python skit. I could not tell if the guys were serious or joking. No one was laughing and no one appeared to be joking, but it sounded crazy, almost like a state penitentiary. Could they be telling the truth? As Tom and I headed to the bussing stations with our plates, he leaned over to me and said, "We really have it easy compared to the good ol' days around here, huh?"

So they were NOT joking. Wow, maybe the whole place was paranoid.

As unbelievable as it seemed, I could see how they could think this way. Instead of comparing the security rules to the freedoms most civilian people had, they were comparing it to past Int Base Sea Org members. According to most of the staff who had been around for years, compared to past times at the Int Base, we were living in a veritable Disneyland!

After studying all day, I was heading home on the bus when Tom started telling me stories about people who had been at the base for years and how we had much more freedom than anyone before.

He told me, "In the early 1980s, Hubbard was being hunted by FBI, CIA, IRS, you name it. No one knew where he was. No one in Scientology knew where he was except a few people that worked directly with him or received advices from him."

"Advices?" I ask.

"Yeah, you see LRH did not want anyone to think that he was running the organizations or any of its management. The government were trying to show that he was profiting from the organizations and that he was making all this money from Scientology. So even though he was still directly involved with telling people what to do and how to run things, "officially" he was not. So anything that he wrote was called an 'Advice.' It was not actually a directive or an order; it was just 'advice.' None of these advices were even signed or had any of his writing on them anywhere. They just had '###' at the bottom and they were from LRH. There are hundreds and hundreds of these advices on everything from the IRS, to new organizations, to how to deal with people that blow from the base."

"He wrote an advice on what to do with people that blow from the Int Base?" I ask.

"Oh yeah," Tom said without missing a beat. "You know how LRH talks about how you always leave the door a crack open for people that leave Scientology, in case they ever want to come back?"

"Yeah, that is in some ethics policies, right?" I said.

"Well in this one advice, he talks about the people that leave and says, 'If they leave from the Int Base, we close the door completely and bolt it shut!' Anyone who leaves almost automatically gets declared a suppressive person based on that one LRH advice alone."

"That is why there was all this cloak and dagger stuff going on around here. No one could know that anyone from the Int Base was in touch with LRH or they could possibly find out where he was based on this," Tom explained. "So it was decided that the best way to make sure that the people from the Int Base did not talk about anything to anyone, was to keep them all locked up here on a full time basis. That solved the problem altogether. But then there were a few cases where people went crazy and then ended up blowing or breaking out or whatever."

"What happened to those people?" I asked, preparing for what might be my future fate someday.

"Those guys get sent out to the Happy Valley," Tom said happily with almost a chuckle in his voice. "It was nicknamed that because the people that get sent out there are crazy. People who want to leave and think that Scientology is bad or doesn't work."

"There used to be a Rehabilitation Project Force here at the base too. But it was recently disbanded and most of the people were transferred to the Estates Division. A few people had to go out to Happy Valley and some even went to the Rehabilitation Project Force in Los Angeles."

"Are there a lot of people out there at Happy Valley?" I asked.

"Well, not really. There is this one gal that was out there forever, Annie Broeker. She used to live with Hubbard and in 1986 she was moved from the ranch in Creston to Happy Valley. She lived there for three years and never left for any reason. Finally she got okay to come back to the Int Base and now she has a house that she lives in here. She never leaves the base, though. She has been here for at least a year and I don't think she has ever left!" Tom explained.

"Why?" I asked, wondering if I will be stuck here for years on end.

"I think it has something to do with her ex-husband, Pat. He used to work for LRH and there was supposedly an issue about Pat and Annie from LRH. Dave Miscavige had the issue cancelled, Pat disappeared and Annie showed up at Happy Valley. That's all I know. Either way, she does not ever leave the base – EVER."

How could I have gotten myself into this? Was this going to be a nightmare? I told myself if for any reason I was not fully comfortable with anything that happens that I would get the hell out of here any way I can. I was not going to end up like Annie, locked up here like a prisoner for the rest of my life.

"Don't worry about that," Tom said. "You would have to lose all your Team Share cards before you start worrying about that stuff."

Team Share cards was a system of privileges that existed throughout the base. It operated on advices from LRH and each staff member was given five cards. You had a Social Card, Bonus Card, Allowance Card, Chow Card and Berthing Card. If you screwed up or your statistics went down, you would lose a card. They were also lost in the above order. If you wanted to get a card back, you had to increase your production. Any one of your seniors could revoke a card from you at anytime if you were disrespectful or simply pissed them off. Each time you lost a card, you also lost the privileges that went along with that card. There were rarely ever any social activities or bonuses, so those two cards were just buffers to keep you getting paid and fed with a place to stay.

Each week a list of who had what cards was issued to the crew. You could see the guys in the hot seats were the ones with the least number of cards. Most people had three to five cards. There were a few crew members that had one, two or no cards at all.

The crew members with zero cards had to sleep wherever they could find a place. They had to scrape up leftovers to eat and they did not get paid at all. The system was arbitrary and if you were in any way threatening or nonconforming to what your seniors wanted, you could lose a card.

Between all of the new rules and rumored advices that had been written, there was no way that I was getting out of this place without a fight. Dave Miscavige was rumored to have said that the Int Base was like Disneyland! And I guess that if you took away all of the trains, rides, giant characters running around, food, happiness, kids, parents or anything else pleasant, and the ability to leave whenever you wanted, the Int Base could be compared to Disneyland.

Just Can't Get Enough

On the Base Orientation Course, I had to learn the lingo for the different buildings around the Gilman Hot Springs property. There were hundreds of abbreviations and names for buildings that made no sense, but everybody was required to learn them all. It seemed impossible to learn the different buildings since the base was a huge, sprawling compound that took at least an hour to walk around. It was something like 500 acres.

In the course pack, there was a list of all the buildings on the base with descriptions of each (*see map printed on the endsheets of this book*):

BV: Bonnie View or Beautiful View – This is LRH's house that sits at the highest elevation of the Int Base property and has a beautiful view of the property. The house was built from the ground up based on LRH advices. The entire house has different furnishings for each season that are routinely swapped out. Furniture, drapes, beds sheets etc. are all custom designed to match each season of the year.

Studio Two: This is the studio where all film mix downs are done by the Audio Division of Gold. There is also a Post Lip Sync studio located in this same building, as well as the film sound transfer facilities used by manufacturing.

Villas: This was where Religious Technology Center was located. There were three buildings, the upper, middle and lower villas. Not only was RTC located here, but top executives also lived here.

Star of California Clipper Ship: The Star of California is a giant clipper ship that was built into the property to be used as a local attraction for people from nearby Hemet and San Jacinto. Promoted as a movie set, local residents were given public tours on Sundays to see how a real movie set looks. The Star of California also has an Olympic size swimming pool, Jacuzzi, sauna and other facilities that could be used for entertaining and local events.

The Spa: The Spa is now the location of the Qualifications Division of Gold. The Spa used to be the main location on the property where the hot springs would surface and several large steam bath facilities were located here. After the United States Government drilled a large underground tunnel through the back side of the mountain, they hit the underground river that fed the hot springs and the springs dried up. Old Man Gilman, who had run the hot springs resort since 1913, had several boilers set up beneath the Spa, and continued to run the hot springs resort for several years before finally retiring in 1978 and selling the property.

Del Sol: This is where the Commodores' Messenger Organization and Executive Strata International, and Watchdog Committee were located. Del Sol used to be the main hotel unit for the Gilman Hot Springs Resort.

The 200s: The 200s were where network units for several areas of CMO Int were housed. These included LRH Public Personal Relations Office International and LRH Technical Research and Compilations.

Ranchos: This is where both the Translations Unit, and the LRH Book Compilations Unit were located. They took approved manuscripts from LRH Technical Research and Compilations and turned these into courses and books for Scientology organizations around the world. They had typesetting, book design and even did glossaries and other book items here.

119 & 40s House: This is where Commodore's Messenger Organization Gold was located and is the unit directly responsible for making sure that Watchdog Committee programs for Golden Era Productions get done.

G Units or Gs: These are houses that were converted to luxury accommodations for VIP guests that stay at the Int Base.

Building 36: Building 36 was the brand new state of the art manufacturing building that was built for Golden Era Productions. It houses production facilities for Hubbard E-Meter Manufacturing and both 16 mm film and Cassette Tape Production. Bldg 36 also houses the Executive, Hubbard Communications Office, Dissemination, Central Marketing Unit, Treasury, and Port Captain Division offices of Golden Era Productions.

Tavern: The tavern is a VIP facility where actors brought to the base for Cine or Audio productions could be serviced. It is done up in the motif of the Knights of the Round Table complete with a large sword embedded in a stone as you enter the building.

Gym: This was the building where the Cine Division had their shooting stage. Originally called the "gym" because the activities of the base were confidential even to the local residents. As a result, the permit to build the studio was applied for under the guise of a "Basketball Gym." Any and all references to the building were to be specified as the "Gym". The Gym also housed the make-up, costumes, camera, lighting, and set sound departments.

F&E: This is where the film and equipment branch is housed, and contains the personnel responsible for maintaining Hubbard's wealth of personal photography equipment and his photos and having them ready in perfect order for use at any time. They also oversee programs being run in the Cine Division of Gold.

Upper Lodges: This is where Gold's entire film editing department was housed. It has a large 35 mm film theater where the shoot crew watch their daily footage as well as feature films.

Lower Lodges: This is where pre-production areas were housed. Logistics, art department, research and assembly, scriptwriting, casting, and pre-production director are all located there.

MCI: Massacre Canyon Inn, or MCI, is the dining facility for the entire base. It has both crew and officer dining hall areas that service all organizations located on the property. It also houses the offices for Gold's Domestic Services Division staff.

Garage: The garage used to be a public gas station that was converted into the maintenance facility for the entire property. Motor Pool Gold is located here as well as the entire Estates Division. The grounds, electrical, construction, engineering and building maintenance departments of the Estates Division are all housed here. Cine's sets and props departments took up the west half of the building. It also contains the International Landlord Office.

Trailers: The trailers were a collection of temporary buildings that were set up to accommodate the Central Marketing Unit (CMU) as well as the tape editing and technician departments of Audio. These trailers later housed LRH Technical Research and Compilations unit and the International Finance Office.

Studio One: This is the LRH Music Studio Complex. It has a state of the art music studio and is one of the most advanced music studios in the world. Adjacent to the main studio are music scoring, and storage for all of the Golden Era Musicians' equipment. Also in this same building are very upscale conference and dining facilities for visiting musicians that are brought up to the studio for recordings.

Lecture Mix: This is where all Hubbard's lectures are restored, mixed and made ready for high-speed duplication using Clearsound technology.

Music Rehearsal: This is where the musicians rehearse for upcoming concerts and performances.

Upper RAV: This is where LRH's Audio Visual Unit, or RAV, is located. This is the unit that is responsible for maintaining LRH's arsenal of personal audio equipment. They are also responsible for running all of the programs in the Audio division of Golden Era Productions. They are the unit that produces any LRH special edition audio releases that Gold is not allowed to produce.

Lower RAV: This is the mixing studio that RAV uses to mix special edition products.

12 Mic: This is the recording room located in Lower RAV. It is called the 12 Mic because it has 12 separate microphones that are used to get the most realistic recording possible.

Horwich House: This is where Jon Horwich and his daughter Roanne lived. Roanne is LRH's granddaughter and lives on the property.

OGH: Old Gilman House is the house that the family that owned and ran the property for most of the early and mid 1900's lived. This house was used for temporary staff lodging.

ISO: This building was right next to Old Gilman House. This is where you went if you were sick. Isolation. There was a men's section and a women's section. If you had a cold or got sick, you would have to stay here until better. You could not go back home or do any work on your post or with the general crew because you might make more people sick. The smell that came from isolation was enough to keep most people from ever getting sick.

M&M or Maintenance Man House: This house was originally the place where the maintenance man for the resort lived. It is now used for staff berthing.

The Lake: The lake is a huge man-made lake just west of Building 36. It even had fish in it. It was more of an eyesore than majestic, with dead animals and several feet of sludgy muck beneath the few feet of water. There is a small island at one end of it with a stone veneer bridge that allows access to the island and has a huge cottonwood tree on it.

Golf Course: This is the public golf course located to the east of the main Golden Era property.

Sublet Road: This is the public road that is adjacent to the main property and runs along the golf course. Several houses are located along this road. Some were purchased and used as staff housing units while others had local residents living in them who had nothing to do with the base.

For my orientation, I would go to each and every building on the property and answer a question about each. This exercise took me two days.

For the most part, it was business as usual in most buildings. People were generally uniformed in the Sea Org garb and people were at desks and computers working away. There were, however, a few exceptions. Most of these exceptions occurred in Gold.

When I went into Studio Two, the mixing facility at the top of the property, a man was sitting at the main mix board console. He was in boxer shorts and a T-shirt. He was sitting in a large leather chair and had his feet up on the mix board. He was wearing socks but no shoes and seemed rather unresponsive to my entrance into the room.

"Hello," I said.

"Hey," he answered back. "Who are you and what are you doing here?"

"My name is Marc Headley and I am doing my Orientation Course." I answered back, almost laughing.

"Well, Marc, I'm Jesse Prince and this is Studio Two. Now - get out! I am trying to work here!" he said, half joking and half serious.

I walked out of the studio and laughed. Of all the areas I had been to, this was the only one where someone was out of uniform and kicking back during post hours.

Beside a few random characters on my route, my orientation was pretty uneventful. I walked around to a bunch of buildings and headed back to finish the course.

My next course was a technical course, the Audio Basics Course. No Scientology stuff I thought – wow. This would be the first thing I would study that was not filled with LRH issues from 20 years ago. I opened the course pack. The first issue was Keeping Scientology Working #1. Okay, well that issue was in the front of every course in Scientology. I came to the first nontechnical issue; it was written by Hubbard in the 1980s and was all about nano webers and magnetic flux and how these all make audiotape possible. There was no escaping it. Hubbard had something to say about everything and no matter what, I would have to study it if I was to get through these courses.

It took me only a few days to plow through this last course. As soon as I was done, I went on my first post.

My Secret Garden

I was told where to go and that I would meet a girl named Clarisse. I arrived in Building 36 in what they called the Gauss line. Clarisse was a short girl in her 30s and wore a long sad puppy dog look most of the time. She gave me the tour of the whole cassette production facility. The Gauss line was the high-speed cassette manufacturing facility at Golden Era Productions. They had two giant master machines, both of which would load master production reels that would play back on a huge loop. The signals from the master machines were transferred to 16 high speed copying "slave" machines that had huge reels of cassette tape on them called "pancakes." Both the master and playback machines ran the tape through at 32X normal speed. In 30 minutes you could make 30 cassettes on each machine. With 16 machines, depending on the length of the lecture being copied, you could crank out 400-500 tapes every hour including setting up and reloading the machines with new tape.

The huge reels were then checked by a special Studer brand tape machine that was designed to play them.

The pancakes were loaded into cassette shells that were then labeled, stuffed into binders, shrink-wrapped, boxed up and shipped out. As we entered the packaging area, there were stacks and stacks of cassettes everywhere. There must have been a few hundred thousand tapes, easily. They were in red plastic bins piled high throughout the entire room. None were in binders, just loose cassettes piled into big plastic bins.

After Clarisse showed me the production facility, I could not help but notice that the place looked like a ghost town. Everywhere else I had been on the property there were people working and desks with baskets filled with papers and trash cans with trash in them. This place had nothing. No papers on any desks, no people working in it, no duffle bags under the desks with the occasional pair of shoes sitting around, nothing. It was as sterile as could be.

Clarisse, or "CB" as she stated she preferred to be called, said that she was the only person posted here and that I would be taking the job as the Tapes Packaging In Charge. More people would be coming to take over the other ten posts that were empty.

Okay. Weird but okay.

When I got to dinner, I told Tom that I was being posted in Tapes Manufacturing. He said he knew that. He told me that all the people coming up to Gold from the mission down in LA would be posted there.

"That is why there was a mission to get a bunch of people up here from LA," Tom said, "to man up tapes with NEW personnel."

"Where did all of the people that worked there before go?" I asked.

"Either declared or sent to the Rehabilitation Project Force," Tom said matter of factly while eating his last bite of dinner.

"What?" I asked him as we got up and headed towards the bussing station, "How?"

"Well, they made about 300,000 overt product cassette tapes," Tom said, "And a lot more that probably went out to public that we never found."

"Holy crap!" I freaked. "How many people are we talking about?"

"Oh, I don't know, maybe eight or nine. CB is still over there though, right?" We finished bussing our dishes and headed out for a smoke.

"Yeah, she was the one who gave me the tour of the place," I answered, thinking about all of this.

"Yeah, well she used to be a Lieutenant junior grade. She was the only one that did not get RPFed or declared. She was lowered in rank to a Chief Petty Officer and has hundreds of hours of amends to do or she will get sent to the Rehabilitation Project Force anyway," Tom explained.

"Why didn't she go to the RPF or get declared like everybody else?" I asked.

"Well, she is David Miscavige's sister in-law," Tom finished.

After muster I went back to tapes.

"So, what should I do?" I asked CB as I walked in.

"Well, we need to set up for all hands tonight," CB said as we walked into the finishing area. "All of these bins of tapes have to have the labels removed." She waved her hands at all the red bins I had seen earlier during my tour.

"All of them?"

"Yeah, all of them," she said. "We've been doing this with the entire crew for a few months already. Each night for at least an hour, all of Gold comes down here and peels these paper labels off the tapes by hand. Then any sticky residue gets wiped off and the tapes get brought up to the 3rd floor warehouse."

"Why not just throw them out?" I asked, dreading spending the rest of my adult life peeling labels off cassettes.

"Because each tape is worth about $1.50. We can't throw that away. That is about a half a million dollars in materials," CB said, almost so softly that I could barely hear her.

I totally understood CB now. She was the only one in this whole place that did not get busted and she knew it was only because she was related to the boss's wife. She would have been mincemeat any other day of the week if it were not for that fact.

It also explained the constant long face she wore. She was miserable. She had been in the Sea Org her entire life and was actually working for L. Ron Hubbard when he died in 1986. She had risen up the ranks and was an officer and here she was after 20 years, just a staffer back at the bottom again.

I asked CB if there were any write-ups or directions on how to get the labels off.

"No, everything was burned," CB replied.

"Huh?"

"Anything that was here from the previous crew was burned, any items that could be burned were burned, log books, daily Battle Plans, directions and procedures, training materials, any correspondence, anything. All of the desks were emptied out into a fire and burnt. There is not one scrap of anything left from the previous people. It is as if they never existed," CB said.

"Okay," I replied, not knowing what I could possibly say in response to that. That was plain nuts. They burnt everything, as if the evilness was somehow going to be transferred onto the next batch of people through the paper.

Weeks went by and we de-labeled cassette tapes each night with the entire crew. It seemed like it would take forever. We'd maybe get a few thousand done each night with a few hundred people helping us. Then one day it happened. A guy named Luigi came into the packaging area and told me to come into the room where all the duplication equipment was.

"Hold this for me," Luigi said as he soldered some part to a circuit board he handed me.

You would think that with a name like Luigi, he would have been a big Italian guy. Luigi was as far from that as you could imagine. He was a small thin Asian with jet-black hair and a Fu Manchu moustache. He spoke perfect English and had just a tinge of "Los Angeles attitude" in his accent.

Bruce, the technician I had met earlier in Ray Reiser's office, was in the room as well. Bruce looked as though he could fall asleep any second. Both he and Luigi had been in and out of the duplication room for weeks. They were trying to fix the machines that made the cassette tapes. This is the exact part of the line that made all of the bad cassettes.

"This is the Gauss line," said Luigi while continuing to solder. "All these machines are made by a company called Gauss."

"What's wrong with them?" I asked.

"Well, they are not making the tapes sound as good as we would like," Luigi answered.

"Why can't you just make the company that made them fix the problem?" I asked, thinking this is just a warranty issue.

"Because the problem is not that the machines do not work, they do not work as well as Chairman of the Board would like them to," Bruce chimed in. "We have to make the machines better on our own with modifications."

CB came in and said she needed my help in the next room and I went back to moving bins around in the finishing area.

"How long will it take those guys to fix the machines?" I asked CB.

"It has been months already, I don't know," she replied. "COB has been down here a ton of times asking them as well. They always tell him something that they have pulled out of their asses and then get assigned a condition of Doubt for false reporting."

The next day I was told that I would not be posted in the final packaging area but would instead be posted as the quality control for the Gauss line. This was huge. The guy that did this before was the one that caused the whole flap that got everybody busted. Wow, I did not know about this. This seemed like a big deal and could end up being a catastrophe.

I had to study a bunch of manuals for the technical equipment I would be operating. In the Sea Org, if you operate any piece of equipment that you are not checked out on, you get assigned a lower condition. You have to read the manual from beginning to end and get someone else to quiz you on the operation of the equipment. The first of the operation manuals I had to study was several hundred pages long. It was a Hewlett Packard 8562A Spectrum Analyzer.

It took me a few weeks just to get through that one manual. The manual itself was written by an engineer for an engineer and I had no business even attempting to read this thing. I eventually got through the manual. After I had learned how to operate the machine and was fully versed in its capabilities, I tried to get a check out. Turns out that no one at Gold had ever read the manual for this machine and those that started had never finished.

"It's not even ours," Luigi said to me. "Church of Spiritual Technology sent it over when we needed something that was well beyond the analyzers we had around here. That analyzer costs around $85,000. These things are used at NASA to test space shuttle crap."

"So I am the only one who has read the manual for this thing?" I exclaimed, after three weeks of having my head buried in five different technical dictionaries and reading about wavelengths and demodulators and radar frequencies!

After that first manual, the rest I had to read took me one day to get though and get checked out. They were a powered speaker, Studer tape deck, OKI data printer and a test generator/analyzer by the Gauss M2 company.

After reading the manuals, I was told to go down and help Luigi and Bruce get the machines fixed.

There was no science to what Bruce and Luigi were doing. Luigi would try something, and then test to see if it worked. When it didn't, they would try something else. We would get all of the machines tuned up and spend all night getting them perfect. After, we slept on the floor for two or three hours right next to the machines, the next morning we would run tests on the machines and they would all be out of whack again. This had been going on for weeks and no matter what we did, the machines were not predictable and would change overnight.

Finally, after weeks and weeks of trying everything possible, it boiled down to several points:

1. The Production Masters – The production line that made the masters had faults on it that were introducing low quality directly into the masters being used to make the cassettes.
2. The master playback machines in the duplication facility – The actual machines that played back the production master to the slave machines had faults with it that needed to be modified.
3. Tape shedding – The cassette tape would shed particles as it passed across the recording heads of the slave machines and this created a loss in sound reproduction.
4. Temperature – The slave machines would have a variance in frequency response based on the temperature of the room. Even a 5-degree change could drastically change the quality of the recordings being duplicated.
5. Quality Control – The Quality Control was done by objective decision and was not computerized.

Dave Miscavige had visited us in the tapes area at least 50 times over the course of all of these discoveries. He had told us that once we fixed everything, we had to be able to produce 50,000 cassettes per week in order to catch up the backlog of cassettes that were needed by public Scientologists.

With the production line now working we had to document everything and take pictures of all of the electronic components and every single piece of equipment. This was so that if anything went wrong, the original documentation could be referred to. If anyone changed any procedure, modified any piece of equipment or changed anything on the production line whatsoever, they would be instantly declared a Suppressive Person. The charge would be a "high crime" and suppressive act — Unmocking a Working Installation.

As we documented everything and got the machines running smoothly, more and more people were starting to show up from LA. Even my sister finally showed up. We were supposed to have enough people for both the day and night shifts and run the line 24 hours per day. We had:

1. Rosi Kamman
2. Clarisse Brousseau (Barnett)
3. Tony Cifarelli
4. Agnese Bertolina Johnson
5. Lynnea Baker
6. Marc Headley
7. Bob Ferris
8. Stephanie Headley
9. Dan Crocini
10. Jessica Thompson
11. Caroline Buri
12. Carlo Russo

My job was to check the pancakes of tapes after they came off the copy line. My official post title was Pancake Quality Control Officer. My boss was a girl named Lynnea Baker. She essentially did the exact same thing I did but also had to spot check stuff from the final packaging area as well. We were running the line 24 hours per day and we were not producing 25,000 cassettes per week. Jason Bennick was the General Manager and he was the one who would report up to COB on how many cassettes we were producing. Even though there were over 10 people working in the area, it was decided that it would only take three people to run the night shift. It ended up being Clarisse, Tony and me.

We would come in on the bus around 4:45 P.M. and leave at 8:00 A.M. to go home. Our full schedule was as follows:

4:45 - 5:00	TRAVEL TO BASE
5:00 - 5:30	DINNER AND MUSTER
5:30 - 6:30	PRODUCTION
6:30 - 9:00	STUDY
9:00 - 11:30	PRODUCTION
11:30 - 12:00	MIDNIGHT RATIONS (MID RATS)
12:00 - 7:30	PRODUCTION
7:30 - 8:00	BREAKFAST
8:00 - 8:15	TRAVEL TO BERTHING

Based on this schedule, if you went straight to sleep after getting home and taking a shower and got up and got dressed quickly, you could somehow get in seven hours of sleep. We were working over one hundred hours per week. On paper it looked okay and comparable to the day shift schedule. But there were a few things not factored in.

Daylight – When we went home to go to sleep, it was daylight. I had blankets over my windows in my room to try and black out as much light as possible. Still, the light would leak through a few spots and that alone could light up a room without effort. Also, Hemet, California, in the summer is completely immune to clouds. It is bright during the day.

Temperature - When we went onto the nightshift it was anywhere from 100-120 degrees in Hemet during a summer day. No matter what kind of air conditioner you had, it was not meant to successfully counteract temperatures that hot. I can remember sleeping on top of my sheets with the A/C set to 70 degrees and still breaking a sweat.

Daytime Activity – The area where we had our housing in town was being developed all around. An entire community was being built across the street from where I lived and during the week, there were hammers, pneumatic nail guns, cement trucks backing up, or kids screaming and playing outside during the hours I was supposed to be sleeping.

After I had been on the night shift for some time, I had perfected how to keep out of trouble and fly below the radar. I was even getting a serious tan! Since I was on the night shift, I would go home each day and sleep out on a lawn chair by the pool at the apartment building where we lived. There was no one from the base to see me and, as long as I turned over every once in awhile, I would get a good amount of sun each day. I thought I was doing fine. Yeah, I had to work long hours, but it was better than not being able to talk to my family and I was not on the Rehabilitation Project Force. That was the only way you could avoid going crazy at the Int Base. Instead of thinking how bad you had it, you had to think of how much worse it would be if you decided to go against the grain and try to escape.

There was always a bunch of people every so often who would lose it and either blow or say they wanted to leave. The few that got away we would never see again. We would hear rumors about how they were in jail or living on the street. The ones who were caught would be made dishwashers or assigned to a job that no one would ever want to do or get assigned to the Rehabilitation Project Force.

I had not done many services as a public Scientologist and had not completed any major levels. I had done the Purification Rundown and some other introductory services before becoming an employee and that was about it. One day, I was told that I might be able to get some auditing. I was not that excited about doing it and was much more interested in doing car school. I thought that driving would be much more fun than auditing. I was pressured to do the auditing first and was told that this was a "once in a lifetime opportunity." I was given a short interview on what I was doing and how work was going; I was instructed to go up to the Villas. The Villas is where Religious Technology Center was located at the time. I was told to go see the Inspector General Ethics, Marty Rathbun! When I went up there, I was met by a staff member who led me in to see Marty. I sat down in front of his desk. He started off by saying that I was one of only two people on the entire base who was qualified to receive this auditing. He told me that I was not allowed to tell anybody about my auditing. I was not to tell my co-workers, I was not to tell my family members, nobody. I would be going in session every day and under no circumstances was I to be un-sessionable on any given day. I would be doing this for weeks and I would have to do whatever was needed so that I could go in session at the same time each day. He told me that all of my seniors were briefed that I would be on "study" on a special program and that Religious Technology Center would be directly overseeing my progress.

This was a lot to swallow in one go. I was a bit shocked by it all, but nevertheless, I was game. Oh, yeah, one other thing, my auditor was going to be Tom Cruise. The penny dropped. Staff had been working day and night for weeks to get the houses (G Units) ready where Tom Cruise would be staying. It explained all the flowers being planted down by the G Units. He was supposedly coming to stay at the base for several weeks or months and was bringing Nicole Kidman with him. It was all starting to make sense now. Tom Cruise was coming to do his Academy Levels. He was going to do his auditor training and he needed someone to audit and this person had to be very low on the bridge. That was me.

I went back to post and worked all night like I always did. The next day was the big day. I came in for dinner like I always did. I ate and then after dinner muster instead of going up to the course room like everyone else, I headed over to Studio One.

As I walked up to the conference room, Tom was standing outside in the hallway.

"Hello, I am Tom," he said. He grabbed my hand with one hand and grabbed my arm with the other. Double handshake. Okay.

I thought to myself, sure, like I'm going to say, "What's your name?" Of course you are Tom Cruise! Everyone knows who you are.

"I'm Marc," I said.

"Hey, Marc, nice to meet you. Come on in." Tom led me into the conference room. My eyes scanned the room to see who was here. The conference room was converted into a course room and an auditing room. On one side of the room at the large table studying were Kirstie Alley and Nicole Kidman. Bruce Hines from the Senior Case Supervisor office was supervising. Another girl from the same office, Heidi Stahli, this sort of hot European girl with a large set of headlights and long blonde hair was supervising as well. Nicole and Kirstie were reading when I showed up. No one else was there.

I followed Tom over to the other side of the room where another smaller table was set up with an E-Meter. The last time I had been on the E-Meter was when I was getting my clearances. I had not even been on study that much since first coming to the base.

Tom had me sit down. He asked me if the room was okay and if it was too cold or too hot. He gave me the metal cans that were hooked up to the E-Meter. He had me give the cans a squeeze a few times. This is done so the E-Meter can be set to the individual you are auditing. Then he asked me to take in a deep breath and let it out. This shows if you have had enough to eat and sleep. It is called a metabolism test. If the needle on the E-Meter dial does not fall a certain amount, then you can't go in session.

Tom gave me a puzzled look. "Let's try that one more time," he said.

I took in a deep breath and let it out.

"Hmmm. We are not getting a metab," Tom said.

"Did you get enough sleep?" he asked.

"Yeah," I nodded.

"Did you get enough to eat?" Tom asked.

"Yeah."

"Did you take your vitamins?"

Is this guy kidding, I think to myself? I never take vitamins.

"No," I shake my head.

"No? Oh, well, that might be the problem," Tom said in surprise as he got up from his chair and made his way around the table.

"I never take vitamins," I said as we headed over to the kitchen area next to the conference room.

"Well, we have some stuff in here that might help," he said as we walked into the kitchen.

There was more food in the kitchen than I had seen all year. Sandwiches, snacks, drinks, three different types of entrées, rice, vegetables, fruit. You name it, they had it in this room. And this was the "just in case someone got hungry food."

Who knows what they were feeding these guys for dinner? I stealthily chomped down a cream cheese danish while Tom was digging through some vitamin boxes.

He pulled out a small plastic pack that had about five or six vitamins in it. "This should help."

"Cool," I took it and went to grab a drink.

"Do you take a lot of bee pollen?" asks Tom while I carefully picked which drink I should choose to wash down my delicious danish and bitter vitamins.

"Like from a bee? Never." I answered right before taking a swig of Snapple.

"Never had bee pollen?" he said, almost excited. "Oh, that will do the trick for sure."

Wow, this is the guy from Top Gun and bee pollen is what gets him excited.

"Where can we get some bee pollen?" he called to Heidi from the kitchen.

"I think they have some in the Canteen," she said. "I think we can have someone get some."

"Oh that's okay, we can go get it," Tom said and motioned me to follow him outside.

His blue and black Yamaha TW200 Motorcycle was parked right outside the studio door. He got on and started it.

"Get on. We can just zip down there and get some bee pollen and be back in a few minutes," Tom said without a worry in the world.

I got on. So much for the super confidential part of me being audited by Tom Cruise. People were going to see me riding on the back of the bike with him on the way to and from the canteen. In fact, it was dinner time and they would all be down around the canteen. Well, if this becomes some sort of flap, I am throwing Tom under the bus for this one.

We headed to the canteen. Every time we passed someone, I thought about how this was going to flap and I would hear about it.

We pulled up to the canteen. Everyone was staring at us. Tom walked into the canteen and asked the person at the counter if they had bee pollen bars.

"Yeah," the person said, stunned, "they're over there. "

"Thanks." Tom said as he grabbed the bar, handed it to me and headed back out.

He didn't even think about paying for it. I wondered if I was supposed to pay. I just walked back out looking at this thing they call a bee pollen bar. He started the bike, people stared at us, I got on and we drove off. At least fifty people had now seen me riding around with Tom Cruise. The entire base would know by the end of the night with the way people talked.

We got back to the conference room. I ate the bar. It tasted like shit. Now I know why I had never had one. I would eat a Snickers bar any day of the week over one of these. I washed the bee pollen down with the rest of the Snapple.

We chit chatted for a few minutes to let the bee pollen take effect. He asked me about what I do and where I work. Then the conversation took a turn.

"Do you know Greg Wilhere?" Tom asked me.

"Yeah," I said, having no idea where this is leading.

Greg Wilhere was the father of a kid that I used to go to school with, Darius. Darius was in Gold now and I lived a few apartments away from him at berthing.

"Ya know, when we were making *Days Of Thunder*, you know, he was with us when we were shooting and we named this one doctor in the movie after him." Tom laughed. All I could think was that Greg Wilhere was out palling around with Tom Cruise on movie sets. Nice.

Well, you wanna try again?" Tom asked.

"Sure," I said as we headed over to the auditing setup.

I picked up the cans. We redid the can squeeze and I gave the breath check another go. I took in a huge breath and let it out.

"That's fine," he said.

"Okay," I say amazed that there was such a trick as bee pollen, knowing full well it was probably the cream cheese danish that did the trick.

We went ahead and started the auditing and it went on for about an hour. Half the time I would space out and think how Tom Cruise could possibly be auditing me. Finally, we ended and Heidi came over to give an end of session exam. After each auditing session you have to get one of these to show that the auditor is not falsifying the session notes or saying that the session went awesome when it sucked. It went fine as far as I could tell and said so.

We said our goodbyes and I left. I was done for the day. Hopefully I could just go back to work and not have to deal with anybody in my department who may have heard about my little excursion to the canteen earlier.

I walked back into tapes and everybody wanted to know how it went. They knew. I told them I was not supposed to talk about it and that I would get in trouble if I did. I went back to work and pretended everything was the same as it had been.

This went on every weekday for a few months until he was done with his introductory auditor training. It was a very interesting time. After that, I was watched over to make sure that I did not end up in big trouble, because after all, I was the guy that Tom Cruise audited. If I went south, or god forbid, some out-tech had occurred; it would be blamed on my auditor, Tom Cruise. That could never happen.

Tom would come to the base off and on. You could always tell when he was there because we had to clean for a full week and make sure that the place was perfect.

One night in late June, around 1:00 A.M., we saw a car carrier pull into the main gate and all it had on it was a single car. It was a brand new Mercedes. As soon as we saw it, we knew whose it was. There was just no question. As we headed over for breakfast the next morning, we saw Nicole looking at the car. It was a birthday present for her. Tom came speeding up on his motorcycle and screeched to a stop inches away from Nicole causing her to scream. Apparently Tom was a bit of a prankster. That was the last time I saw Tom or Nicole in the 1990s.

After that, he just stopped coming to the base at all.

The rumor was that someone at the base had been telling an outside source that Tom was not only in Scientology, but that he was coming to the Int Base and getting Scientology training. It was true, but Dave Miscavige did not want the broad public to know this. Part of the idea of having Tom get trained and do all the courses was so that, when everyone did find out he was in Scientology, he would be in far enough that the onslaught of criticism would not affect him and he would stay in.

After a few days, the leak was found. A guy named Brad Kugler in the central marketing unit was running around on the decks. I knew Brad because I went to Delphi with his younger brother Ryan. When I was at ABLE, I knew his father, Ben, because he was regularly a source of high figure donations. So Brad was getting sec checked full time. Brad being security checked out of the blue at the same time as the Tom Cruise leak was a sure sign something was up. The word on the street was that he was talking to his mom on the phone and telling her about Tom's visits. She was then, in turn, giving the data to someone at some grocery store gossip magazine. Brad was gone within a few days. He was offloaded from the base and his mom was supposedly declared an SP. Brad's wife Tasha was made to divorce him. Whether any of that was true, there always had to be a "head on a pike" when some flap occurred. That was Dave's way of getting closure. You could count on the pain and agony dragging on until someone got RPF'd or declared suppressive. Then we would all concentrate on the next flap on Dave's plate.

Anyone who had phone access at the time lost it. Since one guy used the phone to secretly tell his mom some data, no one on the property could call out without going through reception.

To top it off, Tom Cruise was not showing up anymore either. His secret garden was not so secret anymore.

Sea Of Sin

I t was August 2nd, 1990. It was like any other day. We had gone home at 8:00 A.M. and I was quick to get to sleep. At noon I was awakened, not by someone, but by the noise of the rain. It had been deathly hot out and, being August, rain was the last thing I would have expected. I got some shorts on and went outside. It looked like what you would imagine hell would be like if it was located in the town of Hemet. The sky was literally black with clouds. The rain was coming down in sheets. The water had no place to go. It pooled up where it fell. The apartment complex parking lot was flooded and the side-walks were covered with water and it was starting to come inside the front door of the apartment. This was crazy. I could not believe this was happening. I headed back inside. I threw a bunch of towels on the floor inside of my door to keep any water out and soak up what had already made its way inside.

I fell back to sleep, got up at 4:30 P.M. and headed outside. Tony and CB were outside and we talked about the rain that had woken all of us up. The bus usually picked us up at 4:45 P.M. It was now going on 5:00 P.M. and no sign of the bus. At 5:15 P.M., I called in on a pay phone in the manager's office. Someone would be sent out to get us.

At 5:45 P.M. this Italian guy showed up in his car. Marcello was his name. He did not speak English very well, but for the most part you could understand what he said.

"What the hell is going on?" I asked him. "Why didn't the bus pick us up?"

"I was come get you," Marcello said. "The base flood all over. Roads not open."

Oh boy, this wasn't good. Marcello had actually been in town picking up someone's stuff and got stranded because he could not get back to the base on the closed roads. When he called in, they told him to go and pick us up and try and get back to the base somehow. Sanderson Street was flooded out in Hemet so that way was no good. The other road to the base, State Street, was flooded though not as bad, but the road towards the base from that direction had been completely blocked with a mountain load of mud.

After about an hour, we finally managed to get through on the Sanderson side and come around the west side of the base. It looked like a war ravaged country. There were trees down everywhere. Not just branches and leaves, whole trees toppled over and uprooted. There were huge palm fronds all over the place.

As we drove into the main gate, it hit me. There were people all over the place, covered in mud. Everyone was wet and dirty and it looked like chaos had broken out. We stopped at the main booth. Security grabbed a bunch of stuff out of Marcello's trunk. It belonged to Jacques Boucher. He was sitting at the back of the security booth looking rather down. He was on his way to the Rehabilitation Project Force in Los Angeles. He was the guy in the audio division who made all the production masters for the Gauss line, it didn't look good for Jacques.

We went straight into tapes. The day shift staff filled us in on what had happened. The whole base had been completely flooded. The villas were flooded. The mountain above the G units turned to mud and flowed over the highway and straight into the G's. Supposedly, at least two or three units were destroyed. There was damage all over the base from trees falling on cars, buildings and other structures. The rain had caused several million dollars worth of damage.

Just as we were getting filled in, we were told there was a mandatory muster in the dining hall for all crew.

This was never a good sign, the only time there were random musters called with all the crew was when someone was going to be roasted.

When we got there, hundreds of people were already clearing out the tables and chairs and moving them to the crew side. We were going to be piling into the officer side and standing as a group; the crew side was used for storage of the chairs and tables. The entire base was in the dining hall. Everyone was lined up by their individual organization. Gold was in front and all the others were lined up in back. There was a podium and microphone set up in front of the room facing us. This was for Dave Miscavige – COB RTC. He was going to address us.

After everyone had been accounted for and were all lined up, we waited there at attention for what seemed like forever. It was probably 10 minutes, but when you are standing there with the noose around your neck waiting for the hangman to throw the lever that drops the floor beneath your feet, time stands still.

The doors by the officer's side shook a little. Dave Miscavige came storming in. He went up to the podium and started screaming at us. We were the heathens responsible, we had caused this flood, we were scum, we had sabotaged everything that he or LRH had ever tried to do, we were the reason security checking was developed, we were the reason the drug rundown was developed, we were the reason why the purification rundown was developed, we were scum, and the entire org was assigned a condition of Confusion! 15-minute meal breaks, no canteen privileges, no liberties, no nothing. And everybody automatically lost two Team Share cards and weren't able to get them back until the entire organization was upgraded out of lower conditions.

He had yelled a lot of other things while we were standing there. It was so intense and loud that two crew members standing in line fainted while he was screaming. They literally fell over while standing there, passing out as they hit the floor.

Religious Technology Center staff filed in from all directions and passed out a goldenrod issue that had been printed up.

It was an official printed version of Dave Miscavige's lashing without the vulgar profanities laced throughout. It also had a shopping list of all the things he wanted done in order for us to be upgraded from lower conditions. It was a list of all of the things that he had been trying to get done for years. Now that there was a flood, the list contained repairing all the damage the flood had done as well. One of the items on the list was that the Gauss line had to produce 50,000 tapes per week.

After the issue was passed out, COB stomped out and we all stood there motionless. Everyone was in shock. The place already sucked when we had all our "privileges" in place. Now it would really suck. The Commanding Officer told everyone to go back to their areas and write up their condition formulas. He gave us a pep talk about how if we did this standardly, we would be upgraded and out of this in a few weeks.

There was another muster at Building 36 that night. Everybody was going to be up all night getting the mud out from under the buildings that had flooded and patching up other damage. The Tapes staff were typically exempt from these sorts of things since we had to produce tapes no matter what, and if we were off somewhere digging out mud, no tapes were being made. We went back to our areas. One good thing about being on the night shift, we were staying all night anyway! Some of the day shift crew were made to go and dig out mud while the night shift crew stayed and worked.

Everyone also had to get condition formulas written up and submitted before anyone was allowed to go home for the night. We just went back to work as usual and did our thing.

The whole organization ended up staying up all night. No one went home.

In the morning, we went to breakfast for only 15 minutes and went to get on the bus. We were told that we were not going home and that we had to stay for morning muster. If we did not get on the bus, we would not have a ride home and would end up being stuck at the base all day.

We went back to Building 36 to wait for muster. As the crew gathered, tension rose. Not only were people in a bad mood from having lost the privilege to sleep, having a shortened breakfast and being assigned lowered conditions, there were a few crew who considered themselves above the rest, as they began calling out staff for being more out-ethics than others. Someone made a wise crack while standing in line, and one girl called him on it saying he was a joker and degrader and that he was to turn in a Team Share card. They started arguing and people were telling them to shut up and get back in line.

Just then roll call was started. The master at arms called out the divisions as he always did. As he was reading them out, someone very loudly interrupted him. He was an officer I had never seen before. He was dressed in a different Sea Org uniform than the rest of us. It was the uniform a Sea Org member wore while on a mission into another organization. It was Greg Wilhere, an officer in Religious Technology Center. Standing next to him was another guy that I did recognize. Greg began addressing us:

"We are on a mission in your org. We are being run by COB directly and we will be reporting back to him daily. Obviously, you all read yesterday's issue. Well we are here to enforce that issue and make sure it gets done. We are also going to have some new rules around here in regards to how you guys operate.

"Everyone is to be where you are supposed to be when you are supposed to be there. There are going to be several musters each day. If anyone is late to any one of those musters, even by ten seconds, you will be assigned an all night amends project.

"If that same person is late a second time, they will be instantly assigned to the Rehabilitation Project Force in Los Angeles – no exceptions.

"Each day you will all participate in team drills as an organization.

"Each day you will participate in marching drills as an organization.

"Each day you will participate in Chinese Schooling key L. Ron Hubbard data.

"This is the only way you guys will be able to become a true organization and get out of your lower conditions.

"I will now turn this over to Mr. James Byrnes who will run you on Chinese school and marching."

The other guy walked out in front of the crew. He looked down the lines of crew and told people to get straightened up and to stand in straight lines. Then he went back to the middle of the muster site. He started barking out commands.

"Ten Hut!

"At ease!

"Ten Hut!

"At ease!

"Ten Hut!

"At ease!

"Ten Hut!

"At ease!

"Ten Hut!

"Right face.

"Left Face.

"About face.

"At ease.

"Ten Hut.

"Left face.

"At ease.

"Oh, my god! You guys are pathetic! Are you still asleep? You are horrible. Half of you don't even know your left from right! You are sloppy. You look like crap. You look like you don't care. You don't care, we know that. You guys are losers. We are here to make you into winners and team members. When we are done, you will not still be here if you are a loser as we will weed out the deadwood and get rid of those who can't make the grade."

"Actually, is there anybody here that does not want to be here? Is there? Raise your hand if you do not want to be here right now. This is going to be rough. If you do not want to be here, then just raise your hand and you can leave."

Everyone was looking around. Was anyone brave enough to raise their hand? I wish I had raised my hand. I didn't though. Just then a few people raised their hands! People were actually raising their hands. Wow! I sure thought about it. I did not dare raise my hand. Nothing happened around there without giant strings attached.

"Good," Mr. Byrnes continued. "You guys go ahead and go into the Hubbard Communications Office and we will make sure you guys are out of here right away.

"Anyone else think that they cannot make it here? This is it. This is your chance to get out now. You will get a one-way ticket out of here right now, with no questions asked.

"Okay, no more people. More of you will be leaving. We will find you and the weak will be sifted out of this group and gotten rid of. Only the tigers will survive this evolution.

"Ten Hut.

"Dismissed."

By now it was 9:00 A.M. and we, the night shift guys, were stuck here. We were standing there talking to the day shift trying to figure out what we were going to do.

"Well you guys should at least stay all day because we had to stay all night," Rosi said.

"Now, why would we do that?" I barked out.

"Well, we all had to stay here! Why should you guys not have to stay as well?" answered Rosi immediately, as though she had been planning this all along.

"Good. It's decided, you guys are staying," Rosi said, and walked away towards the building.

All three of us on the night shift crew stood there deciding what to do.

"Get into production! What are you guys doing still standing around here?" Greg Wilhere barked out at us.

We scurried off towards the building, not wanting to risk any trouble.

Since we were rarely on post at the same time as the day shift guys, we were not going to be able to do anything that would benefit us so we decided that we would do preps for our shift. There was the matter of competition between the day and night shifts. Even though we were only three people, we regularly out produced the day shift because we had a lot less distractions during the night shift. No phone calls, no hour-long musters, no executive inspections, no people coming in asking for stuff, overall we worked more and got more done. This always pissed off the day shift and they would generally leave stuff for us to do to try and load us up with more work.

Taking out the trash and doing the shredding was almost always left undone when the day shift crew ended. If the shredding was not regularly done, security could come by and assign whomever was responsible for this a condition of Enemy for violating the security regulations. If it was paper and had writing on it, it had to be shredded and could not be thrown away or leave the property for any reason.

So we did the shredding, got supplies in place for our shift and used the time to prepare to get more done later on that night. This was going to be a long shift.

At lunch muster, we were told about a new procedure that was being put back into place, "overboarding". Mr. Byrnes read an order from Hubbard that covered the exact procedure for being thrown overboard.

Something about having oneself blindfolded and being thrown into the ocean, someone was even supposed to read a short passage as this was being done.

"We commit your sins to the depths. May you arise a better thetan!"

I was wondering if I was the only person in the mustered crowd who knew that we were about 100 miles to the nearest ocean. No sooner had the thought crossed my mind when Mr. Byrnes said that we would be doing all of the overboarding at the lake on the property.

The lake was a sludgy disgusting body of water about 200 yards from Building 36. On a hot day, you could sometimes smell the lake from far away. The dead birds and fish that floated in it could stir up quite an aroma. This is where we would now be thrown "overboard" if we upset a senior or did anything that was in violation of the many rules and regulations. Lovely. Things were really looking up.

I Sometimes Wish I Were Dead

After a few weeks, I was starting to buckle with all the new restrictions being enforced. I had been down to two Team Share cards and had not received any pay for almost two months. I was not sleeping much and not studying either. When we did have study time, it was more like two and a half hours of rest, as one would usually end up falling asleep in the course room for a majority of the time spent there.

Nodding off while sitting at my station checking the tapes as they came off the line was a regular occurrence. Since no one was ever around at night except the other guys on the night shift (who occasionally did the same), it was not that big of a deal.

One day, when I arrived at the base from my daily bus ride, I was told I needed to go straight to the tapes department. When I got there, people were crowded around my station.

"You are toast, mister!" Jason Bennick barked out as I walked in the door. "You violated the production line and you are going to be declared a suppressive person if I have anything to do with it."

I sat down at my station attempting to figure out what they were talking about. I was shown several test results from the pancakes I had passed the night before. The test results were marked as "passed" by me, but two out of the 300 pancakes checked had a very slight frequency out of specification that I had not caught. The specification was +/- 2dB on the 20-20,000Hz frequencies and one frequency was about 1/10th of a decibel out of spec on two pancakes. I was being interrogated and yelled at by roughly four people at once who questioned why I had passed these on to be packaged. Jason Bennick was still yelling and screaming about getting me declared for my supposed attempt to sabotage production. I could see through his act a mile away. The last General Manager was taken off post for allowing the past crew to produce faulty cassettes. Jason was going to declare me a suppressive person and I would be the fall guy and everyone could go back to business as usual.

"There is no question about it. You violated the production line. You are going to be declared!"

I stood up and simply said, "Well if you are going to declare me, then I want to leave. I am out of here."

I walked out and went to the Hubbard Communications Office. Jason Bennick followed close behind. As soon as I got there, Jason came in yelling, "This guy needs to be declared suppressive. He violated the production line in tapes! Get a declare issue drawn up right away!"

I sat down and said nothing while Jason explained everything to the HCO Area Secretary. She listened and when he was done, she said, "Okay, we will see what we need to do."

Jason pointed to me and said, "YOU ARE A SUPPRESSIVE PERSON!" and then stormed out.

I could've cared less, I had already decided this was completely crazy and that I would get the hell out of here. I had no intention of sticking around.

The HCO Area Secretary looked at me and said, "What do you want to do?"

"I want to leave," I said, "give me a Leaving Staff Routing Form."

She reached into the desk and pulled out the exit form. She filled out my name and gave it to me. I looked it over.

It was a long list of all sorts of things I had to do before I would be allowed to leave. It had a list of people I was required to see, documents I had to sign, I had to be security checked, I had to write a list of my overts and withholds, the list went on and on. I did not care what it took, I wanted out of here. I was not interested in getting no pay, no respect and putting in over 100 hours of my time each week, being tortured and mentally abused the entire time.

Jason came marching back in. He went up to the HCO Area Secretary and started yelling at her. "You had better make sure that this guy gets declared a suppressive! He violated the production line documentation and COB said that no matter what, if anyone violated the production line – they get declared an SP." He didn't wait around for her response; he just walked right back out.

"I am out of here!" I got up as if to walk out and was grabbed by a security guard.

"No, you have to do the routing form in order to leave. You can't just get up and walk out of here. You have to do it properly, per Hubbard policy," the guard said. "Meanwhile, you are restricted to the base."

The guard's name was Jackson. He was actually the Security Chief. He told me to go to the Grounds Department and tell them I needed to be put to work while they sorted out what they were going to do with me.

I went to Grounds. A guy gave me a broom and told me to sweep up leaves on all the roads. I happily took the broom and swept leaves. My mind was reeling. All I could think about was how much I wanted to get the hell out of this place. I would go back to LA and get a job somewhere. Anything would be better than this. I would go live with my mom or even move to Nebraska and live with my dad, I didn't care. Anything and anywhere would be better than this hellhole.

No one bothered me for the rest of the day. I swept leaves and at the end of the night I went to the main booth and asked where I was supposed to go. The guard slid the little window on the side of the booth open so I could talk to him.

"Where do I sleep?" I asked.

"Old Gilman's House is packed. When you find a place, just tell us where it is so we know," the guard said and slid the window closed before I could ask him anything else. I stood there looking in the booth as if to get him to open the window again. He just looked forward and pretended I wasn't there. The guard's name was Danny Dunagin. Danny was rude and came across like he did not care about you at all, this might have had something to do with the fact that he didn't. I had only talked to him a few times before and every time, I got the impression that he was put here on earth to make enemies. He also walked like he had something stuck up in his backside and it just added to his whole persona.

I wandered around the base for about an hour before I came across a small camping trailer. It was maybe 10 feet long. It had a small table in it that was set up for auditing and had a small bench in the back that could be folded out into a bed. It stank like mildew and vitamins but after looking for a while, I realized that I was not going to find anything better.

I made my way back over to the main booth. Danny slid the window open.

"What?" he said as though I was taking him away from his important job of watching cars drive by.

"I found a small trailer by Old Gilman's House that is empty, I'm going to sleep there," I said sort of questioning if it was okay.

"Whatever." Danny slid the window closed.

I don't think he cared at all. As I walked back to the trailer I wondered if I even should have told him. He would probably tell somebody that I was here now and have me kicked out.

In the morning I woke up and headed over to the muster site. I lined up with the Hubbard Communications Office staff instead of with tapes. As soon as muster was over, I walked off and went back over to the garage and grabbed a broom. I went right back to sweeping leaves. No one bothered me and I did not have to report to anybody. I was just taking a break as far as I was concerned.

Good thing I was working outside all day, because I had not had a shower and was pretty ripe from working the whole day before and sleeping in my clothes at night. I didn't shave that morning either. No one cared anyway. I had decided that I would do whatever I wanted until I got out of this place. No more rules. No more doing what I was told. I would just live by my own rules and get the hell out of here as fast as possible.

Jackson drove by on his security motorcycle and asked me if I still wanted to leave.

"As long as I am getting declared or sent to the Rehabilitation Project Force, I might as well leave," I said.

"You know that if you leave and get declared, you can never talk to your sister or parents ever again?" Jackson said. "You can't just go back to LA and live life like this never happened. You will have to go live somewhere else and never see your family again. Or at least not until you pay back your freeloader debt and get through all the steps to get undeclared."

"I guess I don't really have a choice then do I?" I said in apathy.

Jackson drove off and I thought about my situation for hours. If I tried to play nice, I would still be stuck here, but would be able to speak with my family. If I did ever get out of here, I would have to start over and find a place to live and somehow find a job to make a living. I could barely do that before with a few connections. Now I would have to somehow start my life over and make a living with no friends or family. That seemed like a daunting proposition. I thought that I sometimes wish I were dead.

My options were limited. I could go to the RPF and live a miserable existence there, but still get food and housing. I could play nice and try and stay here and live a slightly less miserable existence with food and some sort of housing. Or my last and final option was get the hell out of here, do whatever the hell I wanted to, never being able to talk with any of my friends or family ever again, owe these people several thousand dollars and most likely live like a bum, starving to death and without a roof over my head.

At 17 years old, after having spent close to a year at the base, I had no idea what I should do. I was not able to talk to anybody and it was up to me to decide what I was going to do. It seemed like no matter what door I picked, I was going to be walking into a nightmare. I had no idea what I was going to do. I figured I would just go along and see what happened. Maybe an opportunity would present itself and I could miraculously escape the pain and suffering my future had in store for me.

I had to go into the garage to get another broom. On my way in, I had to stop and help a guy move some stuff in the garage. We were down behind a large table and were pulling out some stuff when we saw Dave Miscavige come in. He was with a security guard. As Dave walked in he took off his Ray Ban sunglasses and handed them to the security guard. He walked across the room towards another guy that was in the garage. It was Mark Fisher. Mark Fisher had been in Religious Technology Center just a few months prior. Mark did not stop to show that he saw Dave was there. He just kept doing what he was doing. Dave started yelling at him.

Mark Fisher looked back at him and said "What do you want, Dave?" Mark was much heftier than Dave and at least a foot taller as well.

I had never heard anybody ever call him "Dave" to his face. It was always "Sir."

Dave did not like being talked to in any other way than as if he was the most important guy in the room. Mark just scowled at Dave. He did not care who Dave thought he was, he was talking down at Dave and telling him he did not care what he thought or what he did. Dave started punching Mark with the guard standing right there. Mark did not hit back, he just put his arms up to block as many punches as he could. Dave hit him over and over again. When Dave was done, Mark just stood there, bloodied a bit by all the punches. Mark, although physically attacked, maintained his composure and attitude.

"Make sure the medical officer sees him and gets him patched up," Dave said to the guard as he took his sunglasses back and walked out.

Mark Fisher went back to what he was doing like nothing had happened.

I got my broom and got the hell out of there. I was already in enough trouble without getting involved in this mess. Guess it was not a good day to be called "Mark" no matter how you spelled it.

Later that day, Greg Wilhere came to see me while I was sweeping leaves behind the mess hall. Greg seemed like a nice guy. Besides being the guy that hung out with Tom Cruise a lot, I knew him as one of my close friend's dad. Darius, his son, had gone to Delphi in LA with me years before and now that Darius and I were both at the base, we would hang out sometimes. I had no idea if Greg knew that Darius and I were friends.

"Hey, Marc," Greg said as he approached.

"Hello, Sir," I replied while continuing to sweep.

"Go ahead and take a break, Marc, and talk to me for a second," he said, and motioned me to sit down on a nearby bench.

"What's up?" Greg asked.

"Well, I am supposed to get declared an SP and as long as I am getting declared, I want to leave," I answered.

"You are getting declared an SP? I don't think so. Who said that?" Greg asked, half laughing.

"Jason Bennick."

"Not gonna happen," Greg said. "I am running this organization and I say what goes and what doesn't and I say that ain't gonna happen."

"What about the production line violations?" I asked.

"What violations?" Greg said, "The faulty tapes were caught before they went out, right? Maybe you could not see properly or maybe you were tired and missed those two that were bad. Who knows? But no harm was done. The only thing that I can see that was done wrong is that you were taken off post for no reason."

"Maybe," I said, still wondering how this would play out.

"How long did it take for you to get trained to do your post?" Greg asked.

"I don't know, a few months at least."

"Well, do you think everybody in Gold wants to wait a few months to get out of lower conditions because they need to train up another quality control to replace you because you could not see a few pancakes that were barely out of spec?" Greg said.

"Okay? You wear glasses. We are going to get your eyes tested and make sure your prescription is correct. If not, we will get you new glasses and get you back on post. Go get cleaned up, you are going back to work. I will talk to Jason and tell him not to give you a hard time. Okay?" Greg knew I did not want to get declared. He knew I did not want to be cut off from my family permanently.

I went over to the garage and turned in my broom. I got a shower and changed back into my uniform. I went to see the medical officer. As soon as she saw me approaching the building, the medical officer grabbed me and said that I was supposed to be in town getting an eye exam! She told me that I needed to go to a specific address, it was already paid for and I just needed to get the exam. The phone rang and she picked it up and shooed me out of the office.

I knew the address. It was in Hemet off of Florida Avenue. It was not far from the Kirby apartments. But how would I get there? Right outside the medical office there was a small parking area where people parked their motorcycles and mopeds. Tom Pope's moped was parked right there. It was small and could do maybe 45 mph, it worked, it had some gas in it and I could probably get all the way into town with it. I grabbed a helmet from inside and got on the moped. I put the helmet on, started the moped and slowly crept towards the road leading to the motorized security gate. I waited until another car was driving out the gate and then took my chances on sneaking out right behind it. Chances are that with the helmet on they wouldn't have a clue who was driving out.

I went out the gate and down the highway! I was out and no one was following me. Hah! I made it all the way into San Jacinto before I saw the security rover bike coming up behind me. I had a 50cc moped. The security bike was 650cc dual sport. There was no chance I was going to out run him. I pulled into the ARCO gas station, pretending I had not seen him.

"What the hell are you doing?" the guard asked. It was Bob Champagne.

"I'm going into town to get an eye exam. It was just ordered by Greg Wilhere," I said with a straight face.

"No way, you have to come back to the base," he said, not believing me for half a second.

"Well, I have to get gas to make it back," I said.

Bob got a call on the security radio. He answered it then put his helmet back on. "I have to go back right away, you better come straight back." He drove off towards the base.

I went in to AM/PM. "Can I get one dollar on pump #4?" I handed over the dollar.

The clerk looked at me then turned his head towards the pumps. He saw the moped, gave me a receipt and shook his head.

I pumped the gas. Decisions. Decisions. I had made it this far. Should I go to the optometrist? Should I make a run for it? Should I just drive back? If I take off with the moped, are they going to throw me in jail for grand theft auto? I don't have any money to get a hotel, food or cover any sort of living expenses for more than a day or so.

I decided to get the eye exam. It was paid for and it was my only chance out of this whole mess. I drove the rest of the way into Hemet keeping an eye out for any security guards who never appeared. Maybe they would be at the doctor when I got there. They weren't. I went in, filled out some paperwork, gave them my glasses to test and then got the exam. They gave me a prescription and I picked out some glasses I liked. I also picked out some contact lenses and they gave me some samples on the spot. The doctor showed me how to put them in and explained that my eyes would have to get used to them.

When I put them in, I could not believe how much better I could see. Wow! My eyesight had really gotten a lot worse since I had first started wearing glasses. The doctor told me my prescription was double what I had before. Twice as bad. Wow.

I thanked the doctor and left. I went next door to In-N-Out burger and got a bite to eat. As long as I was out I might as well live it up. I had $4 to my name. I got a Double-Double and a coke. It was pure heaven. There was something about In-N-Out, either it was the crap food on the base or because I had not been properly nourished in the last few weeks. Whatever the reason, the euphoria I felt while eating that burger was memorable.

I got back on the moped and headed back. I knew that security would be steaming mad when I arrived. I had blown the base and taken off without okay, without a license, without okay to drive and against orders to return immediately. As far as they were concerned, I had probably blown and was on my way to Mexico!

I pulled into the main gate. Danny opened the window. "You are toast, dude!" He said it with a smile.

"Go ahead and meet me in Tapes," I said as I squeezed through the slowly opening gate.

I drove over to Tapes, took the helmet off and headed inside. I could see Danny rounding the corner as I walked in the building. Greg Wilhere was in Tapes as I walked in. Danny was now just a few feet behind me. He looked pissed and ready to lay into me.

I walked up to Greg Wilhere. Danny had just made his way in and was approaching me.

"Did you get your eye exam, Marc?' Greg asked.

"I did even better, Sir. Even though no one could give me a ride, I managed to borrow a moped and made it into town myself. I was able to get temporary contacts and glasses ordered, Sir. My new prescription is twice as strong." As the words came out of my mouth, I half smiled at Danny Dunagin who was ready to pounce on me and drag me up to the main booth.

"Wow." Greg said, "See, it was your eyesight. I told you! Well done on making it go right and getting into town and back."

"Thank you, Sir," I said.

"Did you need something, Danny?" Greg asked.

"No, Sir. I was just passing through."

My every fiber wanted to flip Danny off and tell him to go stick it where the sun didn't shine, but I kept my cool and just smiled at him as he walked out.

In the meantime, Lynnea Baker was the only other person who could run the quality control station, besides myself. She had tapes backed up all around her. It was a disaster zone and she had been up for days doing both of our shifts. I could imagine she was pissed off at me, she said nothing and let me sit back at the station. I went back to work like nothing had happened. No one said anything. Even Jason Bennick managed to walk through without saying much.

"You are lucky people in high places like you, Marc." That was all Jason said as he passed by.

I had managed not only to weasel my way out of getting in trouble, but had also made a few friends in high places. I would still be stuck in the hellhole called the Int Base but I had graduated from being the "new guy" to knowing that I could get away with a bit more if I played my cards right.

Sweetest Perfection

We had been running the high-speed copy line for a few months and were getting better and better at figuring out what caused the tapes not to pass through quality control. Soon, we were up to almost 40,000 cassettes a week and were able to do that week after week. It was November, four whole months since the flood and since the organization was assigned "Confusion". It had been an extremely rough time.

We lost Bruce Ploetz to the Rehabilitation Project Force in Los Angeles. He had been up all night in Tapes on two different occasions and no one knew he was sleeping under a desk until he missed morning muster. He was sent to the RPF and we had not seen him since. We could not believe they actually sent him. There were tons of people that missed one muster and ended up staying up all night, but no one missed a second. Except Bruce. I never thought he should have gone. He never slept and was probably the smartest person on the entire base. You could explain a type of electronic device you were trying to make and Bruce could write the circuit board schematic for it right there! I think he was the smartest person I ever met in my life. He was a cool guy that was just around to help. I thought that people took advantage of him. He had helped build and wire almost all of the audio and video production lines on the base. He had also helped design the E-Meter and even held one of the patents!

Either way, we had been having a few tiny problems with a few machines that neither Luigi nor Bob Ferris (the technician assigned to our area) could figure out how to handle. If we could fix these last few machines for good, we could hit our 50,000 target.

Then one day it happened. Bruce Ploetz walked into Tapes. He was back. Bruce had lost some weight and had gotten a haircut, but other than that it was the same old Bruce. Bruce was told what problems we were having with the last few machines. He listened to what Bob told him was wrong and walked off into the technician room. He came back a few min-

135

utes later and started to tinker with one of the machines. If Bruce could fix these last machines, we might have a chance.

It was the third week in November and, within a week of his return, Bruce had managed to fix the last few machines giving us problems. We ran the line day and night and managed to reach 50,192 cassettes produced by Thursday, 2:00 P.M. November 22, 1990. We were pumped. We had done it. We had literally accomplished the impossible.

Mathematically it was almost impossible to do what we did. We could produce around 25 cassettes on average from a single pancake factoring a bit of loss and the few that flunked here and there. It took 2000 pancakes to produce 50,000 cassettes and it took around 5 minutes to check each pancake. That is 23.8 hours a day worth of quality control, and two staff assigned to do it. That means that there is 20 minutes each day where we do not have to be sitting in the chair checking pancakes. There are 168 hours in a week. We spent at least 120 of those working or on the way to work and the rest sleeping. Physically there was no time for anything else.

That afternoon we were all called into the mess hall around 4:00 p.m for a briefing. Hopefully we were not going to be yelled at. We were not in the mood. We had made our target. We wanted to be upgraded into normal conditions again.

We set up the mess hall for a briefing and moved all the tables and chairs out of the way.

We were lined up just like on the day when we were assigned Confusion. COB walked in. He announced that we had made the target of 50,000 tapes in one week on the Gauss line. Our names were all read out. We all went up to the podium and were given chocolates and flowers. After we filed back in line, Miscavige announced that we were upgraded out of lower conditions and that we could have an hour dinner to celebrate Thanksgiving.

It was Thanksgiving? That was one of the things about the Int Base. It was like in Vegas where they don't have clocks. At the Int Base, there were no seasons, there were no holidays. Just weeks that ended on Thursday. You knew when it was Thursday and that was about it.

We had Thanksgiving dinner and gave thanks that we were going to have our 30-minute meal breaks back and would be allowed to purchase snacks and sodas again and maybe even get paid. Sadly, we were happier than we had been for most of the year.

Waiting for the Night

We had spent almost 2 years on the night shift. It was Tony, Agnese and I. Several hundred staff members worked on the base during the day and about ten staff worked at night.

There were both pros and cons to being on the night shift.

Cons:
1. No one is around.
2. Sunlight is only visible when you are supposed to be sleeping.
3. If you miss the bus from berthing to the base, you are stuck at berthing with no means of transportation.
4. Same thing going home, if you miss the bus, you will be stuck at the base all day.
5. You are tired all the time.
6. If any executive comes through and does an inspection during the day, the day shift blame anything they can on the night shift because we are not there to defend ourselves.
7. If you are single, the chances of meeting a girl on the night shift are very low.

Pros:
1. No one is around.
2. No standing around during lengthy breakfast and lunch musters.
3. No mid-day inspections.
4. No snoring roommates keeping you up while they sleep.

Being on the night shift was a lot different than working days. Sure, there are tons of jobs all over the world that are done at night. But working on the night schedule at Gold was different. There were very few areas of Gold that had an official night shift. Most divisions would have day shift people that often stayed and worked through the night, but they had to be there the next day as well. The other areas that had night shift people were Security and the galley. That was it. Security night shift was made up of Danny Dunagin, the Night Watch Chief and whatever guard pulled the smallest straw that week. They would rotate the second night shift guard. The galley night shift consisted of a few cleaners that did all of the really dirty cleaning work that no one else wanted to do. These people were regularly cycled out with the latest person that had really managed to screw something up on the base.

Now in addition to the night shift staff, there were those that lived on the base. The list was not long, but it was interesting. You had:

1. COB RTC - Dave Miscavige. He lived in the Lower Villa with his wife Shelly, COB Assistant.
2. Inspector General for Admin - Marc Yager and his wife Michelle Yager. Lower Villa.
3. Inspector General for Tech – Ray Mithoff and his wife Gelda. Lower Villa.
4. Inspector General for Ethics – Marty Rathbun and his wife Anne. Lower Villa.
5. Annie Tidman (formerly Broeker) – She lived in a small house near Old Gilman's house.
6. Gary and Carmen Wiese. They lived in what was called the Maintenance man's house.
7. Security guards. Just about all of the guards lived on the property in Old Gilman's house in a room packed full of people.
8. Jon Horwich, his second wife Stephanie and daughter Roanne. They all lived in the Horwich house.

So in addition to the night shift, these people were sometimes seen out and about at night.

I remember hearing a story about how Hubbard used to do inspections aboard the Apollo and that he had an uncanny ability to walk into a room and go straight to the drawer where there was something that shouldn't be there. One of the stories I heard was that one of the cooks had put a pair of boots in an oven and Hubbard walked into the kitchen during the day and went straight to the oven, opened it and found the boots. I heard this story because it was rumored that Dave Miscavige had this uncanny ability as well. Staff would tell similar stories about how, during inspections, if there were one thing out of place, he would find it no matter what. Before I was on the night shift, I really did not pay much attention to this and thought it was just another one of those mysteries that goes unexplained.

Well, one night on my way back from eating midnight rations, I was walking past a building and out of the corner of my eye I caught a glimpse of Dave Miscavige in one of the offices going through desk drawers. I did not see anyone else, the room had all of its lights on and you could see into the room but if you were inside you could not see people outside. It was 12:30 a.m. Why the hell would he be going through people's desks in the middle of the night? I paused for enough time to process the scene and not an instant more. I knew better than to stop and ask questions. I walked on as if nothing had happened. I also did not bring it up to my fellow staff. This would be my little secret. I would take note and go from there.

The next day after dinner, there was the single muster that the night shift crew attended. It was one of those musters that we dreaded. Someone had gotten in trouble with Miscavige and now everyone was being punished for it. Turns out one of the staff members had hidden old and unanswered despatches, some of which had been from Miscavige.

COB had done a surprise inspection in the area earlier that day and he found the unanswered stale dispatches as soon as he walked into the room.

Now everybody had to answer every dispatch they had and each person's senior had to inspect and make sure that there were no other stale dispatches anywhere else in the area.

Every person had to get a pass before they could go home that night. Another perk of the night shift. Whereas everyone else had a few hours to comply with the latest order, we had all night!

As I was walking back to Building 36 from the mess hall, I noticed a crowd of executives yelling and screaming outside of the office of the staff member who had just been brought up. There were people jammed into his office and you could tell that it was a bunch of executives trying to make it look like they were doing something to get COB's orders complied to. It was a show. As soon as they were done yelling at this guy, they knew they had to get back to their office and hide their own stale dispatches before

COB came by again.

But then, as the moment was being filed in my head, it hit a previous "COB going through office drawers" moment on file. He had been in there just last night. He was going through drawers last night. He was looking for that stuff last night! He then did his "inspection" today with his whole entourage and of course he walked in and went straight to the hidden dispatches. Sneaky bastard. I immediately pictured Hubbard running around the Apollo ship in his slippers at 2:00 A.M. going through the kitchen and finding boots in the stove. Maybe Hubbard had taught Miscavige this tactic. Maybe this is secret upper level technology that I would find out about years later. Or maybe not.

From then on, every time I heard about situations where COB found so and so, I would laugh inside and wonder how many offices he had to hit before finding the "booty" the night before. If the crew only knew.

Surrender

At the Int Base, there was a drill for everything that would possibly happen. No matter if it was manmade or an act of God, there was a drill for it. The severity of the situation determined how many people were involved in the drill. This was loosely based on Hubbard's Introduction to the Sea Org tapes. He said a well prepared for emergency is not really an emergency because you have anticipated it. So we had our list of drills that would go into place based on various emergencies. These were:

1. Flood Drill
2. Fire Drill
3. Earthquake Drill
4. Power Outage Drill
5. Blow Drill
6. Intruder Drill
7. Protest Drill

Now, there were also varying severities of any one of these drills. Each Saturday the entire crew would play out one of these scenarios as if it were happening. Sometimes they would mix it up and combine drills. Like say for instance there was a power outage, that called for the Power Outage drill but also since there would be no power, the security systems were down, which meant there would be a Security Drill happening at the same time.

Most of the drills were slight variations of each other and depending which drill was called, you would go to a specified location and wait for instructions.

For a Flood Drill most people would go to their work areas and be on standby to make sandbags.

Fire Drill involved pulling out all of the fire hoses and hosing down the building.

Earthquake Drill was a no brainer; check your local gas feed, know where the water and power feeds are, get under your desk and wait for instructions.

Power Outage Drill was a pain in the ass. Each area had to turn off everything in their area and then wait until instructed to turn everything back on. For us, this one was the worst, because most of our equipment was electronic and had settings that were stored in memory. Shutting them off for ten to fifteen minutes would wipe them out and we would need to reset everything when we next went to work. As an added bonus, the security system, lights and sensors would be down in the event of an outage, so every male staff member had to spread out along the fence of the property and form a human perimeter all the way around the property. You would have to be within, say, 100 yards from the next guy or at least be able to see him. If you encountered an intruder, you had to make it known and get others to respond to your location.

Blow Drill was to recover and bring back runaway staff. This drill mainly involved Security. The security guards would try and figure out when the person blew, from where and how. Then Qualification staff would go through the person's folders and find out if the person had confessed to any recent crimes or was in any kind of trouble. Security would go through the person's personnel file and try to find out where their closest relatives lived to provide locations to check for the person. Recent mail and phone logs would be checked to see who that person had last spoken to. Teams of people would go to bus and train stations, airports and local hotels to look for the person. This drill would remain in full effect until the person was located and brought back to the base.

Intruder Drills and Protest Drills were very similar. All staff were to go inside, close the blinds and windows and wait there until the drill was over. No travel between buildings was allowed. Wherever you were when the drill started, that was where you had to stay. No exceptions.

If it was an Intruder Drill, when the intruder had been apprehended, the drill would be called off and crew could go back to normal activities.

If it was a Protest Drill, once the protest was over, the staff would be alerted when they were free to go about their business again.

We practiced most of these things weekly. The entire time I was at the base over a fifteen year period I think there were two trashcan fires and two floods. There must have been twenty protest drills and only a few intruder drills. The undisputed chart topper was the Blow Drill. You could go a full year or so without any of the other drills yet have thirty or more Blow Drills. Sometimes you would have back-to-back Blow Drills. Someone would blow and a Blow Drill would go into effect, which meant the security personnel were under the gun to find the person who had blown and were not watching everybody else as closely. This turned out to be a great time for someone else to blow. One time, someone who went out to check a train station for someone that had blown, got on a train themselves and was never seen again! It took two days before anyone had even reported him as gone because his superiors thought he was still on the Blow Drill! Soon there were only so many people that could be on the Blow Drill as too many people were blowing. Preventative measures were taken to prevent blows in the first place. Musters were held four times a day instead of three. Every single person had to be present and no one was excused for any reason whatsoever. If you weren't doing well, you would get restricted to the base and would have to sleep on the property somewhere.

Quarter Masters were added to berthing. This was a staff member deputized as a security guard who would walk around the apartment complexes at night and make sure no one blew. To the general crew and local Hemet citizens, the quarter masters were passed off as extra neighborhood watch personnel. As more and more staff blew from berthing this seemed to be the solution. All male crew members would hold watch one night per week at any one of the various apartment complexes that were being used in Hemet. Of course the natural progression of this included having the quarter masters themselves blow while on watch! Then there had to be two staff at each location so they could watch each other! Then the quarter masters would sleep in during the day after being up all night and one of them would blow during the day whilst the other was sleeping. Eventually, there would be two shifts of QMs at every apartment complex during the entire night and all day!

In my opinion the Intruder Drills were the only ones that were any fun.

There were four memorable drills that occurred while I was on the base. Then one time, there was a Blow Drill and Power Outage Drill on the same day at the same exact time!

INTRUDER DRILL #1

It was the middle of the day. A guy had committed a crime in Hemet and was chased by Hemet Police squad cars to a location south of the property and across the river. He got out of his car, ran across the levee and jumped the perimeter fence of the property. Not only did he get very badly sliced up by the ultra barrier as he scaled the perimeter fence, but he set off the ground microphones and fence shakers. The booth had already heard the police traffic on the radio scanner and now they had the alarms going off, signaling the intruder drill. Kenny Seybold (former security chief and current Exercise In Charge) was mowing a lawn down on the sports fields when he saw the intruder running across one of the lawns. He offered to help the guy evade his captors and jogged with him towards the main gate. Once they got within a few feet of the security booth, Kenny tackled the guy to the ground and held him until the cops came around to gather him up. This was the only intruder drill that the Security guards would remember as a "win."

INTRUDER DRILL #2

We were on the night shift in Tapes. It was Tony Cifarelli, Agnese Bertolina Johnson and I. It was just like any other night and we had been back from our meal for about an hour or so and I needed to use the facilities. It must have been around 2:00 A.M. The bathrooms are no more than 20 feet from where Tapes was.

I was sitting on the toilet when Tony came in. I could tell it was him because he always checked to see if someone was in the head when he entered. "Marc?" he said, knowing I had just left to go to the bathroom one minute earlier. "Yeah," I answered back. He was taking a leak. I could hear him humming as he did so. I am one of those people who needs some privacy in order to do my business. Tony coming in and humming had chased it back up and I was not about to be able to go.

All of a sudden Agnese came busting in the door and screamed at the top of her lungs that there was an intruder drill and we needed to get back into the Tapes area right away! Crap! Without even standing up, I pulled up my underwear so quickly that they literally ripped right off my legs into my hands.

I pulled up my pants and zipped up as I ran back towards Tapes. Tony was right in front of me. We ran into Tapes and got under the desk. Agnese

CHAPTER FOURTEEN – SURRENDER

had already drawn the blinds, closed the doors and was under the desk when we got back in there. The phone rang! I answered. It was the security booth. "You and Tony need to come to the main booth right now!" Danny Dunagin blurted out.

"Tony, we have to go to the main booth right now!" I yelled as I headed for the door. I was at the main booth within a minute. Tony took an additional minute to get up there.

As I showed up, Danny was in the booth and had a phone in one hand and was talking on the radio with the other. He was trying to reach the guards sleeping at Old Gilman's house and was having no luck. Danny told us a perimeter alarm had gone off up above Bonnie View at the top of the property. Danny still couldn't get any of the sleeping guards on the radio and Tony and I were the totality of the security force besides him and the rover who he had sent to go wake up the other guards. Not only could he not get the other guards on the radio, he could not reach the rover either. The rover was the one who was supposed to be waking up the other guards. Danny, frustrated with the no answers, told me, "Run down to Old Gilman's house, wake up the other guards and tell them we have an intruder. If you run into Deacon (the rover), tell him to answer his damn radio! I ran. Since this was a security drill, I ran straight down the highway as opposed to taking all the many paths that weaved through the property. Normally, security would bust your ass for being on the highway for any reason. As I was almost to Old Gilman's house, I ran into the rover, his radio was dead and his bike was out of gas! Talk about Keystone cops.

I told him that that I was going to wake up the other guards as I ran past.

I busted into the security dorm, started yelling for them to get up and that there was an intruder drill happening. I turned on the lights and told them that I was heading back to the main booth.

As I got back to the main booth, I told Danny that Deacon was down by Old Gilman's house out of gas and that the other guards were on their way. Just then, a few guards pulled up on one of their bikes. Tony was sitting on the curb by the booth watching me catch my breath. Turns out that the security radios were deader than doornails and that most of them did not work unless charged all night long. Well they'd only been on charge a couple of hours, so the radios were mostly still dead from the prior day's use. Between the bikes being out of gas and dead batteries, this intruder picked the perfect time to bust onto the property! Danny had seen something on the cameras but lost it and now Tony and I needed to help patrol the villas until they located the intruder. Awesome! Some excitement. The adrenaline was pumping.

"You and Tony go up to the villas and keep an eye on things up there," Danny said. "And take these." He handed us two long flashlights.

"What are we supposed to do with these?" I asked. "Illuminate him to death?"

Danny was not amused, "Only turn those on if you see something, and then get a hold of the booth and let us know - and be QUIET when you go past the lower villa!"

Tony and I crossed the highway and walked up the path towards the villas. We had to be real careful as we passed the lower villa because the last thing we wanted to do was wake up COB.

For the next three hours, we walked around and tried to spot the intruder. It was pitch black around the villas. There were a few lights outside the doors that led into the villas but the surrounding roads and bushes were pitch black. Around 5:00 A.M. we saw something moving way down near the lower villa. It was definitely a person and they were heading straight for us. We could make out the outline of the body and it looked like they were carrying something. Maybe the intruder was a thief trying to steal something? We didn't have time to make any calls to the security booth, we had to deal with this guy on our own. Tony and I decided that we were going to step to either side of the foot path and as he came by, we would whack him a few times with the flash lights and then call the booth. He was now about 50 feet away and we were right up by the upper villa waiting for him on either side of the path. 40 feet. 30 feet. 20 feet. 10 feet. 5 feet. "Oh damn!!!!" Tony and I cried out in unison. "What the hell are you doing up here!?!" I asked. "Bringing a submission to COB's office," she answered in her condescending French accent. It was someone from the Hubbard Compilations unit, Denise Delderfield.

"You came a split second away from getting your friggin' head cracked open, you crazy lady!" I told her.

She looked at me like I was high and said, "What the hell are you talking about?"

"Hello? There is an intruder drill happening right now! There is some dude running around the property and you are walking around all 'Ho-de-hum' and we almost beat the crap out of you with these flashlights," I said, just about calmed down from the adrenaline rush you get right before you are about to bust someone up with a flashlight.

"Go back to your office and stay inside! Tony, maybe you should go with her," I told them both.

"Okay. I will be back in a bit," Tony said, walking off with her back towards her office.

By the time Tony got back, it was starting to get light outside. "Damn dude, what took you so long? The sun beat you back up here."

"I had to use the restroom," he answered defensively.

Damn, I thought to myself. I still needed to take one. I never did get to go a few hours back and now that I was thinking about it, I REALLY needed to go.

"Besides, it was a good thing I did. I called the security booth and the drill is over for now," he added.

"Wow, dude! Thanks for telling me! You could have told me that before you took a thirty minute crap!" I said as we walked back towards our building.

We got back to the security booth and told Danny about how we almost killed Denise and asked him what the deal was.

"We found the intruder on the other side of the property when the sun started coming up," Danny said.

"He is walking down the highway now," Deacon added.

"Well, we're going back to work," we told the guards as we walked off towards our building. It was almost 7:00 A.M., so in reality, I was going to take a crap, clean up my workstation, eat breakfast and go home.

We got back to our areas and did our normal end of shift work, cleaned up and took out the trash. We went and ate breakfast and told Agnese about our lame adventures. Denise was in the dining hall and we told everyone around how we almost killed her with our flashlights. She was not amused. We got on the bus to go home and JB was our driver. JB told us that HE was the one who spotted the guy coming down from the mountain above the property while he was driving a bus in and alerted the Main

Booth. Good thing he did or we would have been up at the villas indefinitely. So in the end, he never even climbed over the fence! What lame ducks the security guys were. We asked ourselves what would have happened if there actually was an intruder with all of the Keystone cops stuff they pulled with the dead batteries and no back-up guards, etc. God forbid. At least we had some fun.

INTRUDER DRILL #3

This Intruder drill will go down in the books as the one that changed the security force forever. It was a normal Tuesday night, around 10:00 P.M. There were staff on post and it was not yet time to go home. Danny was in the security booth. Deacon was on the rover bike driving around the base. Danny saw an alarm outside the perimeter by the garage and dispatched Deacon to check it out. Deacon drove down the highway and pulled up in the area where the alarm went off. Almost 90% of the alarms they got on gates were from wind and small animals passing through. Deacon left the bike running and pointed its headlight at the fence. He saw something move by the fence. Danny called and told him the alarm had been tripped again. Deacon got off the bike, put down the kickstand and approached the fence slowly. He got up to the gate and confirmed there was nothing there. Just as he turned around to make his way back to the bike, he saw someone dressed in black drop out of the large tree by his bike, get on and take off!

"Danny, my bike has been stolen!" he shouted into the radio.

"Oh no!" was the message that Danny's brain sent to his mouth. Just as Danny's mouth was processing the message, his brain received a message from his eyes. Two more alarms had just gone off! One on the South side by the levee and one by the east entrance to the property!

"Repeat last message to mouth," Danny's brain commanded.

"Deacon, we just got two more alarms!" Danny said into the radio. As if Deacon could do anything, he was huffing and puffing his way back to the security booth on foot now that someone had practically jacked the rover bike right out from under him.

Deacon made it back to the booth and hopped into the security truck.

"Get to the east entrance!" Danny yelled to him.

Deacon headed out to the east entrance to check out the alarm down there. As he climbed out of the truck, he decided to take the keys with him this time. Good thinking Deacon. You would not want to have two vehicles jacked in one night. There was nothing there.

"All clear here," Deacon said over the radio.

While Danny and Deacon were freaking out and trying to catch the intruders setting off the alarms, unbeknownst to them, someone was climbing over the fence above the villas and carefully NOT setting off any alarms. He was dressed in black like a Ninja. He had a gun and seemed to know where he was going and what he needed to do.

Meanwhile, Danny and Deacon had received back up guards and vehicles. Two guards headed down to check out the alarm at another location. Who knows where the guy on the bike went? Was it the same guy setting off the other alarms?

"Eagle, do you see anything?" Danny asked.

The guard at Eagle could see the whole property from the perch on the mountain. If there was a motorbike driving around anywhere on or near the base, you could see it from Eagle.

"Guy on Rover Bike has been spotted; he is driving around in the riverbed on the south side!" Eagle answered.

Two guards raced down to apprehend Rover Bike Guy.

Meanwhile the Armed Ninja Dude up by the villas made his way to the middle villa, where the Religious Technology Center offices were located.

As the guards came closer to getting the guy on the bike, Deacon reported that he couldn't find anyone at the east entrance. Deacon headed down to the river to meet up with the other guards and get his bike back.

The door to Warren McShane's office in the middle villa opened. Armed Ninja Guy entered. Warren McShane was sitting at his desk typing on his computer. As quietly as Armed Ninja Dude entered, he took out his gun and came up behind Warren's chair.

Back to the riverbed. "Where is this guy?" the guards asked themselves.

"Looks as if he has turned the bike off!" Eagle said. "I don't see him anymore."

"We have the bike!" The guards exclaimed over the radio, as if they had anything to do with getting it back. It was parked in the riverbed with the key in it. Rover Bike Ninja Guy was nowhere to be found.

"We are heading back to the booth," the guards told Danny.

Back to the villas.

"Bang – you're dead!" were the words Warren McShane heard at the precise moment the cold gun barrel made contact with the back of his head. Of all the words in the English language, those three are probably not among the few that you would want to hear while the cold muzzle of a gun was being pressed against the back of your head.

Back at the booth, the guards were just starting to catch their breath and recover from what was probably the equivalent of having your shorts pulled down in front of the whole school at the championship basketball game.

The hotline phone in the booth rang. This was the direct line that is used only by Religious Technology Center staff in urgent emergencies or serious security situations. The guards in the booth looked at each other. Danny picked up the phone knowing that no matter what the reason for the call, no good would come of it.

"You guys are toast!" the voice said. "Someone just broke into Warren's office in the villas with a gun!" He hung up.

You could picture the look on Danny's face and the steamy pile that he dropped into his pants as the words hit his ears. I can imagine it probably took place somewhere in between "toast" and "gun."

Danny put the phone down and the guards gave him the "Well?" look. Danny told them that someone broke into Warren's office with a gun. Before they could even do anything, the phone rang again. It was Warren's number this time on the phone's digital display.

"Hello?" Danny picked it up hoping to hear Warren's voice and then immediately realizing that if he did, that they would all soon be dead instead.

"WHAT THE HELL?!" Warren screamed. "You guys have royally screwed up! You are ALL assigned a condition of CONFUSION! Oh yeah, the security chief is OFF POST!" Danny did not need to say a word. That was the end of the conversation. Warren hung up.

"We are screwed," Danny said. He was right. They were in fact screwed.

Turns out that Religious Technology Center hired some private investigators to break into the property and "pretend kill" Warren McShane. They were not told how to break in or given any information on the base. They were provided with a picture of Warren and an "X" where his office was located on a crude hand drawn map of the property.

These private investigators weren't even superfragelistic former criminals or anything. They were a bunch of yahoos that follow people and do your normal P.I. stuff. Well, Security got tested all right. As a result of this disaster, Security got a new truck, new rover bikes, new radios with spare batteries and about ten more security guards. Like that was going to make a difference.

FIRE DRILL #1

When we came in on the bus, it was like any other day. The only exception was that on this particular day the entire hillside behind the base was on fire!

The base crew were in a frenzy. People had fire hoses out at every building. All buildings on the entire base were being hosed down. By lunch time the fire was still going strong. The fire department had brought in several truck loads of fire crews. These particular firefighters had a unique quality: they were convicted criminals that were used to fight fires. There must have been four or five busloads of these guys right outside the perimeter fence making their way up the mountain. Because of this, the fire drill was turned into a security/intruder drill at the same time and we had people spread out all over the base with radios in case any of the prisoners decided to break into "Desert Disneyland" as they called it.

The state prisoners saved the property and got most of the fire out by the time the sun had gone down. It was actually kind of ironic: here you had the "most ethical people on the planet" and they were being saved by people that had been convicted of crimes serious enough to get them locked up. The fire was now burning on the other side of the mountain and the base was in little danger. The mountain was still smoldering and glowing with a bit of a red hue to it.

Marc Yager, Commanding Officer of the Commodore's Messenger organization, had been in the main booth running the fire drill and was telling everyone what to do. At around 8:00 P.M. it looked like several smaller fires had started back up on the hill above the base. From the ground, it looked like there were firefighters near the fires. Marc Yager wanted it checked out. I was asked to go up there and see what the hell was going on. Another guy, Erick, was sent with me. We were given a radio and were told to drive up to the top of the mountain, find out what was happening up there and report back.

We jumped in a Jeep Wagoneer and made our way up Lamb's Canyon. There was an access road that you could take to Lamb's Canyon that eventually made its way around the mountain and placed you directly above the base. It took us a bit to get up there. From the top of the mountain, we couldn't see anything. No fires, no base, no nothing. All we could see was lots of smoke. We would have to run down the front of the mountain a bit before we would be able to see what was happening with the fires. We did. After about five minutes of running, I started puking my guts out. I had, after all, been working a desk job for the last several years and running down mountains in thick smoke was not my specialty. While I stopped and puked, Erick had a chance to catch up.

Finally, we got to the edge of the mountain and we could make out what was happening. The firefighters had taken a break and were sitting around large camp fires that they had made and were keeping warm and resting. And to think that I threw up a perfectly good dinner to find this out. We radioed back and told the security booth that the fires that they could see were ones keeping the firefighters warm and nothing else.

Marc Yager would have none of it. He wanted us to talk to the fire captain and find out what the deal was.

When we got up close to the firefighters, we talked to the first person we saw.

"What do you guys need?" he asked as we made our way down the mountain towards him. He had a rifle in his hands and I got the impression that he was not one for messing with.

"We're from the property down there and we just did not know why the fires had started back up," I said, thinking it was the stupidest thing I could have said.

"Yeah, we're just taking a break," he said. "Did you guys figure out which one of your guys started the fire?"

"Don't know anything about that," I answered. "Okay cool, thanks."

We radioed back and confirmed that the fires that they could see were camp fires and that the mountain was covered with people still. Erick and I headed back up towards the Jeep. It took us an hour to get back up to the Jeep.

We wondered who the hell would have started the fire from the base. Did the guys at the base know this is what the firefighters were saying?

Wow. This was huge. We got back down to the base and everyone had gone back to their areas and the commotion had died down.

A bunch of people were yelling and screaming over by Building 36. The fire crews had to sleep. The place they had come from was hours away. They had to be back up on the mountain at sun up and needed somewhere close and secure so the prisoners could not escape during the night. Well, Muriel DuFresne, the public relations officer had freaked out about the fire crews/prisoners being on the property, so she had offered for them to stay out with the Rehabilitation Project Force at Happy Valley. Well, that would not have been such a big deal, but all of the kids were out there as well. As much as we wanted the base secure, sending a bunch of rapists and thieves to sleep next to the kids was not the brightest plan known to have come out of the public relations office in a while. The problem was that the deed had already been done and the crews were already on their way there.

So now we had a bunch of screaming parents trying to figure out how they were going to get their kids off the Ranch for the night, while convicted criminals slept a few hundred yards away on the football field.

We still hadn't found out who started the fire. Setting a trashcan on fire is one thing. Setting a mountain on fire is quite another.

The next day it would all come out.

Kevin Posten, one of the night watch security guards, had been on watch up at Eagle the night before the fire. When he got off watch in the morning he decided to take a crap before coming down. Not being in security, I am not sure how they normally handled such situations, but apparently Kevin did not want anyone to know that he had popped a squat up there and tried to burn the toilet paper he used, so as to destroy the evidence. Well, he ended up burning the whole mountain down instead. So, he was security checked and interrogated. Turns out that taking dumps up at Eagle was not his worst secret.

Security had a long range rifle with a scope on it up at Eagle. Kevin confessed to loading it and following Dave Miscavige around the property with Dave right in the cross hairs. He had seriously considered pulling the trigger but had never done so. Kevin's future as a security guard was not looking bright. He disappeared from the base and was never seen again. We didn't know if he was sent to the Rehabilitation Project Force somewhere but he would never be up at Eagle again, crapping, setting fires or otherwise.

Power Drill & Blow Drill

It was Saturday night during the summer and it was hot out even for Gilman Hot Springs. It was close to 95 degrees outside and it was pitch black. The past few weeks had been extremely hot day after day and with temperatures over 100 degrees every day the air conditioners on the base had been running constantly.

The base got its electricity from Southern California Edison. When the temperatures got into the triple digits, it was guaranteed that the base would max out the feed coming in from Edison to the property and whenever that happened, the power would shut down completely.

There was some sort of safety mechanism installed that would blow the power out. It was like a giant circuit breaker for the entire property.

We had been told earlier in the day that on Sunday it was supposed to be over 110 degrees. The power was sure to go out.

Whenever the power went out, anybody who had anything to do with the power drill, would jump up from whatever they were doing, spread out all over the property and turn off everything in their assigned building. That way, when the power was ready to come back on, we would not have such a huge load on the overall base power feed and the people assigned to each building could turn some things back on in each place and keep the power lines from overloading. All in all, this involved about sixty people.

With a Scientology event coming up in a few weeks, there were several areas of the base that were going to be up all night. One of these was Special Effects. They did all of the special video effects for all event videos. Flying through space, fancy graphics, fire, smoke, flyovers, you name it, they did it. There were about five people in Special Effects that did the work of about twenty-five. When it got close to an event, these staff could be counted on to be in their offices all day and all night.

A kid by the name of Power Coleman was one of two people in Special Effects who could crank out shots. Power was a mix between a surfer dude and a computer geek. He was very talented and smart when it came to computers, but had the apparent intellect of a waterlogged tree branch and although he never did drugs, you could swear he was high on something. He had an awkward glee about him that made you like him, but not take him seriously.

Power was sitting at his computer when he got a call from his girlfriend, Elsa. Elsa wanted to "talk to him", which most likely meant that she wanted to break up with him. If you are not married in the Sea Organization, you cannot have any sort of sexual relations with anyone, and if you do you will be assigned to the Rehabilitation Project Force when it is found out about. If Elsa broke up with Power, there was a good chance he would not be getting laid for years. Elsa and Power had loosely planned to get married in the next few months. So while Power was concerned about what the outcome of the meeting would be, if he wanted to salvage his relationship with her, it was a must. As he was going to be up all night, it would have to be in the morning when he went home to take a shower. Power lived at the Kirby Apartments in Hemet and Elsa lived about two miles away at the Vista apartments in San Jacinto. He decided he would walk over to Vista from Kirby in the morning after he got home. They would meet at Vista at 10:00 A.M.

Even though it was still very hot outside, the night went by quickly and Power managed to get on the 8:30 A.M. bus to the Kirby apartments where he lived. He hadn't slept a wink all night and was really tired. He walked into his room where a few of his roommates were cleaning. It was Sunday morning, so most people were supposed to be cleaning from 8:30 A.M. to 11:45 A.M. even though most people slept in or did their laundry for the week. Power was going to take a shower and head over to meet Elsa. By the time he had taken a shower it was already 9:30 A.M. He had to hurry if he was going to make it to Vista by 10:00 A.M. It would take at least 30 minutes if he walked fast or even ran some of the way.

He made his way out of the Kirby apartments toward Menlo Street. He was starving. The last food he had was at midnight the night before. He stopped at the Kirby market on the corner and got himself a jug of orange juice. He chugged the whole thing right there. Not only was it 100 degrees outside, but he had to get to Vista in the next 15 minutes. He would have to run the whole way to make it on time. He started running. After only five minutes of running, he had made good progress and was almost at the halfway point. Then it happened. As Power was running along the sidewalk and just about to cross an intersection, he passed out. Now, most of the time when you see someone pass out in a movie or on TV, they are either standing or sitting. Not very often do you see someone pass out while running full speed. That was exactly what Power did. Hitting the ground at that speed did a fair bit of damage. If he would have landed on the concrete sidewalk, it would not have been that bad, but the normally grassy area next to the sidewalk was gravel. Hemet is big on its gravel and small pebble sized rock lawns. These rocks were not friendly to his face as he came crashing down. Power laid there unconscious and bleeding for a few minutes, before an elderly couple on their morning walk spotted him. They called 911 and an ambulance was dispatched to pick him up.

Once he was loaded into the ambulance, they were able to bring him around. He appeared to be delirious, but otherwise not seriously injured. He was on his way to the hospital.

Meanwhile, at the Vista Apartments, 10:00 A.M. had come and gone. Elsa waited for Power until 11:00 A.M., and then left to get ready and catch the 11:45 A.M. bus to the Base.

As Power was rolled into the Emergency Room, the nurses had already found his wallet in his pants pocket. He had no identification and no money. The only thing in his wallet was a Blockbuster Video card. It was not even Power's card. He had borrowed it from another staff member weeks before. Even though renting videos was not a regular occurrence, some staff managed to sneak off during the night and get a video here and there. Power was one of these people. But as he did not have any ID or a bank account or credit card, he had borrowed someone else's Blockbuster card. The card belonged to a Peter Cook and there was a phone number listed. Although probably a common name, Peter Cook was a guy that worked in marketing.

"Okay, Peter, what seems to be the problem today?" The nurse asked Power as they took vital signs and got him cleaned up.

"My name is not Peter. It's Power," Power told the nurse.

"Okay, honey. So what happened to you?" the nurse repeated.

"I don't know. I was running and the next thing I know I was in the ambulance," Power told her, truly not knowing that he had face planted while running full speed down the street.

"Well, honey, you got pretty banged up, but we are going to get you some help and the doctor will be here in just a few minutes," the nurse gave him a smile and walked off.

Power laid there in the gurney and wondered what had happened and how he ended up in this mess.

Back at the base, the buses were pulling up and dropping people off near the dining hall. Elsa got off the Vista bus and spotted one of Power's roommates.

"Hey, did Power come home?"

"Yeah, he left to meet up with you this morning! We haven't seen him since and he was not on our bus."

"When did you last see him?" Elsa asked, worried.

"He left around 9:30 A.M.," Power's roommate said as he walked off toward the dining hall.

Elsa knew what had happened. He had blown. He never showed up at her place and he was not on the bus. It was not like him not to show up and he would have had no means of transportation to the base if he missed the bus. Elsa had to let someone in HCO know right away. She found Gerald Duncan, the Director of Inspections & Reports. She told him about the whole break up talk and Power not showing up for their meeting. Gerald could not take any chances. A text message was sent out on the pagers and phones to initiate the Blow Drill.

It was about 12:15 P.M. by this time and most people were inside the dining hall getting some lunch. Then, as sure as the sweat dripping down our foreheads, it happened – the power went out. You could immediately see who was on the first string of the power drill; they popped out of their seats in the dining hall tables and dashed out through the exits. They were going to turn off the power in their buildings.

The rest of us finished lunch and got ready for lunch muster. Muster was held right outside the dining hall. All the staff would line up and hopefully the muster would be quick with the heat being what it was. It was not unusual for musters to go on for 30 minutes. In the heat of summer, a 30 minute muster would mean that people would get heat stroke. Just in the past few weeks there had been several faintings during lunch muster. People would literally pass out from the heat. It was a combination of the intense heat, lack of food, sleep and overall exhaustion. Either way, most of us were hoping for a very short muster.

After everyone was noted as present or accounted for, the Commanding Officer Gold, Lisa Schroer (Allen) made an announcement.

"Okay, anyone involved in the Power Drill, stay behind."

Now, on any other day, this would have been a clear statement. It had probably even been said before on different days and had not been misunderstood. Today, this statement was confusing.

After the crew were dismissed to go back to post, it was like muster was still happening. A few people left, but most of the staff remained there.

"Let's go people, back to post," the Commanding Officer barked.

"But we are here for the Power drill, Sir," a girl from the qualifications division answered back.

"You guys can still work with or without the power coming back on," the Commanding Officer told her.

Gerald Duncan leaned over and whispered into the Commanding Officer's ear. Apparently Lisa was not aware that two drills had been called.

Yes, there were people waiting to be told which bus station they would be driving out to and people who were wondering if the electricity was going to be coming back on in the next hour or so.

"Okay, if you are here for the electricity outage go over there. If you are here for the Power Drill come over to this side," the Commanding Officer said while motioning to the two groups to move into different spots. If people were confused before they were certainly VERY confused now. After a few minutes of people still standing with the wrong group of people, eventually everyone made it into their respective mob.

Back at the hospital, the doctor had arrived to deal with Power and was asking him a few questions.

"So, what is your name?" the doctor asked, knowing that there had been some discrepancy with the nurses on this subject already.

"Power"

"That's it. Just Power?"

"Well, Power Coleman."

"But, your first name really is Power?"

"Well, it is actually my middle name, but that's what people call me. I go by Power."

"What is your actual first name?"

"My first name is actually Pure."

The doctor let out a small chuckle. "Your full name is Pure Power Coleman?"

"Yeah."

"Okay, Pure Power, where do you live?"

"Kirby."

"You live on Kirby Street?"

"Well, no I live at an apartment on Kirby."

"Do you know the address of your apartment on Kirby?"

"No."

"You don't know your own address?"

"No."

"Okay, what about a phone number? Do you have a phone number?"

"Um, oh, yeah, I have a phone number! It is 1-800-I WANT HELP." Power was excited; finally, he had an answer to a question that he knew.

This was the phone number that Gold staff were told to use if they were ever in a situation where they were out in the world and needed to call someone. The 1-800 I WANT HELP number rang directly into the main security booth.

"You don't have any ID, no driver's license, you don't know where you live, but your phone number is 1-800-I WANT HELP and your name is Pure Power Coleman?"

"Yeah," Power answered matter-of-factly.

The doctor got up and walked over to the nurse. "Let's get a tox screen done on Peter over here and find out what he is on."

Back at the base, teams had been sent out to check the bus stations and to drive around town. Power had no known identification or credit cards so he was not going to get far if he was on his way anywhere. His mom worked at the base. His younger sister worked in the Sea organization in Florida and other than that he did not have anywhere to go to. He might have had a grandfather somewhere. The only reason we even knew that was from a story that went around about how, when Power was little and was just about to get on an airplane, his grandfather took him to the little boys' room. Both he and his grandfather used the urinals in the airport bathroom. After being seated on the plane with his mom and grandfather, at the exact moment when everyone is quietly waiting for the plane to take off, Power yelled out in the little kid voice that reaches any and all ears on the entire plane at once:

"Hey, mom, when I get older, is my wee-wee going to be as huge as granddad's?"

While Power's mom was thoroughly embarrassed and said nothing, the whole plane burst into uncontrollable fits of laughter.

And just as the laughter started to die down, and Power's mom had still failed to answer the question, Power asked, "Well is it? I want to know!"

So maybe Power was on his way to his well endowed granddad's place, nobody knew.

As if the day had not started out odd enough, in the middle of the power drill and looking for Power, the receptionist received a strange call. Someone was calling from the hospital in Hemet; supposedly Peter Cook had been admitted to the Emergency Room. Gerald Duncan was notified and immediately the marketing secretary was questioned as to why she reported Peter as present at lunch muster if the hospital had just reported he was injured. Someone was sent up to marketing to check into it further.

When the Hubbard Communications Office staff got up to marketing, there was Peter Cook sitting at his desk, clearly not at the hospital.

Just then the electricity came back on.

Two people already driving around town looking for Power were told to head over to the hospital and check out the Peter Cook imposter. When the guys from Gold showed up, and saw that it was Power, they claimed him and talked to the doctor to find out what had happened. The doctor said that it looked like he had either gotten into a fight or fallen off a bike, and was high on something they had yet to determine. The doctor referenced the unfamiliarity with his surroundings and the strange names and phone numbers he had told them about. The doctor was told that all of these things were actually true and that Power's real name was in fact Pure and his phone number really was 1-800-I WANT HELP and that he lived on Kirby street in Hemet.

After Power got some sleep, they let him leave the hospital. Subsequently, Power was required to get an ID card with his full name listed. He was made to learn his address and the local phone number to the base. Elsa was so impressed by his devotion, that she decided not to break up with him and they got married a few months later. Too bad that he eventually cheated on her with another married girl at the base and both Power and his mistress ended up on the Rehabilitation Project Force for having sex.

Years later, Power Coleman was spotted in Clearwater, Florida on the Rehabilitation Project Force. Not sure if he knows his new address or telephone number.

It's No Good

t was 1992. We had been running the Gauss high speed tapes copy line for a few years now. We had produced so much overstock that it was becoming a huge situation. We were producing hundreds of thousands of cassettes per month and only a small percentage of these were being sold. Most of the staff that were in Tapes had been transferred to new positions or had been removed from their post. Agnese went crazy and tried to blow but was somehow caught. Rosi got pregnant and refused to have an abortion. Unfortunately, I was still there.

It was around this time that I met a girl at the base that I really liked. She was a cute girl who was a supervisor where people studied. She was about five foot five, very slender and had long red hair. I was always a sucker for redheads and she had the longest red hair I had ever seen. Her name was Claire. Her parents were Scientologists and lived in Los Angeles.

The thing about the base is that there is no "drive it before you buy it" clause. If you get caught in anyway whatsoever messing around before you get married, you will go to the Rehabilitation Project Force. It had happened with this one guy who sat at my dining room table. He and his girlfriend had sex once and he went to the Rehabilitation Project Force in Los Angeles. Another girl that I knew had sex with someone and she met the same fate.

So Claire and I were careful not to have any romantic interludes that would wind us up on the RPF. After a few months of being together, we decided that we would get married in August of that year.

Because Claire was under 18 years of age, I had to get her parents to sign a waiver and my dad flew out to LA and drove us up to Las Vegas to get married in the state of Nevada.

In California, if you want to get married and you are under 18, you have to be interviewed by a psychologist and as that was strictly forbidden by the Scientology organization it was off to Vegas where they had no such requirement.

We had a total of three days off for the wedding. We went down to LA and met up with my dad, he took us to the jewelry district in downtown LA to get some rings. Claire and I were broke as a joke so my dad got us some really inexpensive rings which was his wedding present to us. My dad was not loaded with cash, but without him I would have had no rings. Afterwards, it was off to Vegas. We drove up in the afternoon, got the license in the all-night courthouse then went to a chapel where they did the ceremony and we drove right back to LA that night/morning to prepare for the ceremony that would take place the next day.

Since most of my wife's family and friends lived in LA, we had the wedding at the Celebrity Centre / Manor Hotel in Los Angeles. My mom and Claire's mom took care of whatever arrangements were needed. Neither Claire nor I had anything to do with the invitations, flowers, cake, etc. We just showed up.

It was clear that Claire's mom had done more on the wedding invitations than my mom, because I only knew about ten people who attended the wedding and that included my family!

We stayed at the Manor hotel that night. The next morning we got a call from the base. We were informed that we would not be getting a room together back at the base because no more couples' rooms were available! As if that was not bad enough, Claire's seniors were canceling her honeymoon day and said that she had to come back to work right away.

We went back to the base and while Claire went back to work, I went out to the apartments in Hemet and scoped out our chances of getting a room. Claire lived with several girls in a dorm. It was strictly forbidden for girls and guys to live in the same apartments. I did not care. Claire lived in an apartment with seven other girls. One of the girls had just blown the week before, which cut the number down to six. This was a small number of girls living in a two-bedroom apartment. Most two-bedroom apartments had four girls in each bedroom and maybe three to five in the living room as well.

I decided that this was our best chance at getting a room together.

I moved all of the belongings of the two girls that were sharing a room with Claire into the small living room and moved all my belongings into the room that Claire was already in.

In a few hours we had a room. And I was living in an all girls apartment! When the girls came home that night, they were none too happy. After a few weeks, all the girls were moved out and a couple moved into the other bedroom. Corinne Smith and Henning Bendorf moved in. Corinne was Maureen Bolstad's twin sister. Maureen Bolstad had tried to leave the base and was not allowed to. There were a lot of rumors going around about Maureen and that she was crazy because she tried to leave. I think it took her at least two or three years to finally escape from the Int Base.

Besides getting married, not much was happening on the base. The only noteworthy event was that Dave Miscavige had been playing basketball with some other guys and broke his leg. He was PTS! Now there were different rumors about what happened. Some said Dave broke his leg playing basketball with Tom Cruise and Dustin Hoffman. Must have been a short man's league on a seven-foot basket. Throw in a few flying monkeys as mascots and you could have had the Lollipop league from The Wizard of Oz. That one went over real good. The girl in Religious Technology Center who was responsible for Dave's handlings promptly disappeared. She went to a doctor's appointment in town and never came back. Smart girl if that is really what happened.

Anyway, Dave Miscavige had been buried in some major legal proceedings and we didn't see him much. We liked it that way. If he was occupied, then the base staff could get on with their work. It was a pure nightmare when he was around. People would blow, would get sent to the Rehabilitation Project Force and would exist in a constant state of terror. When Miscavige was at the base, it was like the place had frozen over and nothing would get done. It was weird because when he was there, the big push was always to get MORE done. It never worked out that way. So it was fine with us that he was off in Washington D.C. and Florida dealing with legal situations.

I was bored as hell being in tapes and any chance I got, I would help in the Audio Visual Systems department. They had these two old crusty technicians who worked in there and needed help badly. I loved making cassette decks and projection systems so they let me help whenever it was slow in tapes. Systems was another department in Manufacturing so the Manufacturing Secretary would pressure my senior to let me help. It worked out really good for me; my division head would go to bat for me to work in another area! I had gotten so good that I had even gone out to some organizations to install audio visual systems. One of the systems included two cameras and microphones that were installed in every single auditing room. All the cameras were fed to central locations where auditing sessions were watched and recorded.

Anyway, one day the guy who was over all quality control in Gold came to see me. I held one of three quality control posts in Gold. Well this guy was responsible for quality control of everything produced at Gold. He could walk into any area of the organization and do a spot check inspection of a product and if it was low quality or had any fault with it, he could shut down the entire area until it was sorted out to his satisfaction. He was a god. Even though he was quality control for Gold, Dave Miscavige had to approve all film rushes, videos and final film prints.

Well, this quality control guy, Randall, really wanted to be a mixer and had been in training for that before he was assigned the quality control position. He still wanted to be a mixer and if he could get himself replaced, he could become a mixer. He wanted me to replace him.

I liked the idea. In fact, I loved the idea. I could finally get out of tapes and I would be posted in the Executive division of Gold! My senior however hated the idea. My senior was Lynnea Baker. Before working in tapes, Lynnea had been in Religious Technology Center. She worked for Greg Wilhere and had been dismissed from Religious Technology Center by Dave Miscavige. After the Gauss line was cleaned out of all people and needed more, she was posted in tapes. This girl had risen all the way to the top and now she was as low as you could go. And here I was getting promoted out of there. There was no question that she was the better staff member, that she was more dedicated than I was, that she was more in-ethics most of the time. None of these weighed in on the decision. It was purely the fact that I had experience with systems which made me more qualified to do the job! So because I was bored with my assigned job and loved messing around in another area, I was more qualified! I loved that. She was pissed she ever let me do that systems work.

After all kinds of kicking and screaming from Lynnea, I got the job. I was now over all quality control. I would walk all over the base and check different tapes, films, videos and systems. I would spot check some items, and others, like systems, required that I check each and every one before they were sent out to Scientology organizations.

My wife was very proud of me. She was a real strait-laced Sea Org member compared to the wild unconformity I was known for. Now that I had a respectable position, I am sure she was happier. She no longer had to tell people her husband's post was the Pancake quality control. I remember that when I told her family that I was the pancake quality control they thought that Gold had so many people they needed a dedicated post to check the pancakes being served for breakfast!

From my new position, I had a tiny bit more freedom. I was posted in the executive division of Gold. My direct senior was Claudia Olander. She had been promoted up the ranks from the security clearance office and was now an executive in Gold. Claudia had no idea what I was doing because my post was technical and hers was administrative, so I did whatever I did and she left me alone.

We had a big event coming up in October at Saint Hill, the big old organization in England where Hubbard had lived for many years, and that meant we would have cassette releases and films and some other items as well. I would be busy quality control checking all of the products that would be released before the event as well as the videos of the event that would be distributed.

About two weeks before the event, a big meeting was called. The event was not going to be in the Great Hall at Saint Hill after all. It was not even going to be in Europe or England at all. It was not only going to be in the United States, but would be held at the LA Sports Arena! This was a huge deal. Every year there was an event at the Shrine Auditorium in LA and it was a nightmare trying to fill the venue, which held around 6,300 people. If we squeezed 4,000 people into the lower seats and blocked off the balconies, we were lucky and that was with all LA staff in attendance as well!

Well, the Sports Arena held well over 15,000 people. I am sure that everyone in the meeting was thinking the same thing, why are we doing this? We were not told why. We were told that a very big announcement would be happening and that this would be the biggest event Scientology had ever had. Well in Gold there was a saying: The bigger the event, the more chances we have to screw it up!

The event preparations were crazy. We had all the Rehabilitation Project Force members in Los Angeles building the huge sets that would be loaded into the Sports Arena. All the event crew were barely able to pull off a decent event at the Shrine. This place was easily five times bigger than the Shrine and the acoustics were much worse than the Shrine. The Sports

Arena sounded like a giant bathroom. It had so much echo that the sound guys were totally baffled (no pun intended) on how to deal with it.

Tons of lights were brought in. Tons of cameras were brought in. We even had a flying camera that was on a huge high wire that would fly back and forth throughout the event. They called it a "sky cam" or "cable cam". There were enough speakers to fill the Shrine auditorium and have no room for people. The speakers barely made a dent in the Sports Arena. The budget for the event was inevitably going to be in the million dollar range. It was like there was a money hydrant turned on to put on this event, and money was pouring out for anything and everything that was needed.

The stage being built for the event had a giant gold background with huge pillars. There were two teleprompters built into the stage that would allow Dave Miscavige to look out at the audience and read his speech reflected on these two mirror devices while being scrolled on a TV beneath the stage. This was standard for any type of event where a speech was prepared ahead of time.

People were being brought in to attend the event from all over the United States. They had people flying in from all over the world. All the rich Scientologists were being told, "It does not matter where you live, you have to come to this event and be there live." And of course, in true Scientology style, this was all being done at the last possible minute with the least amount of warning possible.

The event would take place on October 8th, 1993. As the date approached, more and more staff members were staying up all night to complete the preparations. Everything had to be perfect. We still did not know what the hell was even going to happen. A few people in the editing bay knew something was up. They were putting together graphics for the event but they were completely random. It looked like things from the past 40 years of Scientology's history.

A week before the event rumors were flying around the base. Documents were being brought in to be photographed and made ready for the event.

We had one week left before the biggest event in Scientology's history. This was either going to be the best thing to happen or the worst. Most of us at Gold had our money on the latter.

All the cameras at the event were TV style cameras. They had at least seven cameras throughout the Sports Arena plus the cable cam flying overhead. All these cameras were fed to the large production truck that was controlling all of the audio and video recordings of the event. There was a huge control station inside the truck and banks and banks of video recorders.

The audio and lighting inside the Sports Arena was being controlled from a large platform in the back of the arena facing the stage. There was a huge audio mixing board with a few people at it and a huge lighting board with a few more guys at it. The guy controlling the cable cam was also situated there and he had a TV showing the cable cam feed.

The night of the event came. The Sports Arena was about two thirds full. In addition to the public Scientologists, all West Coast organization staff and Sea Organization staff were in attendance which made up at least 2000 people.

The event opened with a laser light show and a flag twirling honor guard procession. Then Dave Miscavige talked for two hours. Most of us couldn't understand a word he said. The audio in the Sports Arena was horrible once you got up past the floor seats. So a thousand people heard what he said and the rest of us just clapped when we saw the people in the floor sections clapping. I knew that the audio staff would be losing at least one or two people to the Rehabilitation Project Force after this event. But that would be a small portion of the fun we had in store for us.

At the end of the event, Dave Miscavige announced that the war with the IRS was finally over. There was a big fanfare, falling confetti and standing ovations which continued for at least fifteen minutes. Dave then handed out some Waterford crystal awards to the tax attorneys.

Then Marc Yager, Guillaume Lesevre, and Ray Mithoff each gave a short five-minute speech and the event ended with David Pomerantz singing a new song called "Nothing's Gonna Stop Us Now." Cheddar had less cheese in it than this. From our perspective, besides the horrible audio, it was anyone's guess what would happen next.

The next day back at the base trouble was already brewing. There were unseen problems that had gone on throughout the event and Dave Miscavige was furious.

It seemed like anything that could go wrong did.

We all knew the audio was horrible in the arena, was it was also horrible on stage? Supposedly Dave was losing his voice because he was fighting to even be able to hear himself throughout the entire event.

When Dave got up to start talking on stage, the teleprompters were not properly aligned. So instead of having two teleprompters for him to read his speech from, he had one third of one teleprompter and the other was completely unreadable throughout the entire event. Also, the lighting was screwed up and a spotlight was trained directly on Dave the entire time making him sweat like a pig and barely able to see.

The staff editing the event had cut away from Dave before he could utter the words "The War is Over!" Dave had a big deal with this and had wanted to have the cameras focused on him when he said this. He was adamant that this was the most important moment of the entire event and he wanted the event re-edited so that the cameras stayed on him while he said, "The War is Over!" Simple enough request. Well, the video deck recording the camera that was on Dave when he said that line had a problem with it. Apparently it did not properly record that part. It recorded the rest of the event fine, but during that one single phrase, the deck was faulty and did not properly record. This meant they did not have Dave Miscavige saying the most important part of the entire million dollar event.

In addition to cutting away from his big line, the lights had moved off him when he said it. This meant that even if the footage was in some way salvageable, it was too dark and would have to be fixed at an expensive visual effects post production house in LA.

People were being security checked all over the place. Dave was going to get to the bottom of all of the problems with the event. He wanted answers. A list of people that would be receiving a Committee of Evidence was drawn up. It had five people on it so far and as more and more people were security checked, the list grew.

And as people were sec checked, rumors started to fly about what had caused the problems.

The teleprompter story was the first to hit the base rumor mill. The teleprompters were poles with one-way glass mirrors that were raised and lowered by hand, which was done by two staff positioned under the stage. Those staff had to live under the stage throughout the rehearsals and during the entire event. These two guys had to maneuver their way to the front portion under the stage and sit there for several hours and then raise or lower the teleprompter poles on specific cues. Well the poles didn't only move up and down, but if the person raising them wasn't careful, they could rotate the pole in its shaft which threw the angle off and made it unreadable to the person on stage. This was the basic problem. Also, the glass on these devices would be cleaned with special cloths for at least 20 minutes before each event. If the glass had so much as the slightest blemish, it would make the text very hard to read. These glass panels were highly sensitive and had to be handled with the utmost of care. You could only clean the glass above the stage because there was no available light below the stage.

Turns out that right before the event, Dave Miscavige had come out on stage for a make-up check. When he stood at the podium, Shelly Miscavige stood in front of the podium to make sure that his make-up looked good. Shelly was wearing a long flowing dress. She stood right above one of the holes in the stage where one of the teleprompter guys was camped out. Now I can't speak for every guy out there, but if you have a girl that is half way pretty standing above you and she is wearing a dress, chances are you are going to sneak a peek. Now we have a stagehand that is a bit excited, works up an appetite and proceeds to eat a big, juicy green apple. Eating an apple is not the best thing to do when you are sitting inches away from a piece of glass that despises even the slightest hint of bad breath. Well the guy ate the entire apple. A few minutes before the event was to begin, he noticed that he had sprayed apple juice all over his teleprompter glass and in three minutes he would be raising it above the stage. He took off his shirt and tried to wipe the juice off. This made matters even worse and the juice covered the entire glass with smudges which no amount of spit and last minute cleaning was going to save.

Meanwhile the guy on the other teleprompter was asleep. He had been up for a week straight and sitting in a small, cramped place in the dark for more than two minutes will do that to you. The sleepy guy had the teleprompter that was one third usable. The apple juice guy was a wipe out on his.

Upon being told about the disastrous occurrence with the video footage, Dave Miscavige wanted to review the video tapes himself and verify what was being said. He went down to the editing bay to review the footage. While he was waiting, he noticed the footage from the cable cam at the event. One of the operators in the bay tried to get him to come over and look at the footage he had been waiting to review. Dave Miscavige would have none of it. The poor video editing staff member cringed. This staff member had already watched the tape that Dave Miscavige was now watching, so he knew what was coming. The cable cam operator was doing the sweeping crowd shots of the arena and the stage and then after the shot he would point the camera straight down, bring the camera back up and do it again. Well the cable cam guy had given himself a bit of a challenge. There was a halfway good looking woman sitting in the front row of the crowd wearing a long flowing dress that was low cut in the upper frontal region. The cable cam guy would point straight down and get a really close up shot of her breasts, focusing right in on them before going onto the next shot. After two hours of practicing this, he had gotten very proficient and some would say that he had it down to an art. It really was art after all. Too bad the woman in the front row was Shelly Miscavige, Dave's wife. Anyway, so there was Dave, at the end of the tape and watching his wife's breasts up on the screen in video editing. By the time Dave finally turned around, the editing staff had braced themselves for the inevitable onslaught of profanities that ensued. To top it off Dave Miscavige was assured that the footage of his monumental phrase "The war is over" was in fact completely unusable.

Dave Miscavige said that unless they fixed the footage, no videos of this event would be sent out to the Scientology organizations. This was a big deal as usually Gold made video tapes the week after the event and had them sent out to all organizations around the world to play at events that had already been scheduled.

Something like this always happened at events and it was routinely a problem getting the videos edited and sent out for the organizations to play for the local public. COB would want all the speech flubs fixed, bad live edits fixed and a plethora of other errors corrected in the "final" copies that were sent out. Most organizations were supposed to have their local events the week after the live event but usually they were told to hold off for weeks and sometimes months until they got their video copy of the event.

One day I was sitting in my office on my computer. The computers we used in the Sea Org at the Int Base in 1993 were completely state of the art - for 1980! They were green monochrome monitors that were connected to a giant, room-filling VAX/VMS mainframe system. We had our own super fruity word processor system that had been upgraded to be able to print on Laser jet printers! We had a primitive message system that would spit out reports on you if you did not answer someone within a certain amount of time. And you could also get telexes on this super high-falutin' system.

I got a telex from one of the organizations in Los Angeles. They were writing to me to report that their video copy of the recent event was low quality. This did not make sense. Dave Miscavige was in the video editing bay screaming and yelling because no videos were ready to send out and here I was reading a telex from LA about a video they were watching that was low quality. I had to drive to LA to check some laser discs that were being made, so I made a note to check into this further.

The next day, after checking some laser disc masters in Pioneer's plant in Carson, I made my way over to the organization I had received the report from. I went into the lobby where they had a big screen TV with VCR set up. Sure enough, they were playing a video of the recent event! I was amazed. The event was playing on the TV but not one person was there watching it. The video was off color, had horrible audio and looked like it was copied over a football game that hadn't been erased. You could even hear the football announcers during portions of Dave Miscavige talking. I removed the tape from the machine and was immediately confronted by one of the local staff members.

"Where are you going with our event video?" he demanded.

"I'm confiscating it," I said as I walked away toward the lobby exit.

"You can't do that, it's our only copy!" he exclaimed.

"Sure I can. I'm the quality control and I just did." I answered.

I was amazed that they even had a copy. How did they get it? Where did they get it? There was more to this story than I knew.

On a hunch I walked across the street to another organization. As I entered the lobby, sure enough, the event was playing there as well. It was not as bad as the first video but it was definitely not something that I would ever pass off as okay. I went over and removed the tape. Again, a staff member came over to try and stop me.

"Can I help you?" he asked me.

"Yeah, you can tell me where you got this video tape," I told him.

"Well, we got it from the events unit like we always do," he said, trying to grab it back out of my hand.

"Well, it is being confiscated for being low quality. It's no good. I am from Gold and you are not getting this tape back," I said as I walked out.

I didn't even look at the video playing in the next lobby I entered; I removed it from the machine and made my way outside to my car parked in the lot.

I have to get back to Gold and find out who is making these videos, I thought to myself. I wondered how many videos were out there and where they had come from.

When I rolled into the base, it was starting to get dark. I made my way back to my office with the confiscated videos. The Commanding Officer, Wendell, and the Watchdog Committee member for Gold, Ken Mortensen, were both sitting in the next door office and they saw me as I walked in.

"Marc, can you come in here for a minute," Ken said.

I walked in. There were several executives standing around the room.

"We just got some telexes from LA. It appears you stole all of their event videos in a single afternoon. Why would you do this, Marc?" Ken asked.

It appears that during my trip home, the staff down in Los Angeles had been busy little bees.

Before I could even answer, Wendell chimed in with his two cents. "You know that this is the most important event in Scientology's history and you are directly cutting across COB's message to the public by taking those videos."

Now I was confused. The videos were shit. It was my job to take the videos. I was the quality control for all Scientology videos!

"The video copies were sub-standard and faulty at best," I told them, "And they were not made here and no one authorized them to be made. They were pirate copies."

"It doesn't matter, Marc, you are cutting across COB's message to the public. You can consider yourself off post if you do not give video copies back to those orgs tonight! Go sort this out," Ken told me, while Wendell nodded in agreement.

I left and headed down to video editing. I was distraught to say the least. Here it was my job to control the quality of videos being made and if one single video was found that was not okay, it was my butt. I found some bad videos and then was told that I would be taken off post if I didn't give them back.

I walked into video editing and sat down to try and figure out what I was going to do. No sooner had I arrived, COB and Marc Yager came walking in. COB looked at me and saw I had a very worried look on my face.

"What's wrong with you?" he asked in a pissed off voice.

I could tell that these would be my last few minutes at the base.

"Well, Sir, I heard about a video playing down in LA that was bad quality. I went down to LA, verified that it was bad quality and then found a few more at the other LA organizations and I confiscated them. Now I was told by Wendell and Ken that if I do not give the videos back to those organizations tonight I am off post, Sir." I said and braced for the inevitable.

COB turned to Marc Yager. "You get Wendell and Ken down here right now! They are both toast!"

"You," he said looking at me, "are the only one around here that is doing what I want. You find out where any of these other videos are and get them all rounded up and sent to you. Do not stop until you get every last one that exists."

"Yes, Sir," I said, thinking I must have dodged another bullet meant for me.

Just as I was making my way out, I could hear Dave Miscavige laying into Wendell and Ken. If there was one thing that Dave Miscavige seemed to love to do it was yell at people. He had obviously been doing it for years as he did it effortlessly and could be heard from over a hundred feet away. Oh well, better them than me, I thought with the typical dog-eat-dog base mentality.

In the end, it would cost about $90,000 to have a high-end visual effects company in Los Angeles fix the 12 seconds of footage of Dave saying, "The war is over." It would take months to get an edit of the event approved by Dave.

At least ten people from throughout Gold were given a Committee of Evidence and two were sent to the Rehabilitation Project Force. Most of the staff involved in the event lost the remainder of any rank they had achieved in their decades of service to the Sea Organization, and they were assigned hundreds of hours of amends to do (in their sleep time) to make up the damage they had caused. It was a blood bath. It was the worst situation since the 1990 flood.

1993 would spark the beginning of a new era of cruel and unusual punishment.

And it took me more than a year to gather up every one of the 1235 copies of that video that were passed around. It turned out that a "pirate copy" operation had been in place for years. I say "pirate" as everybody knew about it besides COB. The night the events were held, one SVHS copy of the event from the video production truck would go to COB and one other SVHS copy would go to a guy who would make a bunch of video copies locally in LA. Those copies would then get sent out, copied again and distributed to the smaller organizations. Turns out that because Gold took so long getting the final event videos approved by COB, this shadow operation had been put in place. Since I was the new guy and hadn't been grooved into the whole system, I ruined it for everyone. Up until that point, COB thought the events being watched were high quality edits that he was approving weeks after the event. Instead, most Scientology public were seeing all the errors, bad audio mixes and crappy speech flubs made in the live event that Dave would spend weeks having staff at Gold cut out so that the public wouldn't see them!

Behind the Wheel

After the 1993 International Association of Scientologists event and the deal with the IRS, it seemed like Dave Miscavige had nothing to do anymore. He was getting more and more involved with everything happening at the base. From technical revisions of courses to the color and type of the carpet in the dining hall, Dave had to approve it or dictate what it would be.

If Scientology as an organization were being driven like a car, who would the driver be? Who was behind the wheel of Scientology, so to speak? The answer is simple, Dave Miscavige. He controlled every single aspect of all operations and any major decisions were made by him.

In 1995, I was sent to Florida to install several new systems at the Fort Harrison hotel and surrounding buildings. I had to install several new equipment items in the Flag Auditorium, Sandcastle, and Coachman training building.

Dave Miscavige was at Flag the entire time I was there. He was running everything at Flag. Because he was there, and he wanted to use the Fort Harrison auditorium to brief the Flag staff on a regular basis, I had to make sure that if I ever unhooked anything or rewired the mix board or other equipment in the auditorium, the system had to be able to work in minutes if Dave Miscavige needed to use it.

I had set up a sound system for an outdoor wedding that took place at the Sandcastle. Dave Miscavige would be attending the wedding of two Sea Org members who worked with him, so because of this, I had to set up the sound system. If Dave had not been attending, then nothing would have been done, but because he was going to be listening, Gold staff needed to set up the sound system. God forbid that Dave would not be able to hear the ceremony properly!

Dave liked to give the entire Flag Technical delivery staff a briefing at least once a week. When I say briefing and Dave Miscavige in the same sentence that is Sea Organization slang for a lashing or toasting.

These briefings would take place in the Flag auditorium and usually it would just be Dave Miscavige on the stage and all the staff seated in the auditorium. Since these staff were dealing with public during service hours, the briefings would take place after hours when they would normally be sleeping.

The first briefing he did while we there was a real toasty one. He had been reviewing public Scientologists' auditing folders and was looking for things that were messed up so he could give the staff some lashings. He was pissed about certain public not being forced onto certain actions. The Flag staff were not being persistent enough and making the public do the services that Dave wanted them doing.

For this particular briefing, all of the Flag technical staff were there.

He started going through individual public auditing folders and saying what the public should be on and was toasting the staff for not having them on these actions. The public that he brought up in this briefing were burned into my mind since they had special significance for me.

He mentioned one particular public named Dan Kingsbury, the very same Dan Kingsbury with whom my mother had a child. Dan was supposed to be moving up the Bridge, but had taken a break to get some dental work and so had not been progressing. Dave said this was an excuse not to get up the Bridge and that Dan should have been handled and never allowed to take a break to get dental work. Now I do not know if there was a picture of Dan's teeth in his auditing folder, but anyone who knew Dan would agree that it might have been a good idea for him to get some dental work. But alas, the picture of his teeth wasn't in there and regardless, Dave was now going to make sure that Dan was forced onto his next auditing and Dave himself would be overseeing it.

Before this time, I had no idea that Dave Miscavige had ever been involved with technical matters of this nature. I knew he knew that some of the upper levels delivered at Flag (called the L rundowns) were the biggest money making service that Scientology had ever had. I had heard those words come out of his mouth. But either way, he said he would be overseeing this select group of people that were doing services at Flag and HE would show the Flag staff how awesome he was by doing this. As far as I knew, Dave was a Class IV Auditor trained at Saint Hill in England in the 1970s when he was 12 years old. He was not a case supervisor.

Dave continued with the next public person. He prefaced it with the fact that this girl had paid for a large amount of services and should be treated well and made sure that she continued on the Bridge no matter what. Her name was Lisa McPherson. He read through her auditing folder and pointed up things that had been done wrong on her case and told the staff that he was going to review her folders and make sure that she was being handled correctly and not being let to chase butterflies while she could be gotten up the Bridge.

We were up on the balcony of the auditorium while this was taking place. The balcony is near the back of the auditorium, but there were staff within 20 feet of us sitting in the seats below. One guy lifted his arm and looked at his watch as Dave was talking and instantly Dave went into a tirade.

"YOU WANT TO GO HOME??" Dave's voice boomed, "Really? I am here doing your jobs, and you are worried about getting home and getting some sleep. I will come back there and smash your fucking watch! While it is still on your arm!" If Dave Miscavige was upset before, he was genuinely pissed now. That was just the sort of thing that would set him off. Here he was trying to show them how he was doing their jobs and how he was doing what they should be doing and they could give a hoot. They just want to go home and for him to stop talking. We knew exactly what this meant. This was not going to end anytime soon now. And most likely, the guy with the watch would be getting his own reaming, either by Dave personally or one of his staff.

The briefing ended probably an hour later. Before everyone was dismissed, Religious Technology Center staff scooped up "watch guy" and led him backstage. Just the plain theatrics of this one guy being lead off would serve as an example to all of the other staff there that they were on notice. The rest of the staff then quietly filed out.

Someone from the Religious Technology Center came up to the balcony.

"Do you have the tape?" she demanded.

"Yes, Sir, we are just rewinding it now," I said to her.

All of Dave Miscavige's briefings were recorded on camera with the mics on stage being fed into the recording deck. He would probably have this tape sent back to the base and make all of the staff there watch it as well. Why not? He could play this video to them and show them how he was doing all of their jobs as well. After all, he was literally bypassing several echelons of Scientology's command structure all the way from Religious Technology Center, the base and Flag executives by even talking to these people. At a minimum, he was doing the job of the Technical Secretary for Flag. COB was doing a job fifty levels below himself. But this was how Hubbard did it back in the day, so this is how Dave Miscavige would do it.

The briefings were a regular occurrence for the next several weeks. We would play videos of bad sessions, you name it. Dave was going to rub their faces in any little fault he could find anywhere in Clearwater. He was going to keep rubbing their faces in these things until they started doing things his way.

One day, Dave Miscavige asked us to cue up a tape that he was going to play for the Flag crew at that night's briefing.

The tape was a semi-confidential tape called "A Talk on A Basic Qual" I say semi-confidential because it was not broadly released to public and was only available on certain courses. Students could only listen to it in the course room and they were not allowed to take it out of the org.

The briefing took place and afterwards COB called a few of us into the Green Room behind the Auditorium. One of his staff had called up to the balcony and asked us to bring the cassette he had played to the Green Room.

Dave Miscavige was all excited. He had an idea. In the tape, LRH talked about two things that set something off in Dave. LRH talked about drilling auditors and he talked about an E-Meter that had specific qualities that the current E-Meters did not have. This night would "change Scientology forever" Dave Miscavige said. No kidding. He was right.

Over the next few months Dave would live in Florida and tinker with every single area of Flag until it ran like a well-oiled machine. Everything from the way the Sandcastle auditing rooms were set up to how people went in session.

Dave had concluded that if Flag could make perfect auditors — lots of them and rapidly, they could drive the nearly one million dollar a week income at Flag up to two or even three million by streamlining every single aspect of Flag. And if they could do that in every area of Flag, then why wouldn't they be able to do that in every organization in the world? The Golden Age of Tech was born. Dave Miscavige would codify and perfect every single aspect of every single thing in Scientology so that there was no longer any thought process involved whatsoever. The auditors would just be programmed to do the right thing and people would get perfect auditing. Dave would essentially build a huge machine that would crank out Scientology services.

Within weeks the Flag Gross Income was over one million every single week. Dave had 30 people brought down from the base to work on technical investigations and handlings that he wanted done. This mostly involved staff at Flag being busted off post. He met with staff from the Church of Spiritual Technology about designing and researching out a new E-Meter. Meanwhile, Dave had staff at the base compiling new drills that would be put in place for any and all technical training courses in Scientology.

Dave had managed to take anything that involved any part of "friendly" or "personal" out of Scientology. It was now a machine that had one route and one answer, and that answer was being programmed into every staff member, every public, everyone that had anything to do with Scientology. If you did not follow the exact route laid out in the Golden Age of Tech, you went to Ethics, no exceptions. If someone refused Ethics and they were in any way irrational or "nuts", they did the Introspection Rundown or were security checked. Period. There were no exceptions. Dave's new machine was a factory that only had exact options. Gone were the days where you could talk to someone and sort something out or decide what was needed based on what they thought. The thought process had been taken out of the equation. Any talking about it had been taken out of the equation. You looked at the routing form or program and if it said Int Rundown, that is what the person had to do.

The policy on Keeping Scientology Working was quoted heavily. "We'd rather have you dead than incapable," Hubbard wrote in the policy that appears as the first thing you read in every single Scientology course. Well that's just what happened in December of 1995. Lisa McPherson, one of the few people that Dave Miscavige had been personally overseeing and supervising, had died. Dave knew he was personally involved in this one. Anyone that had anything to do with the "LMP" situation, as it was referred to, was watched like a hawk.

The two Religious Technology Center representatives at Flag who had been executing Dave's orders regarding Lisa were brought back to the base and were posted as dishwashers in the galley. The senior case supervisor on her case was made a cleaner at Flag. One of the rooms where Lisa had been held and examined was cleaned out and wiped down completely. Any traces of anything Lisa were erased. People were given an official story of what happened even if they thought differently from what they witnessed.

Dave Miscavige had messed up big time. He knew it, and a lot of people that worked with him, for him or around him, knew it. Some how, some way he had to make this go away. While behind the wheel, he had crashed and although he was surely at fault and there were witnesses, this would be classified as a hit and run and he would not be caught. Not yet at least.

There were people that were there when this all happened. There are at least five people that know the truth about what happened to Lisa McPherson. Those people will eventually tell their stories and the truth will come out. While they might be morally wrong for not having spoken out, I am sure their hesitation stemmed from concern they would end up just like Lisa if they did so.

Monument

The International Landlord Office was located at the base. This was the office responsible for making sure that every single organization in the world was in a building that was big enough, well located and properly designed and set up in accordance with Hubbard policy.

The landlord office had photo binders which contained detailed pictures of each organization around the world. In the front of the binder was a picture of the building exterior and then photos of all interior rooms, walls, furniture, toilets, sinks, broken floor tiles. You name it, they had it.

Now there were about ten staff in the landlord office. A few designers, a few space planners, a few logistics people, some project managers that went around and supervised individual renovations projects and the International Landlord. This last post was the most frequented post in the entire joint. I think that there was a new International Landlord about once a year. I can remember at least seven of them, and I didn't have much interaction with them.

My initial involvement with the landlord office was when I helped build their offices as part of the weekly all-hands renovations in 1990. The landlord office is located in what used to be a gas station adjacent to the main highway that runs through the property, in the "garage" or "estates" building as it would later be named.

In 1993 I spent quite a bit of time in the landlord office drawing up plans for one of their biggest organizations in Europe. This was the Advanced Organization & Saint Hill Europe. This building would be the first to have a new type of auditing session surveillance system installed in all auditing rooms. We were supposed to install a microphone and two tiny cameras in every single room where auditing was to take place. These cameras and microphone would then feed into several central locations where they could be both viewed and recorded. Any number of people would then be able to watch these sessions.

I had installed this same system in Los Angeles already, as well as other audio visual systems at other organizations in the LA area.

The Danish building was almost entirely made up of solid brick walls, so planning the installation of hundreds of cameras and microphone wiring was no small task. It took many weeks to plan and many more months to execute.

While I was working in the landlord office I became familiar with one of the biggest projects that they had been working on. It was the new Flag Building. This was to be the new facility where the Super Power rundowns would be delivered across the street from the Fort Harrison Hotel. The building was HUGE. It was six stories high and entirely covered with glass panels. It looked nothing like the Fort Harrison Hotel at all. They had a full-scale model of the building on display in the office. It was very detailed and even had tiny little cars driving down Fort Harrison avenue and people on the sidewalks.

I was asked to look at the building because they would need to install the same camera and mic systems in that building as well. It was huge and had hundreds and hundreds of auditing rooms. I told them it would cost a lot of money for that kind of stuff. "We spent over $50,000 having this model made," one of the landlord staff told me. "I think we will be able to afford the cameras with the millions of dollars that are being raised to build this building."

Super Power - 1995

There were two girls that worked at the base in the Qualifications Division of Gold. Katie and Melissa. Both Katie and Melissa shared the same last name of Feshbach. They were not sisters, but cousins and both daughters of the famed Feshbach brothers. The Feshbach brothers were famous within Scientology because they were rich. Not only were they rich, but they were still rich after giving millions of their dollars to Scientology. So they were in fact, crazy rich.

Katie and Melissa were obviously not hurting cash wise. Most of us would live week to week on our $35 paycheck. Not Katie or Melissa. My wife was also in the Qualifications Division of Gold and worked with Katie and Melissa on a regular basis. When Katie got married to a good friend of mine, my wife and I shared an apartment with Katie and her husband, Josh.

Melissa had a car (given to her by her dad), but had not done Car School, so I would frequently get to drive it whenever I needed, in exchange for being her driver when she needed one. It was a very fair deal and her new car was in no way a detriment to me.

Well, at one point Katie and Melissa found out that their dads and their uncle were all coming up to the base! This was unheard of. Public Scientologists coming to the base? Only movie stars or musicians would normally come up here, not stock market short sellers! So sure enough, Joe, Matt and Kurt Feshbach ended up coming to the base for several weeks.

Then we found out why. They were all going to get Super Power! Supposedly Dave Miscavige had personally invited them to come and receive the highly confidential level as part of a handling program that was being done with them.

The Super Power pilots had been being done at the Int Base for a few years, in 1991 and 92 but that was it. The rundowns were delivered to about a dozen staff. It was a pilot program, something LRH had written up in the late 1970's but that had never been released. It was sort of like the Star Wars movies. LRH had envisioned the processes, but the earth technology did not exist to do what he had laid out. Then LRH ended up handling all of the reasons he could never release Super Power by dealing with TRs (Training Routines) and then Key to Life (grammar and communication course). The first complete pilots were those in 1991. There were very few Int Base staff that were trained on all of the LRH writings on Super Power and they were the only ones who could audit it. And in order to audit on Super Power, you had to have first been audited on Super Power. It was like the chicken and egg problem. One of the rundowns on Super Power was designed to hone in all 57 perceptions, some of which included: Sight, Taste, Rhythm, Smell, Blood circulation, Gravity, Motion, Balance, Magnetic Fields, Compass direction and Pain.

The processes for each of these were devised based on what the staff in the LRH Technical Research & Compilations area thought would work best. These were then written up for the auditors that were doing the Super Power Pilot program and they wrote up whether or not they "worked" or what happened instead.

I remember seeing one of the Feshbach brothers on the Par Course (fitness trail) one day with his auditor, Gelda Mithoff. The Par Course was an exercise course at the Int Base that had various obstacles and sand pits off to the side of the track where one could work out and check one's heart rate. He was walking across one of the wood balance beams. Hmmmm? Could he have been perfecting the perception of "balance"? Maybe. He could have been doing a whole series of them. If he fell down at any point during the course they could switch over to the "Pain" perception. Anyway, that is where they apparently did a bulk of the perceptions with the Feshbach brothers.

After a few weeks and they had all "completed" the pilot rundowns, the Feshbachs donated at least 4 million dollars between them and their families to the Super Power Building in Clearwater, Florida.

There was very little written up by LRH on what to do on some of the rundowns. On this one rundown, the Perception Rundown, he said that the perceptions needed to be trained and tested. There was very little direction or writing on how to do this. Hubbard had said to have the person put his attention on the perception and then take his attention off it. This was one of the biggest blocks to Super Power getting done. No one on staff was qualified to figure this out. Some of these things were highly technical and required complicated engineering and design work.

The Super Power building plans had been announced in 1991. Five years later they had not even been designed! How would they design and build and test 57 perceptics systems that could be installed and used at the Int base and then perfected and reinstalled at the new Super Power building? In 1998, discussions occurred about how they could properly pilot the Super Power Rundowns in order to know how to build the building in Florida. Would they have to build all of the perceptics systems at Int BEFORE the building could be properly designed? This was a huge situation that needed to be addressed. Not only did it need to be worked on, but it had to be worked on by people that were not already working on some other aspect of Super Power as then that would come to a screeching halt.

Dave Miscavige came up with the solution. Who within the Scientology organization structure had designed and built things that were not already figured out by others? CST. The Church of Spiritual Technology was the organization responsible for designing and building the secret underground bunkers in California and New Mexico. They were the ones that had figured out how to put all Hubbard's writings onto titanium plates and gold records. They had also been able to do all this with an unlimited amount of funds provided by Author Services, Inc. These funds were primarily from royalties of fiction and non-fiction book sales, limited edition artwork, as well as public donations for "Preservation of the Tech". Russ Bellin, the Commanding Officer of CST, was the driving force in getting these things done.

Russ and his crew were brought in and briefed on what was needed. They had to work fast because the new Super Power building needed to be designed around what they were going to ultimately come up with in terms of designs for the individual perceptic systems.

When CST was done testing and devising the perceptics devices, pilots could actually be done correctly for the first time. But when would this start?

Since LRH originally wrote about Super Power in 1978, it had never made its way into being delivered in a Scientology Organization. LRH's original intention for Super Power was that it was for the out ethics unproductive staff that were running Scientology Internationally. It was not originally intended for public at all!

2003 – Cine Castle

The Cine Sec Gold, Lisa Schroer, came to see me in the Cine Castle. Russ Bellin and several CST staff needed to set up a perceptic device for testing at the Cine Castle. By this time, I was the Pre-Production Director over the Cine Castle and thus over anything that needed to be set up in it, since I had the Sets and Props Crew under me as well as the manpower to build and move stuff.

Russ Bellin was going to meet with us along with some of his CST staff. We met in the main Studio. Tom Willis and Tom Vorm, both very tall CST staff came and saw us with Russ Bellin. Russ did all of the talking. He filled us in on what was going to happen. For one of the upcoming *Freewinds* events for the upper level Scientologists (OT VIIIs), we needed to show some of the new perceptics devices in order to get more donations for the Super Power project. Dave Miscavige had directed Russ Bellin to set up and shoot video footage of a few of these devices.

The ones we would be setting up would be the "Orbitron" and the "Zero Gravity Rig". The Orbitron was your basic personal Gyro Spin rig that you can get on at the high-end gyms with one small additional detail. It was motorized and had a joystick installed on it so that you could adjust your spin and axis in any direction while riding it. If there was a perceptic that had to do with perception of puke leaving your mouth, this was the rig to test that. I am cool with roller coasters, but this thing was like the craziest roller coaster you have ever ridden – on crack. It had metal diamond plate panels on every flat surface imaginable.

The next perceptic rig was pretty tame compared to the Barfitron. It consisted of two 18-foot high sets of wire trusses that supported a personal harness over a span of about 20 feet. With a set of weights matched to the person's own body weight, you could walk with the apparency of zero gravity. If you gave a small push against the ground with your foot while in the harness, you would raise several feet into the air. This rig, while cool, was insanely loud. A water vacuum was being used to regulate the weight balance, and motors and pumps were grinding away while the person bounced around in the rig. It also had quite a few moving wires and parts that were sensitive to movement.

When the CST crew showed up with the two rigs for us to shoot, they brought along the guy that helped them build these things. The guy was very cool and had a tricked out truck with metal diamond plates on every surface possible. I was starting to see where the design criteria were coming from for these perceptic rigs. After setting up the rigs and talking with him a bit, it was clear he was just an engineer that worked out of his own shop and was the local guy that CST had found to work on their stuff. I gathered he was from Running Springs or another nearby town to them.

While these rigs seemed fine for a small shoot to pump some people up and get them to dump more money down for the Super Power building, I myself could not fathom how they would be perfecting these to install in a building for regular and constant use by paying public. Just think about how often roller coasters break down and people get hurt. Now just pretend that Billy Bob down the street designed and built the roller coaster. That was what these rigs were. They were home grown projects that had a lot of money behind them.

After we had set up the rigs and shot the footage, Dave Miscavige thought he would show off all the work his CST people had done and started bringing more and more perceptics rigs to the base for people to see and try out. He actually had many of these set up in his newly built 70 million-dollar RTC "Building 50". Funnily enough, the 70 million dollar

RTC building went from design to built in no more than five years. That included the interior work being redone several times and having a lot of very expensive furniture custom built, but still it got done in one fourth of the time as the Super Power building! Once the perceptics were set up, Dave showed us these himself and compared them to what was done before over the past twenty years.

There was the Smell perceptic. Hundreds and hundreds of vials of distinct smells that did not evaporate. You name it, bananas, peppermint, sunflowers, any smell that you can think of, they had it in a vial. There were rows and rows of vials and each one had a number on it. Some of the smells were very similar, like oranges, tangerines, orange peel, orange juice, you had to tell the difference and until you could name each and every one correctly, you did not finish this perceptic.

Dave Miscavige said that before CST had made and designed the perceptic devices, the smell perceptic was done using plates of oranges, apples, lemons and bananas. You could have done the old smell perceptic with a hotel breakfast cart! So that is how the Feshbachs got through the smell perceptic.

We saw a rig for drilling the balance perceptic. It was a small diamond plate platform about 3 feet wide that had a small handle bar that came up from the floor and had three places where you could grab with your hand. You would stand on the platform and it would slightly adjust its pitch randomly to try and get you to fall off. If you grabbed the handles it would shut off and default the platform back to its flat position. Ray Mithoff got on the machine and Russ Bellin turned it on. Before it could even really start to change its pitch, Ray lost his balance and grabbed the handles. Even I lasted around 15 seconds before grabbing the handle on my first go!

While we thought this "show and tell" was very interesting, Dave Miscavige had another reason for showing us all this stuff.

One morning shortly thereafter, he called us all into the main conference room in Building 50. We all knew that this would be one of those six-hour meetings where he would tell us why we were all responsible for keeping this project stalled. He explained that CST had spent many years and many millions of dollars perfecting the perceptic devices for the new Super Power building. Even with that he did not think that would get us any closer to opening the new building. Why?

START OF MEETING: The Super Power building had been redesigned and partially built, but was having to be redesigned again to properly fit the new perceptics rigs and even that was a guess as none of the rundowns had been delivered with these devices, they had just been worked out on paper. They had not been tested or piloted with people and auditing. Dave reminded us that the new designs also meant that all the money that the Landlord office spent on the original "Death Star" Super Power Building design had to be scrapped and the new design would match the Fort Harrison more. That was millions of dollars wasted on the old plans, designs, models, etc.

Now here was the real clincher. There was nobody to do any of the work that was needed to get Super Power ready.

Who was going to do these pilots? The base staff were out-ethics criminals and could not get case gain. That had been the problem all along; you cannot get standard results on people that are out ethics. But it was a confidential program that needed to be done at the base. (Funny, that was the EXACT reason LRH developed Super Power in the first place—to make the out-ethics staff at Int into productive staff.)

So after the pilot Super Power Rundowns are done on a mysterious group of people, who was going to write up the processes and codify how they get delivered? Someone had to write up the course pack that each person receiving the rundowns studies. Someone had to write a Super Power Course Supervisor Course Pack. And a Super Power Case Supervisor Course Pack has to be written up and checksheets had to be written up for all of these packs.

The packs had to be designed, printed, and then they had to be tested in conjunction with the actual devices and how the building was laid out.

How could you have multiple people doing the rundown at the same time? Were people going to be stuck on one perceptic system more than others? Did there need to be multiple rooms for some perceptics and fewer of others? These were all questions that had been unanswered for years and would remain unanswered for many more years.

The whole reason that Flag was being streamlined in the mid-90s was to increase the number of new Ls Auditors. Ls were the single largest source of income of all Scientology services. That was part of the reason the Golden Age of Tech came about. It was an effort to make a machine for creating Ls auditors faster than had ever been done before. More Ls Auditors would equal more money. If it could work for Ls auditors, all tech should be trained that way.

And then, of course there was the Cause Resurgence Rundown, or Running Program. This had been an extensive pilot programs for as long as Super Power and still it was not totally worked out.

Hundreds of people at the base have done the Running Program. It was a very simple program. I know, because I myself did it. A person would run around a dirt track until they were physically exhausted and could run no longer. They would be allowed to come inside a small area with couches in it and rest. As soon as they were rested, they were instructed to go outside and run again. When I say run, I do not mean walk fast, I mean run like you are being chased. You would do this non-stop for at least five hours per day. That was the absolute minimum hours the program could be done daily. Most people doing the program were asked to go for a full ten or twelve hours daily. The length of the rundown was different for every person. I myself took about three months to complete the program. The last day I was on the program, I ran for six hours without stopping. I did the pilot version of the rundown. All of the materials I read while doing the pilot rundown were written in the early 1980's.

The Running Program had been done at the base for years. It could only be done by people who are physically fit or who can work up to it, but even the most physically fit had injuries on this program. How were we supposed to deliver this to the public? Also there was the fact that a large percentage of the people who did the program eventually blew or were declared SP. Why was that? What was being done wrong?

And PC, Supervisor, C/S packs and checksheets would also have to be drawn up for the Running Program and people would have to be trained and gotten through it BEFORE the building was opened so that they could be in place beforehand.

Super Power and the Running Program were not the only things that needed to be released:

- We still had all of the Basics Books and Lectures to be redone.
- The new Mark VIII Ultra E-Meter – 30,000 already produced and sitting in a warehouse in Los Angeles. Only cost $40 each to make but we would still sell them for over $3000. Would not require being sent in for service. Could be updated over the Internet. All public would be

made to buy two and we should be able to sell out in the first year. We only ever made 30,000 Mark VIIs so we knew there were at least that many people that would need the new E-Meter.

- New E-Meter Books – new E-meter would require that all these books be re-done.

- New Grades – with new E-meter we could then re-release the Grades that were incorrectly modified and made 10 times longer than they were supposed to be.

- Key to Life and Life Orientation Course had to be redone as they were not done based on what LRH said to do and took too long to complete.

- Would the Saint Hill Special Briefing Course be released on CD? All those 400 plus lectures had to be re-edited and checked, transcripts had to be re-done. Packaging had to be redone.

- Would the Ls need to be fixed? The issues being used were Board Technical Bulletins written by David Mayo — a past Senior Case Supervisor International who used to be LRH's auditor and was now a declared suppressive — among others. How would we fix these since they were the best money maker, but not written by LRH? How do we solve this?

- Any auditor courses that had references to the E-meter had to be updated. All of these things affected each other. You could not change one without changing another. If you released one thing you might have to re-release four other things as well.

These were the things that had to be figured out. END OF MEETING.

Dave Miscavige then spent 2 more hours telling us how he was the only one who could do any of the above things and how he had to redo all of the new Basics books himself, he had to redo the PTS/SP Course himself, he had to do all of the Golden Age of Tech himself with a few people working directly for him. Then after all that, he had to redo the policies himself and would inevitably have to redo all the Tech Bulletins and new Tech Volumes himself. Everything that had not been redone in the last few years ALL had to be redone because there would be so many new things that the old things would not match up at all, wouldn't make sense and would contradict each other.

The meeting went until about 1:00 A.M. and we all went back to our work areas. Of course, I left out all the name calling, people getting smacked by Dave, sentences laced with vulgar profanities and Dave Miscavige sending people out of the meeting because he no longer wanted to "look at their faces" while talking.

You may wonder how I could sit and recount this in such detail. Well, seeing as this exact same meeting happened at least 30 times in some form or another over several years, I remember it like it happened earlier today. More or less the same people were there and the same things were gone over since Dave had told us to do them on hundreds of occasions—he was the only one who could do these things and any work done by someone other than him was uniformly rejected, so why bother?

Every so often, one of the hundreds of things he had talked about would finally get done and it would be one, single thing that we would no longer have to hear about. Even sometimes that thing we would hear about again, since later on, Dave would decide that it was now flawed based on some new thing he had decided should be a certain way. For example, a book that went with a certain set of lectures and it had been mistakenly paired with the wrong set when re-released.

One would think that a Book Editor would have to have certain skills to edit a book. Well that being the case, can you imagine Mike Rinder (the head of Office of Special Affairs, the Scientology Intelligence operations branch) editing an LRH book while getting no sleep? How about Ray Mithoff (Senior Case Supervisor International and former Inspector General for Tech), the same guy that was declared a Suppressive Person by Dave Miscavige in the year 2000 for the out-tech on KTL and LOC? What about an Audio Mixer, Rick Cruzen, whose sole qualification that got him assigned to edit LRH's books was that he had read all of them — while on the Rehabilitation Project Force for several years! All of these individuals were editing LRH books, the basic books. Dave Miscavige says he ended up re-editing all of the basic books himself. So how in the world could the Super Power Building be completed and filled with staff and public?

(Author's Note: As I write this in 2009 the Super Power Building has still not opened. Over 100 million dollars has been raised to fund the construction of it — and continues to be raised, although more than double the budget has already been collected. The Empire State Building took a year to build! The only thing released from the above list of materials are the "Basic Books and Lectures".)

The Great Outdoors

We had to shoot a film so that it could be released at the Auditor's Day event coming up in September. The film that needed to be shot was Technical Training Film #1 - TRs in Life.

Mitch Brisker was a professional director who was hired on to direct the films and all other staff that produced the films were Sea Org members. Mitch Brisker had been a Scientologist for many years. The story went that years back he used to routinely do drugs and one day he woke up with his dead (cocaine overdosed) girlfriend next to him in bed. He ended up doing the Purification Rundown and years later he would become a commercial director and then somehow he ended up at Gold directing all of the Tech Films that needed to be re-shot. They needed to be re-shot because the existing films were so low quality as to be completely unwatchable and embarrassing. (Note: Dave Miscavige was on the crew that shot the crappy films and only one film that he worked on is being shown in organizations today.)

The rest of the Shoot Crew were Sea Org members. There were about 25 of us. This was the Camera, Lighting, Make-up, Costumes, Props, Sets and Talent staff. An equivalent Hollywood crew doing the same type of film shooting would have had at least three times the number of people we had.

We had four vehicles that all staff and equipment had to fit in. We had a 1979 GMC lighting truck (that routinely broke down somewhere). We had a 1979 GMC Camera truck, a Chevy "dually" with trailer and a white 15-passenger van. There were only five of the twenty-five staff that could or were allowed to drive these vehicles.

In the Sea Org at Gold, there are specific requirements that have to be in place for you to be able to drive. Very few staff met all the requirements:

1. You have to have done Car School, a course that requires you attend study time for a full month at 2.5 hours per day so that you can learn about how a car works and learn how to drive.

2. You have to have a current valid driver's license. One in every twenty Gold staff had a current valid driver's license.
3. You CANNOT be on the Potential Trouble Source (PTS) list. This is a list generated by Perimeter Council. Since all mail going to and from Gold is opened and read by Security, any bad indicators or critical remarks towards Scientology by any relative or friend would land you on the PTS list. Until you formally handled or disconnected from this person, you would remain on the PTS List. Also, if you got sick in any way, you would be added to the PTS list until the person suppressing you was located and handled or you disconnected from them.
4. You have to have read the manual for the vehicle you wished to drive and another person had to quiz you on specific points of the manual until you were able to answer any question they posed.
5. You could not have any accidents or tickets on your driving record. If you had an accident or ticket, you had to redo Car School and pay for the accident or ticket fees to get back "on the road."
6. You have to be insured on the vehicle you wish to drive. If it is a personal vehicle, then you have to cover the insurance costs out of your $40/week pay. If it is an org vehicle, you must get approved to drive it and get added to the overall insurance plan.

As I said, very few staff made the Okay to Drive list; out of twenty-five of us, we had five and that was doing real well. In some parts of Gold, out of fifty people only one or two people could drive. The vehicles were mainly needed to transport the crew when on location shooting and to and from the studio. You see, during this time period Gold did not have its own film studio and the one that was used in prior years was tiny and barely big enough to shoot videos in. Gold did a majority of the film shooting in an abandoned nuclear bunker at the Norton Air Force Base in San Bernardino. The Air Force had just moved out and gave a portion of the base to the local San Manuel Indian tribe as part of some government deal. So Scientology paid rent to the Indians and they used the money to build themselves a casino.

Each day we would load up and travel 40 minutes from Gold to this abandoned Air Force bunker located in the middle of nowhere. At the end of the day we would pack up and head back to Gold. There was no operational air conditioning in the building and on some days during the summer it would be over 110 degrees in the studio. There were portable air conditioning units that we brought in to direct at the actors in between takes so that the make-up would not melt off their faces. Yeah, this is the place where 90% of the Scientology Tech films were shot! Now, if we were shooting on location, we would usually have to get up around 3-4 A.M. so we could pack up the equipment and travel to the location, set up and shoot. Then pack everything up and travel back to the base.

For the TR#1 (Training Routines in Life) film, we had around 30 sequences that needed to be shot. Most sequences would take a full day to shoot. Mitch, the Director, had decided that about half of these sequences he wanted to shoot on location as opposed to in the studio. This meant that we had to stagger the shooting so that one day we would shoot on location, the next day we would shoot in the studio. This would allow for the sets crew to switch out sets while we were on location and so on.

Well, Dave Miscavige wanted to release the TR#1 film for Auditor's Day and that was in September. It was the end of June, and based on how much time it would take to edit the film, get the music and final mix down done, he had arbitrarily decided that the film had to be shot by Sea Org day (early August). That gave us about a month to shoot 30 sequences. Every day that passed was a lost day and starting filming right away was a must. We began within a few weeks after location scouting, budgets and designs were all done and approved.

Our daily shooting schedule went something like this:

DAY 1 - We got up at 6:00 A.M. and left for Norton, we would shoot all day and got back to Gold around 10:00 P.M. We then had our meetings and went over the next day's shoot, which was a location. We went home around 11:00.

DAY 2 - We got up around 4:00 A.M. to leave for Norton. Once at Norton, we packed up the gear and drove to our location. We shot all day and got back to Gold around 10:00 if we were lucky. Had our meetings, and went over the next day's studio shoot. Went home around 11:00. At least we got to sleep in until 6:00 the next morning!

DAY 3 - Repeat DAY 1 schedule.

DAY 4 - Repeat DAY 2 schedule.

And so it went for a full month. By the time we got to the last week of shooting, crew were falling asleep standing up, driving, you name it. Most crew could sleep whenever we were traveling. But, as there were only five drivers and four vehicles, most of the drivers slept 2-5 hours a night on a good day. Some nights we returned from a location shoot at 1:00 A.M. and had to be at the studio at 7:00 the next day.

Well, we got to the end of the film and this is where things became a bit tricky. The end sequence of the film contains all the actors who appear throughout the entire film. So you had 30 plus actors who all needed to be available to drive out into the middle of nowhere and spend six hours on a set that was 100 degrees. Add to that, the script from LRH called for a camera move that was nearly impossible to achieve and had not even been done on the previous version of the film. This sequence was re-shot four times. Each time it was reviewed, Dave said that it was not okay and could not be used in the film. So we would shoot it one last time. We finished very late that night at the Studio and dropped the film off at the base. It was Sunday night and Tuesday was Sea Org day. We were finally going to get a day off and the film was done!

We came in Monday and the shots were reviewed. They were not okay. Dave was pissed. His plan was foiled and the film would never get done in time now. What did this mean? What were we going to do? Organizing another shoot was out of the question as we now had actors out of town, on other projects, etc. We had already shot the sequence four times and some of the actors refused to come back again no matter what. And they were the Scientologist actors! We demanded that, amongst the four times the end sequence had been shot, there must be enough footage to be able to cut together a full sequence and be able to finish the film. No, this was not an option. Dave Miscavige himself had stated that without the end sequence properly shot, the entire film was a bust and could not be completed. We did not know what was going to happen, but we knew it could not be good. We were puppets waiting to be put into motion. Well, no matter what happened, we knew that Dave Miscavige would be pulling the strings.

That first tug happened soon enough. Naturally, first on the list was for all of the Dept Heads to be heavily security checked by RTC staff. This included any and all suspected activities that we could be involved in. Hookers? Theft? Sex with the actors? Goofing off? Sex with each other?

Gambling? You name it, we were asked it. We were asked the exact same questions over and over again, worded differently, anything and everything was thrown at us. This went on for at least eight hours straight. We had screwed up the filming of this one sequence four times and there must be some real crimes below this. No one wanted to hear about us not sleeping for a straight month. No one wanted to hear about the crew pooling their own money to pay for gas for the org vehicles. No, the only thing that was wanted was for us to admit to committing the most heinous crimes imaginable and then it would all make sense. Dave Miscavige said we had crimes so we did, and until we admitted to those crimes, it would not stop.

After hours and hours of sec checking, it was now around 1:00 A.M. It was at this point that we realized that, up until now, we had never experienced anything that would compare to what was to come. We were told to muster outside on the road that was next to the dining room. We were told that wherever we went, we were to run, that we could not speak unless spoken to, we would be on a strict military schedule and that we would not be leaving the property to return to our own berthing until all of us had admitted to all the crimes we were involved in. The six of us lined up on the road. There were four guys and two girls. We were all tired and had not really had more than a few hours of sleep a night in at least one month. It was July and we were not only skinny from not eating much, but the heat and lack of sleep had really taken its toll on our overall energy level. Most staff on the property had long since gone home. Most of the lights on the property had been turned off and it was very dark out. Here we were, just having spent hours being grilled about what crimes we had been committing and all we wanted to do was get some sleep. It was at that moment when three off road motorcycles pulled up. Jon Stumbke, Inspector General master at arms from Religious Technology Center was on one and the others were ridden by Gold Security guards.

"Run!" they ordered. "Stay in the headlights and run until we say stop!"

We started to run. Where were we going? What the hell was this? I had heard of some crazy crap going on at the Int base but this was beyond anything I had ever seen or heard. Motorcycles driving behind us in the pitch black while we were made to run ahead of them like dogs. They yelled out at us every few seconds to keep going and scolded us for slowing down.

They kept driving and yelled out to go left or right at certain points and we just ran all over the property. The Int Base covers over 500 acres and some parts were fairly undeveloped. We ran all over the property and kept on running. When one of us slowed down or stopped, the others were ordered to grab that person and force them to keep going. No matter what, we were not allowed to stop for any reason. We ran across grassy areas, dirt, pavement, through trees, and anywhere else the guys on the motorcycles decided to drive. It was almost as though we were not going anywhere specific, but that we were just going to run until someone decided we had run enough.

Finally, one of the girls collapsed. She could not run any more. She was tired and was crying. The rest of us were made to do push-ups while she was yelled at and made to get up and start running again. She cried and ran at the same time. It was horrible to watch. It was horrible to experience. It was just plain horrible, that sick feeling you get when seeing something awful and wrong.

That moment would be burned into my existence forever. I knew then that I would never forget this for the rest of my life. 2:30 A.M. came and we were told that we were now going to run to where we would be sleeping. Finally the torture was over. We were told to run out to the South end of the property. This did not make sense, because there was NOTHING out there. No buildings, no shelters, nothing. Just some trees and grass fields. But as the motorcycles roared behind us, we ran and ran until we reached the South end. We were ordered to stop and told to stand at attention in the dark. Most of us used this time to catch our breath. The one girl was still weeping and would sniffle from time to time amidst her crying.

About ten minutes passed before we all saw a pair of headlights coming towards us. It was a pick-up truck. It pulled up; someone got out and climbed into the bed of the truck. They proceeded to kick a large bundle out of the back of the truck and throw some poles down on the ground. The person got back into the truck and drove off.

It was pitch black out and if there was any moon out it was a sliver. We could barely see each other a few feet away. The only light was from the stars themselves and a faint glow from the nearby town of Hemet. Jon Stumbke told us that we would be sleeping out here tonight. Two tents were provided for us and that was all we got. We were told that we would be marched to our next assignment at sunrise and that we had better have our tents packed up and ready to go by the time the sun was up over the mountain. He got onto his motorcycle, as did the two security guards that so happily drove after us with him for the last two hours. They drove off and with them left the only light we would see for the rest of the night.

Until this moment in my life, I had never appreciated the Coleman camping tent that I had enjoyed as a child. You put two poles into a fabric sleeve and poof you have a tent! The tents we were given on this night were no Coleman tents. They were what appeared to be very old musty canvas tents from the army. They could not have been less than 30 years old, and the poles that went with them were very old and worn down. It took us at least 45 minutes to even figure out how the tent and poles went together. It was pitch black and we had never even seen these tents, much less set one up previously.

By about 3:30 A.M. we had the tent set up. Turns out that old style tents did not have bottoms like the new nifty Coleman tents either. We had tents, but no blankets, or tent bottom to sleep on. The grass was still a bit wet from earlier that night. Most of the grounds at Gold have sprinklers that are timed to go off around 11:00 P.M. Four hours later there was still a bit of moisture left. Most of us had to just rest our head on our hands or sleep directly on the grass. Luckily, it was summer and it was not too cold outside. That was about as lucky as we would get.

At 4:30 A.M. the sprinklers went off. Not all of the sprinklers on the South side went off. ONLY the ones where we were sleeping. Most of us jumped up and ran out of the area where the sprinklers went off. It was a dirt area not fifty yards from where we were sleeping. Now our clothes were most definitely soaking wet and we had nothing with which to dry off. A few of us managed to just lay down in the dirt and go back to sleep, while one or two just sat there until the sun came up an hour later.

After dragging the wet tent out of the grass and packing it up, we were greeted by another security guard on a motorcycle. Of course, Jon Stumbke and the other two guards were sleeping in their warm beds somewhere and would not be here to rouse us this early in the morning. I am sure we were each thinking that exact same thought as we saw the new guard pull up. Anyway, he told us to run over to the garage and take showers there.

We were given 10 minutes to take a shower and be back outside ready for our breakfast. Most of us just washed our hands and face and went back outside. The water in the garage was freezing and by the time the water was hot enough, it would be time to go. We were told to run over to the galley and see the cleaner in the kitchen. She would give us breakfast and tell us what was next.

We got over to the galley and there was the cleaner. It seems everybody loves it when they are normally the lowest person on the totem pole and they get the chance to boss someone around. The cleaner told us that she had some bread and water for us. We were supposed to eat in five minutes and then get to work. It seemed that no sooner than we saw her leave, she was back telling us that breakfast is over and handed each one of us a toothbrush. She informed us that she and the rest of the galley staff were taking the day off since it was Sea Org day. We were supposed to spend the entire day scrubbing the galley floor tiles with our newly acquired toothbrushes.

You have never felt pain until you have spent sixteen hours on your hands and knees scrubbing floor tiles with a tiny toothbrush. Lucky for us, we got 10-minute meal breaks for lunch and dinner. Because most of the Int Base crew were off for the day, not that many people were around to see us scrubbing the floors. It was humiliating enough that we had the cleaners bossing us around. We looked like utter crap from not having slept or showered.

By the end of the day, we were all nearly physically incapable of doing anything besides sleeping. We were made to run out to the area where we had slept the night before. Knowing full well that the sprinklers had been reprogrammed to coincide with our sleep time, we moved our location out of their range and we had each smuggled large plastic trash bags out of the galley to use as sheets to sleep on. We at least knew how the tents went together, so setting them up did not take as long. We were able to get to sleep around midnight. For the first night in many nights we would get a full night of sleep, or so we thought.

At around 3:00 A.M. we were awakened by another security guard. We were told that we were not allowed to sleep on the grass since we were being punished and making amends and did not deserve such luxury. We were told that we had to break down the tents, carry them over to OGH and rebuild them there. It normally took 20 minutes to walk to OGH from where we were. Getting over there with the tents took a good 45 minutes. Everything around OGH was dirt. There was no grass anywhere. We looked at the bright side, no grass = no sprinklers. By the time we made it over there, we opted to lay the tents on the ground and sleep on top of them. This would give us a little more time to sleep and we would not have to break it back down in the morning either.

Day after day, week after week, we followed the same routine. Not allowed to talk with other staff, not allowed to go back to our own homes or berthing. Not allowed to see our spouses. Out of the six of us, four were married and had spouses who also worked at the Base. Two weeks in, we did get a surprise; the entire rest of the shoot crew joined us. Another twenty or so people sleeping in the dirt. None of them even knew why they had joined us out in the tents, scrubbing dumpsters all day, or toilets, or floors again with toothbrushes. They just ended up out there and who knew how long they would stay.

It was about two months before we were allowed to return to our normal duties and return to our own beds to sleep. Not one of us ever did admit to any crimes and nothing ever came of anything. The TR#1 film was completed and Dave Miscavige himself sat in the editing bay with the Chief Editor and used all of the shots we shot from all four times we shot that last sequence and managed to do what we had suggested before any of the extreme mental and physical torture had taken place. We were given no explanation as to why we were allowed to go back to post, no nothing. Just go back to your life as if nothing had happened.

Oh, but something had definitely happened. Several individuals had been emotionally scarred for life. To this day I think that the night we were being chased around the Int Base by motorcycles in the dark is the only time that I have even entertained the idea of suicide in this lifetime. Only years later, after I had become one of the highest executives at the Int Base, would I find out what had happened and why we were eventually allowed to return to our normal lives.

It turns out that after Dave Miscavige had ordered us out into the tents and for the guards to run us all over the property and so forth, he got involved in some big legal suit and totally forgot about us. He went off to LA and was working on other matters. Because he never ordered us to go back to post, we never went back. Some weeks later, the subject of the shoot crew came up in some meeting and to his supposed "amazement"; we were still out in the tents and scrubbing toilets all day. We were then ordered back into production like nothing had ever happened.

Now, This Is Fun

t was 1999 and Dave Miscavige had been writing down to Int Executives all year about making sure that the New Years 2000 event was the biggest event in all of Scientology's history. Dave even wrote a dispatch to CO CMO Int on January 1st, 1999, telling him that it would take all year to get the next year's event properly planned.

So of course when October 1999 had rolled around, nothing had been done all year to prepare for the New Years 2000 event. Dave had been asking about this event all year and was assured that it would be taken care of. So he did what he does best, he created havoc.

Now keep in mind that the 1999 IAS event had just been held in England and was a complete wipeout. At the start of the event, the 35 mm film projector that was meant to show the opening film went out. Then the backup projector went out and then later in the event during a video, the video projector went out. In addition, somehow the translations got screwed up and the live translators simply gave up trying to keep up with Dave Miscavige's verbose and speedy delivery and just quit midway. Being a predominantly foreign language-speaking crowd from all around Europe, the event was officially classified as a proper disaster. The entire event crew was still reeling from this and the projector guy got an express ticket to the Rehabilitation Project Force. He also just happened to be one of the Gold Visual Effects guys and they were already undermanned before his absence.

Based on the dismal performance in England, and the fact that the entire Int Base had ignored him all year regarding this next event, Dave Miscavige directed that every single person on the entire Int Base work on getting the New Years event produced. Normally there would be a crew of a few hundred up for a few weeks before an event. This time it would be the entire Int Base. Every single, last person was to work on getting the event done and if it was not a huge success then it would be every single person on the Int Base's fault, (except Dave's, of course!).

The New Years 2000 event would have to top the biggest event to date, which was the 1993 IAS event. In order to do that it would require more people and be on a bigger scale than the LA Sports Arena event. Dave decided that the Sports Arena was the venue to hold the event, but that it would be bigger in size and scope. And this time there could be not one empty seat in the whole place. When Dave briefed the event crew on this, it was like déjà vu all over again. We knew this event was cursed for sure. If there had not already been enough bad mojo attached to it, this was now guaranteed to turn into a giant crap sandwich. The LA Sports Arena was like a black omen to a Gold crew member. It held the special significance of being the one place that Gold had produced an event and not one single thing had gone right. We were on course for certain death.

For the next three months Dave Miscavige would go between the editing bays in the Upper Lodges and the Lower Lodges conference room and yell at people and demand better speeches, better video edits, better music scores and better anything else he wanted. He would detail out what kind of video shots he wanted, what types of instruments he wanted in music tracks, how he wanted a video to end and the next one to start, how he wanted a speech to segue into a video, you name it. He dictated every breath that we would or would not take for three whole months.

As the dreaded event grew nearer and Dave constantly changed speeches and videos, it was clear that everything would not be ready for the big night. He had dictated that there be two huge screens on either side of the stage showing moving video footage during his speech. So we essentially had four hours of moving footage that would need to be shot and edited to his speech, a speech that was constantly changing. Even Dave knew this was an impossible task with only a few weeks left until the event date. We knew Dave knew this when he ordered that LED tracking markers be installed in the frames of the screens on each side of the stage. These tracking markers would be used by the Visual Effects crew at Gold to re-insert the proper footage into the video screen after the live event took place. At least the final video of the event would be correct, even if the live show were botched.

The live show was now only a week away. The Sports Arena had an army of Rehabilitation Project Force members from LA and at least a hundred crew from the local stage unions. The RPF in LA numbered in the hundreds by this time. They were like a swarm of ants that would attack giant set pieces on semi trucks and within minutes the stage items would be carried by hand down the long ramp into the arena and handed over to the union crews. It was a sight to behold.

The stage was a bit bigger than the one constructed for IAS 1993. It had a very similar look with the usual giant pillars and tiny podium. This event was for New Years instead of IAS, so a more celebratory motif replaced the earth logo and torches that were historically linked to the IAS.

In addition to the huge projection screens on either side of the stage with moving video footage, two additional even larger screens were placed on either side of the hall to project the live event for the crowd. Then another 20 projection screens and 50 giant plasma television screens were placed all around the arena so the audience was able to see Dave Miscavige clearly throughout the event.

And there was no projection department left to execute it all. I was tapped to do all of the projection and replace the guy that had gone to the Rehabilitation Project Force. Even though I was directly over the Departments that were supposed to build the stage and over the Stage Manager himself, I was also going to have to somehow get all of the projection set up for the biggest event in all of Scientology's history in my "spare" time.

The planned event was to open with a very large flag procession with Sea Org members from all over the world marching around the arena carrying the flags of their countries and their orgs. Then there would be a twirling color guard that would do a dance on the main stage and then Dave Miscavige would come out and speak and introduce a series of videos and have moving footage during his speeches. Dave Miscavige even worked in the phrase "The war is over" into his new speech so that he could say that and get it on tape after being cheated of that pleasure so many years earlier. The event was to end with another Scientology song written just for the event, which would be performed by a giant gospel choir.

As the day of the event approached, the cameras were set up, the production truck was set up, the sound system had been built and giant baffles were installed all around the arena to cancel out the echo that had ruined the prior event in 1993.

The cable cam operator was ordered never to point the camera directly down, and was told that if any breasts showed up in any shot it would be cause for non-payment. The teleprompters were now fully automated with pneumatic risers and tweaked within a millimeter of perfection. The lighting on Dave was to be on him the entire time no matter what and was not to come off him at any point during his speech for fear that any footage might be unusable. Every single detail was being accounted for – or so we thought.

The day of the event arrived. All Gold crew were on pins and needles and again knew that this would either be the best thing to happen or the worst. Based on the prior months and years of experience, most knew what the smart money was on - the worst.

The production truck crew had pages and pages of speeches and most of the visuals that had been prepared were out of order and didn't match up. So the truck crew knew before the event even started that it was going to be a bomb from their department.

Since I was responsible for both the stage and the projection, I decided that I was going to spend the entire event backstage, directly behind the stage where the main projectors for the event were located. This way I could keep an eye on the projectors as well as any flaps that occurred on stage.

The event started out looking good. The stage looked good, the lighting was decent, the sound was okay and the projection and TV screens were all working fine. The flag procession ran a bit long, but we made it through.

Now came the on-stage flag twirlers. It was about twenty young college girls in tights with huge flags that they twirled around. They did a bit of a dance and marched around the stage flinging the flags around in unison.

While they did this, Dave Miscavige got ready to walk on the stage. The stage manager had instructed him to enter from an exact part of the stage. There were only so many spots from which one could enter or leave the stage. Well, the stage manager had been up for six days straight and might have gotten his spots mixed up. As the girls danced around the stage and Dave stood in the magic spot, he started to become uneasy. He questioned the stage manager if the spot was the correct one and said he thought he was supposed to enter from a different spot. Just as the music crescendoed and the flag girls were about to finish, Dave decided to move despite what he was told. As the girls exited the stage, they threw their steel-tipped spiked flagpoles off stage at the exact spot Dave had been standing not two seconds earlier. (He would later say that as he moved from the spot, he could feel the tips of the flags brush past his hair as he moved away!) Now, normally I would have assumed this was his exaggeration, but this time I had seen the entire thing go down before my very eyes. Dave Miscavige came seconds away from being speared to death multiple times by a bunch of hot college girls wearing skimpy outfits! Talk about girls gone wild! It didn't happen. But the next biggest disaster of the millennium was now underway.

As Dave began his speech, you could see that every once in awhile the video footage on the side screens was either too early or too late or had nothing to do with what he was saying. But at a certain point in the event, it was pure chaos. The footage was completely random and some-times footage that had already been played was up on the screen again. It was going to have to be completely re-done in post production, guaranteed.

After seeing the near shish-kabobbing of Dave Miscavige and the vi-suals wipeout, I pondered the turmoil that would ensue. I knew my direct junior, the stage manager, was destined for the Rehabilitation Project Force, that was a given. You cannot almost kill COB and get away with it. He was a goner for sure. But what about the rest of us? We had been up for the last three months day and night. Most of us were too numb to feel pain or even worry about what would happen to us.

After the event, people just disappeared here and there with no expla-nation given as to why or where they were sent. If anyone asked, "We are getting rid of the deadwood," was the reply. Busloads of people were taken to the Rehabilitation Project Force in LA.

Everyone at the base had to re-do a battery of tests; every single per-son at the base received a Fitness Board. If for any reason, you were found unfit for the Sea Org, you had the uncertain fate of being sent to the RPF or dumped off in some foreign country to live with some SPs who had been assigned the task of taking care of you in order to get themselves un-declared.

We were back to shortened meal breaks, no canteen privileges, people being restricted to the base for months on end, sleeping under desks, in at-tics, or wherever you could find a spot that would go undisturbed for a few hours during the dead of night.

While most people on the Int Base were considered the scum of the earth, I had the pleasure of being the direct senior of the guy that almost got COB RTC killed. Not only was I restricted to the base for an unspecified amount of time, but I was considered to be on a very short leash. I would have to grovel, beg and plead to ever make it off the property to sleep in my bed again. Like many other staff on the Int base, I had to fend for myself.

A lot of people had to find a spot that was not already taken and make that their spot. It was very territorial. If you had found a spot, and had any personal effects of yours there, it was commonly understood amongst other restricted Int Base staff members that the spot was taken.

Having been there throughout the construction of the Cine Castle film studio, I knew the good spots that were out of sight and out of mind. I slept in an attic above a hallway behind the castle cyclorama wall for four straight months. I had a thin blanket that I had gotten from costumes and each night around 3:00 A.M., I made my way up above the hallway to sleep with the blanket on the plywood decking until around 7:00 the next morning. Hopefully, the Sets & Props staff that worked throughout the night loading in sets for the next day's shoot would not be too noisy and I could get a good, solid three hours of sleep. I was over all Pre-Production Departments at the time and was one of the highest posted executives at the Cine Castle, so it was not unusual for my staff to see me at all hours of the day and night. I ate leftover snacks meant for the professional actors, showered in the Costume changing rooms, did my laundry in the Wardrobe washing machines and slept in my little makeshift attic bed. The castle was my home. Some of my staff would make the remark that "it is like you never ever leave the castle." They had no idea that for most of the year 2000, I didn't. I lived there.

Now, this is fun.

A Pain That I'm Used To

We had been having meetings up in Building 50 weekly. Building 50 was the new Religious Technology Center building that was built, but was only occupied by Dave Miscavige and his personal staff. So you had a seventy million dollar building being used by about fifteen people. That made sense.

The building was started in the late 1990's and was finished in 2003. The only reason it even took that long is that it got built several times over and parts were redone and redone based on Dave changing his mind. At one point the interior of the building was mostly completed and had a very expensive wood paneling throughout it. Although he had approved the plans, Dave decided he didn't like it and it was ripped out and redone.

Then there were the internal staff issues. The guy that designed the electrical distribution for the building had placed the high voltage panels for the entire building directly behind Dave's personal shower in his office. Dave was not too keen on that. The electrician was sent to the Rehabilitation Project Force somewhere and the electrical plan and existing wiring had to be redone.

Then there was the Gold engineer that was making sure that the water pipes in the building were properly tested after being installed. I will not get into details, but I can guarantee you he brought a whole new meaning to laying pipe! After this was discovered, he was shipped off to some far-away place and never seen again.

When the furniture for the building was being done, a carpenter from PAC, the Sea Org base in Los Angeles, was brought to the Int Base. He was a master in his own right and was brought there to make the main desk for COB's office. After months of working on this desk it was shown to COB. Dave said that it was the most heinous piece of crap he had ever seen. Shorty after this occurred, the carpenter was killed in a freak motor-cycle accident on the highway while leaving the base to go home for the night. Even though he had been riding motorcycles all his life, he crashed on the road that leaves the base and was pronounced dead on the scene.

This also just happened to be around the same time that a girl was killed on the highway by a piece of heavy equipment that was crossing the road. It was late at night and it was dark and the girl drove her car directly into the bucket on the front of the loader and she was instantly decapitated. Her mother was following behind in another car. When the mother got out of her car to check on the daughter she screamed out in horror. It happened right next to the road at the Castle and I could hear the mother screaming for what seemed to be at least an hour.

Then there was the girl that was electrocuted to death in a power transformer vault at the Int Base near Building 50. She had been trying to go see her parents and husband in LA and was told she could not go and that she was PTS. One Sunday morning, she went into a power vault and was instantly killed by electrocution and the power to the entire Int Base went out. The Port Captain at the time, Ken Hoden, told the police investigating the accident that she was going into the vault to save a squirrel. There was quite a bit of controversy over this whole thing at the base. The girl Stacey was not stupid and no one went into power vaults on the base. I worked there for 15 years, was on the electrical team for years and never went in to one ever. Stacey had only been at the Int Base for a short while.

It was also odd that shortly after her death, the guy who told her she was PTS was sent to the Rehabilitation Project Force. And that Ken Hoden, the security guard that responded to the outage and the person who supposedly saw the suicide note Stacey left all disappeared from the base for undisclosed reasons.

Three people died in three weeks at the base. Many more went to the RPF or were offloaded and declared during the construction of Building 50. So it was odd that after all that, it was not filled with people and only Dave Miscavige and his personal staff would occupy it.

Anyway, we would often be called up to meetings at Building 50 and Dave would lecture us and lay out the entire future production and international event releases for the next ten years.

The only difference between today's meeting and yesterday's meeting, or last week's meeting or last month's meeting, was that Dave had figured out a few more ways how we had all screwed something up that was already released years prior and now he was explaining to us how, once again, he was going to have to figure out a solution or work around our latest screw ups and swoop down and save the day in the end, as always.

Somehow, even though most of the facts and figures and key players in this saga were the same, the meetings would always take at least 8-10 hours to unfold. Granted, a lot of those minutes would include us just sitting there in a large room around a table while Dave Miscavige was off in another meeting, or on the phone with Tom Cruise, or eating or even sleeping.

This was a pain that I was used to. We would be reamed out for having gotten nothing done since the last meeting, and now we were in another meeting about something else that we had not gotten done. Tomorrow's meeting would surely be about the previous day's meeting demanding a progress report. What were we supposed to say? "Well, Sir, I did not get that done as I was with you all day getting reamed out." No, it was widely known that Dave was the one cross ordering all of his own orders, but if anyone dared utter the words, it was an express ticket to who knows where.

So, we sat there and listened to Dave lay out his most recent act of sheer brilliance in sorting out this mess called International Scientology Expansion. He had figured it all out, what things would get released at what event, in what sequence and how this would fund the next upcoming releases. He had figured it all out: prices, how it would be packaged, how much it would cost to produce, how many people it would take to make it, you name it. It was like he was handing it to us on a silver platter. After four straight hours of him explaining it to us, now all we had to do was confirm for him that we could do it. We would break for dinner and when we returned, we would have a chance to let him know our plan.

After dinner we would usually get to sit there for 30 more minutes by ourselves to hash out what we were going to do. Most of the time, no one would agree on anything and the biggest item to be nailed down was who in the group would speak on behalf of the group. This was a double-edged sword if there ever was one. If you were picked to be the representative for the group and screwed it up and COB disagreed with what you were saying, the group would surely throw you under the bus and say to COB "we had not gone over that, Sir." Or you would come out with flying colors and Dave would decide that you were the next best thing since sliced bread and you might be the favorite pet for a few weeks.

Usually right as Dave came back into the room, someone would hastily say that they would be the one to talk and we would see what would happen.

"So what did you guys work out?" was the usual question Dave Miscavige would ask as he walked back into the marathon meeting in progress.

"Well, Sir," the appointed sacrificial lamb would begin. After a long-winded interpretation of how to execute COB's brilliant plan was laid out, we would all hold our breath waiting for his answer. If objects in the room did not immediately start to fly at the person who just finished speaking, we were usually in the clear. But then sometimes, Dave would get up from his chair and slowly saunter over from across the room and launch a full out Pearl Harbor sneak attack on the person. So you could never be too sure what was coming.

"No, you guys just don't get it! Let me explain it to you again," Dave started saying. So after getting a second chance to hear his whole plan and then having him tell us as well how we would execute it, we are now another six hours older.

Dave wrapped up the meeting, apparently in a good mood with, "Okay, guys, I think this can really work. Thanks."

He left and we filed outside to light up cigarettes and figure out what was next. It being nearly 1:00 A.M. by this point, most of our crew have already gone home or were about to, so we all decided that we were going to end on a good note, go home and get some sleep.

I headed back to my area and did a few things before heading off down to my house, which was right next to the Int Base. I rolled in around 2:00 A.M. and my wife came home maybe 30 minutes after me. Just as I was almost asleep there was a knock at the door.

It was Karsten Matthias, one of the Gold Security Guards. "COB wants you to come back in. He wants to talk to you up at the Villas," he said in his German accent.

I dressed and headed back in. As I made my way back, I saw a few others who had been at the day's meetings coming back as well. This was probably not going to be good. I made it up to the Villas and Dave was off in the distance dressed in his pajamas, slippers and even had a cup of tea. Shelly was standing there and told me to go over to the ship and wait for Dave there. I went over to the Star of California Clipper Ship and there were already about twenty people lined up. Some were still in uniform and some were in their sleepwear. I was wearing my uniform, knowing that it was always better to show up looking like you never left. That was a golden rule I learned and adopted years ago. Over the years, people had routinely been picked on for looking like they had just been sleeping at 5:00 A.M. when, of course, it was expected that they had just been working hard at whatever Dave Miscavige wanted.

People continued to trickle in and line up, until I heard the buses pull up on the highway, the loud air brakes signifying a stop and the sound of hydraulic doors opening.

As the flood of new people showed up, it was the entirety of CMO Int. Maybe a hundred or so people, plus a few Gold and CMO Gold staff who were at the meetings that had occurred throughout the previous day. Now the pool area was full of people standing around wondering what the hell was happening. The pool was lit up nicely and whoever had been cleaning it lately was doing a damn fine job. You could see every detail of the bottom of the pool surface and even the lines of the drains, etc. I was not any sort of pool expert, but I was quite impressed with this one right here, right now.

Dave came down the steps, still in his pajamas, slippers and still with his cup of tea in hand. I was amazed to see him like this. I had seen him once before in his apartment at the Hacienda near Flag early one morning in 1995 when I was switching out an amplifier that he did not like the sound of. He was in his pajamas then, too. As COB Asst answered the door in her skimpy nightgown that morning, his pajamas were not really what I remembered most, but now seeing him again reminded me of that. I wondered to myself why Shelly was not now, again, wearing her skimpy nighty, and then thought about how I had not worn pajamas since I was a kid.

Was I supposed to be wearing pajamas? I thought to myself. Could I even afford a pair of pajamas? Certainly not super duper silk ones like Dave had on. Definitely not the fuzzy indoor/outdoor sheepskin slippers Dave was sporting. Those were just over the top. They probably cost more than I make in a month, I thought. They were surely straight out of the latest Hammacher Schlemmer catalog and cost a pretty penny. I was not in the market for a pair of those any time soon.

As Dave made his way down the steps to the pool where we were all standing, he took a sip of his tea. Then he started to explain why we had all been called back in.

He was apparently upset that after the meeting broke, some or most of us had gone home. Here he was, now having to do his entire day's planned work that he couldn't do because he had spent his whole day explaining our jobs to us. Now, he was going to be up all night working, while we were nestled snug in our beds while visions of sugarplums danced in our heads.

Dave had decided to vent his frustration on Marc Yager, who lived in a room with Guillaume Lesevre in the Lower Villa, where Dave also lived. However, when Dave got to Marc's room he was gone. Long story short, Dave would frequently tease and torment Yager and Guillaume about being gay becasue they lived in the same room, even though this sleeping arrangement had been set up by Dave. He frequently told Marc and Guillaume that the only expansion they ever personally achieved was in the rear ends. Well Marc Yager decided that he wasn't going to take it anymore. He dragged his mattress out of his room, halfway across the property, and put it in a field of dirt where he decided he would sleep.

Dave promptly ordered someone to go find Marc Yager and to call everyone from the day's meeting back in to the property immediately. He was going to make sure there was hell to pay for this. And to make sure this never happened again, we were all going to go overboard right here, right now.

"Come on, Norman, you read the quote,' Dave prodded. "Come on, let's get this going."

We lined up at the diving board of the pool. Norman Starkey recited the age-old Flag Order for the overboard drill. "We commit your sins to the waves. May you arise a better thetan." Or something to that effect. After Norman said this, a person would jump off the diving board into the pool, swim over to the side, climb out and stand back in line around the pool. It was more weird than embarrassing. The pool was heated. I mean it was not like this was really that horrible. I am sure some people were glad that their uniforms were now going to get a free wash, and as an added bonus they would get a bath in as well.

What was worse about this particular incident was that one gal got up on the diving board — if she weighed less than 250 pounds I would have been surprised. You would have to butter this girl's hips to squeeze her through a doorway. She was not only big but she was very rotund. She was the last person to have to go in. You could see that she was worried and did not think that she should be getting up on the board. She was clearly expecting someone to stop her from doing it, but that never came. When she got up on that diving board and started walking forward, the end of the board was, literally, touching the water. In the back of my head, I was truly concerned that she might get hurt if she tried to walk off, the sheer force of the diving board springing back up would surely catch her in the back as she moved off the end. As Norman read out the obligatory line, the end of the board was literally dipping into the water.

Dave was watching from the side of the pool. Was he really going to let this take place? I was disgusted. I mean, I could care less that I had gotten wet and was standing there in my uniform dripping wet, but making this poor woman do this was just plain wrong. She must have been in her 50s and had been at the base for at least 25 years.

"Wait a minute, Rae!" Dave finally said, "Come back."

She barely maneuvered turning around on the end of the diving board. I was sure she was somehow going to get hurt here.

Wow, that was close. I really thought he was going to make her do it. But then, just when I thought Dave Miscavige possibly might have some tiny shred of decency left somewhere in him, he yelled out, "Go and walk into the shallow end!"

He made her walk back off the board and then all the way to the other end of the pool and slowly walk into the shallow end, down the steps and, holding onto the railing, go under water and then walk back out.

This sucks, I said to myself. There was nothing to be learned here. All Dave had done that night was prove to us that he was evil and enjoyed watching other people suffer. Not only had we all been dragged back in from our beds, we were now wet and presumably we should not go back home fearing that we might get chucked back in the pool a few hours later. What kind of lesson did we learn? I don't even know what lesson we were supposed to learn that night. I just don't know. Even though this was a pain that I was used to, I know that for me personally, another switch flipped in my head and it was not one in favor of Dave Miscavige.

More Than A Party

I t was another day in hell. We had been restricted to the CMO Int/WDC conference room for two months now. The basic explanation was that until all org boards and postings for the Int Base, Middle Management and Class V Orgs were done (the entire management and organizational structure of Scientology), we were not allowed to leave. We had to sleep under our desks each night and food was brought in. We were allowed to go down to the Gold Estates building for showers if we went down real early. We were not allowed to be seen while other base staff were around. We were allowed to go to different areas of the Base only if it had something to do with a specific order Dave had issued. If we were found to cross order COB in any way while we were in any area, it was an immediate RPF assignment. There was nothing we could do. Anyone who had an external facing post was not allowed to send any traffic out. All telex lines and orders from the base were cut by COB. Because all of the traffic coming from the base was cross ordering HIS strategies, he ordered no traffic be passed on to ANY orgs or management units. All of the internal facing posts were involved in the org boards and postings.

The org boards and postings for all of Scientology management had been added to the list of things Dave wanted done in July 1999.

Actually, the New Years 2000 event sealed the deal on these and was the flap of the century if you want to call it that. The entire event had to be re-done digitally after it was held live at the Sports Arena. This took two months to do over, at least.

Following that disaster, Dave's continuing statement of why the event had been such a catastrophe was that NO ONE HAD A POST AND NO ONE AT THE INT BASE WAS RESPONSIBLE FOR ANYTHING. That was in 2000. It was now 2004 and we were locked up in the conference room. This was but the latest in a series of "too gruesomes" meant to make people crack under the pressure, and finally do something that Dave has asked for. Typically, Dave Miscavige asked for a lot of things in any given day. If one someone were to keep track of everything thing he asked for and typed them up, it would take them — oh, wait, he had a staff of eight people that did this as their sole function! They were:

1. COB Asst
2. COB Secretary
3. COB Communicator
4. COB Sec for Correspondence
5. COB Sec for Compliance
6. COB Sec for Incoming Traffic
7. COB Sec for Outgoing Traffic
8. COB Typist

These people recorded everything he said throughout the day and then turned those tapes into streams and streams of orders that were sent out in triplicate to anybody and everybody that had anything to do with any of them. The recipients then had to word clear his orders before they were allowed to do anything on them. There were over 2000 pages of transcripts that dealt solely with the subject of doing the Int Base org boards and postings!

There were lists and lists of every single different possible personnel scenario that could be put into place at the Int Base. Does CMO Gold stay its own org? Does it get put in the Exec structure of Gold? Does it move into CMO Int? Does Annie Tidman stay the CO? If it goes to Gold then she can't still be the head as she and Lisa Schroer, the CO Gold, don't get along that well. Does CMO Gold move across the property, does it stay where it is? All of these issues and about a thousand more had to be taken into account for each org and all of the postings that were being done.

For at least the last seven years, the org boards and postings had gone like this: All of the postings get worked out by a committee of whoever thinks they are the current exec structure in charge. They then order the internal staff to draw up charts with pictures of everybody being proposed so it can be seen who will be posted where. Personnel files and experience are rarely used – this is a "who would I like to do what" drill that gets done by a few people. If the persons doing this drill don't like you, it is likely you will end up on a post that sucks. This drill takes at least a few weeks and the list is nearly done. There are, however, a few Watchdog Committee and higher exec posts like Gold Div heads that are still vacant. Nobody wants to do those posts since they know that these have a very high turnover rate, at which point the whole thing stalls out and cannot be finished. Dave Miscavige calls a meeting and then all of these people who are doing the org boards and postings get hauled up to Building 50 or the WDC conference room for nine hours to hear what people Dave thinks should be on what posts and which people he DOES NOT want on certain posts. After this meeting, they start over on the list and have to somehow put all of the pieces back the way Dave wants them and still be able to come up with rosters that make sense. Add into this that they now have to offload five people and that four people blew since the last list was made. So now they have to somehow get rid of some posts, or name some people who are not even at the base to take these posts once they get to Int. Oh yeah, no new people can come to the Int Base until the org boards and postings are done, so no new personnel arrivals have gone to Int for nearly seven years. There have been over 500 offloads, though.

Oh, yeah, and many things are not allowed until all of the Int Base org boards and postings are done. This applies to ALL INT BASE STAFF unless otherwise noted: liberties (days off); meal breaks longer than 30 minutes; canteen privileges; getting married; bonuses; having rank (all Int Base staff were demoted to a rank of "Swamper" in the year 2000. Swamper is the very lowest rank you start out with when you first join staff); Sea Org Day; promotions; Thanksgiving; Christmas; New Years; birthdays (except COB's – bring on the gifts!); going home to berthing (if you are directly related to getting the postings or org boards done),

Back to the main story here! We were locked up in the conference room and Dave was going to come down and meet with the key execs about the music studio. It had just been redone for the fourth time and Dave wanted to go over what he found when walking through the studio that afternoon. When one of these meetings happened, you had about twenty people who went into a room and did not come out for hours on end. You would see COB come and go as he pleased, but the people in the room did not leave for any reason, no bathroom breaks, no snacks, nothing. When Dave left or was going to be gone for a bit, sometimes they could duck into a nearby room, grab a protein bar, take a bathroom break and go right back into the room for fear that he would return while they were gone. No one was allowed to come into a meeting once Dave had entered the room. Once he was in it was locked down, so to speak. No one came or went unless he directed it. This particular day's meeting was to be at 3:00 P.M. in the conference room in CMO Int. This room holds about 20 people max and that was with ten sitting on one side of the table and the rest standing behind them or sitting in chairs behind those at the table. The other side of the table was for Dave. He usually sat at the table and had a set variety of items that had been placed there by his stewards before the meeting: water (a specific brand that only he drinks. No one would dare drink that same brand of water!), protein bars, ashtray, pack of Camel non-filter cigarettes, pens, paper, tape recorder (unless room is hard wired for recording, which all Int Base conference rooms are). The attendants of this meeting were the CST guys, Russ Bellin and his staff who were running projects at the Base, CMO Int execs, and Gold Execs. Annie Tidman was there as she was directly running the Music Studio re-re-re-re-renovation and up-up-grade that was currently being done.

COB came in and immediately asked who had been into the studio lately. Of course only one or two people had and even they were probably lying, so he told everybody to go and look at the main control room. The music studio was right next to CMO Int so it was a 30 second trip over there. The musicians were in there and they had a look of horror on their faces; obviously COB had been by there recently. They said that he had come in, asked some questions and left.

We returned to the conference room. After a bunch of back and forth questions and guesses from us on what was wrong, we were told by Dave that the mix board was crooked and we were all sent back to the studio control room to see what he was talking about. Okay, back in the conference room he proceeded to give us a lecture on mixing and how it's done. He then asked for a copy of the "Queen's Greatest Hits" CD to be brought down to the conference room. After it arrived, he played the CD for us and told us to listen. You have got to picture this: You had twenty people who probably didn't give a crap about Queen, had not eaten, were tired and who did not care about mixing, or who at least were certainly not going to take away a whole lot in terms of learning about it today; yet, we listened.

While Dave was playing the CD for us, I think it was during "Keep Yourself Alive," he suddenly became ecstatic and jumped up from the table. "I just had a great idea!" he exclaimed. He was the happiest any of us had seen him in months, almost in glee about this new idea that had popped into his head. He said that we should get something to eat, and then get all of CMO Int rounded up and into the WDC conference room for a meeting in about an hour. He said to remove the table from the middle of the room and make sure that there were enough chairs for EVERY SINGLE PERSON to sit down. He was very clear to make sure we understood this part. The room was to be cleared out. Now, the WDC Conference room is much bigger than any other conference room on the base. It is two very large trailers put together with no walls or posts to block Dave's view of anyone in the meeting. That is why he liked meeting in this room; he could be close enough to the greatest number of people in a meeting and could read their reactions.

With the table cleared out, there were a lot of people now in the room. It was all CMO Int crew with the addition of two Gold Execs. No one had a clue why we were there. We knew that Dave was happy about some idea that he had come up with while listening to a Queen album, but other than that the meeting purpose was unknown. It was now around 5:30 P.M.

Dave showed up and talked about the org boards and postings. He also talked about how there had been over 500 people that had been musical chaired off post over the last five years. (He left out the part about most of them being as a result of his orders.) He then asked a few people what "musical chairs" means. About three people answered with the Scientology definition of musical chairs: frequent post changes. No one seemed to know that it meant something else. One guy from Programs said that it was a game. Dave had him explain the game to everybody.

"Good. So you guys understand the game?" Dave asked. "Okay, well today we are all going to find out how the entirety of Scientology feels about you guys playing musical chairs with the posts of international Scientology orgs and the Int Base. We are going to play the game musical chairs, but with a twist. You are all going to walk around these chairs here. While the music plays, a chair will be removed, and whoever does not get a chair when the music stops, well, that person will be offloaded from the Int Base. Those are the rules and that is the game. Oh, and the person who is left standing when all but one chair is pulled out will stay here and help me repost the base and get Scientology expanded. This is not a joke and I am not kidding. You guys have messed with me for the last time. I am going to find out right now and right here, who is the most determined to stay here."

You can imagine the horror on the faces in the room. There were about seventy people in the room and everybody knew that this was going to be a very cutthroat ordeal. And what did "offloaded" mean? There were so many meanings for this word at the Int Base that what he meant was not clear. To most this meant that they were going to be given $500, put on a bus to the middle of nowhere and told never to come back. Some had the hope that it meant going to a lower org, maybe. To some it meant going to the Rehabilitation Project Force in Australia, Canada or Africa where no external trouble could be caused. There was a lot of fumbling around to get the chairs into a giant circle. Dave had the Cine Sec Gold (Fed Tisi) bring up a video camera so the whole thing could be videoed. This was going to be a major production!

Dave played a few CDs. "We are the Champions" by Queen was not the right message for this. The Queen song that Dave ended up using was "Bohemian Rhapsody". Dave Miscavige did not pick this song on a whim. He wanted the lyrics of the song to be burned in our minds. I had never before really listened to or understood the lyrics of the song. Dave had. He wanted us to feel like the guy singing the song. As far as Dave was concerned, we had been bad and this was our execution. We were all about to be blown away into the wind.

Anyway, the first people to go were the usual suspects, the older, more reserved bunch. As people would leave the game, Dave had them lined up in one area of the room. He would jab comments at them and apologize for it having to end up like this. If the person was married or had a spouse in Gold, he would ask them why they had not thought about this before. "Is it real to you now?" he would ask.

One guy, John Oldfield, was leaving the game. He was married to Megan Oldfield in Gold. She was a video editor and they had been married at least a few years. John had tears running down his face. Dave asked him why he was crying. John said that he was going to miss Megan and that he did not want to have to leave like this. Dave said, "Well, you never cried for me!" To prove that he was not kidding, Dave had one of his staff go off and come back with actual airline tickets printed up with the people's names on them. They were handed out to people that had been kicked out of the game so far.

As the number of people still in the game grew smaller, Dave let the music play longer. This went on for hours. When it got down to around twenty people, it started to get VERY physical. Mark Ingber and Mike Sutter actually destroyed a chair by pulling it from each other and fighting and punching each other to let go of it. Mark Ingber actually ripped the seat of the chair from the frame and sat down on it on the floor! That counted and Mike left the game!

As the final people were weeded out, people were being thrown to the ground, pushed against walls and otherwise fighting for a chair. If you could imagine what it would be like if pro athletes played a game of musical chairs, that was what it was like for the last fifteen or so people. It was very sad to watch. People who had been best friends for years were throwing each other to the ground for a chance to get a chair. Those who had lost were made to stand there and wait. Wait and do nothing except wonder where you would end up, what would you do, whom would you ever see again? Many of these people knew nothing else except for the Int Base. They had very little or no family, or at least they had not seen their family in so long, they did not even know if they could go to them. No one had credit cards, bank accounts, or much more than 50 dollars to their name. Very few staff had driver's licenses and fewer had vehicles. And even if they did have a vehicle, it either did not run or it had been years since they had registered or insured it. How would they live, how would they even eat? What would their spouses think of them? Would they be told that they were a suppressive person and never hear from their family or partner again? There were now almost seventy people standing off in this big group. These people were now being referred to as the "Offload Group" by Dave. Fifty percent of them had either been crying or were still crying at this point. The other half might have been happy to get the hell out of there or did not care enough either way to cry. The last four people were Greg Wilhere, Sue Wilhere, Mark Ingber and Lisa Schroer. Mark was literally thrown aside by Greg Wilhere. Lisa beat out Greg for a seat. Sue Wilhere and Lisa Schroer walked around a single chair for what seemed to be an eternity while Queen rang out. Then the music stopped and they fought for the single seat. As fate would have it, Lisa Schroer got the seat and Sue was sent to the side.

"A deal is a deal," Dave Miscavige said to Lisa. "You can stand next to me. The rest of you are not done yet. We still have to figure out where you will all end up going."

At this point, Dave told everybody to split up into groups of seven and that no couples can be in any one group. If both you and your spouse were in the room, you would have to go to different groups so that even once offloaded, you could not be together! The offloads were split into seven separate groups each with ten people. Dave asked the first group where they thought that they should go. Of course none of them could agree on one place as there were ten different people from ten completely different places in the world.

"Okay, I know how to solve this." Dave had Marj Habshied brought into the room from her office. Marj was working in Exec Strata. People would write in to the Executive Director International from orgs all over the planet and she would answer them for him. Most of the time Guillaume would not even see the responses or care to read them. Anyway, Marj was fresh in Dave's mind from a flap that had recently come up, so she would decide the fate of ten people today. Dave was careful to make sure that everyone in the room knew that no one could tip Marj off as to what was going on. Everybody needed to put on a happy face and say NOT ONE SINGLE WORD to Marj when she came in.

Marj walked into the room. Dave asked her if she knew much about the different Continental areas around the world and the state of the Scientology orgs in each. She said that she was very knowledgeable about this as she got letters from all areas and knew the particular complaints in each area. Dave asked her to tell him which one she felt was the worst of all. She hemmed and hawed a bit, but eventually came up with Canada. Dave sent someone to fetch the Org photo binders for Canada that exist in the landlord office. These photos were updated weekly – binders of all orgs and Sea Org units in Canada. Marj was asked to wait until the photos arrived. Little did Marj know that she was actually deciding where ten people would end up going after being offloaded tonight. The photos arrived and, sure enough, there were pictures of black toilets crusted in filth, fifteen beds in a single room at the staff berthing, showers with green mold on the tiles, etc. The photos were horrid. In the binder it said that the management organization had been broken into just a week prior, that they were behind on rent and the staff had not been paid in many weeks. They weren't making enough money to purchase food for the crew and some staff had been working on missions in the organizations so that they could get food and berthing money to at least support themselves.

Dave asked Marj if she was sure that this was the Cont that she considered the worst of all. She agreed and was dismissed. As soon as she left the room and was out of earshot, Dave said that the first group would be going to Canada. Dave then asked the next group who they thought the most out ethics person on the base was. This person was then brought up to the room and then their Cont was picked out. This went on for at least an hour, with Dave reading out things about the Cont, showing the pictures around the room, making sure that everybody could see that any place they went was going to suck and that no matter what, the Int Base was a resort compared to any of these places.

Finally, all Conts were picked: 1. CANADA, 2. AFRICA, 3. ANZO (Australia, New Zealand and Oceania), 4. PAC (Pacific Area Command in Los Angeles), 5. EAST US, 6. WEST US and 7. CC INT (Celebrity Centre International). The CC Int team was given their Cont by Dave. He had asked that he be allowed to decide the destination for one of the groups. CC Int did not seem that bad an area compared to the rest. There had to be a catch. The team assigned to CC INT would be a cleaning team specifically and that is all that they could do. They were a cleaning team that was assigned to ONLY PUBLIC areas and Celeb areas. Dave said that if they were fortunate enough to be going to CC they should be able to see celebrities and that he would make sure that they did. "Ashtrays, toilets, trash cans and celebrities will be your life," he crowed.

Just when everybody thought that the torture was over, Dave said, "Well, you have got to have uniforms, too." Dave then asked the CC INT team if they could think of someone who they thought was hip or cool to design their uniform for them. Becket Wells was brought up as a person that was up on the latest fashions and styles.

"Good," Dave said. "Get him up here." Dave made sure that everyone knew that the same rules applied—NO ONE was to tell Becket what was happening or say anything to him at all. ONLY Dave was allowed to talk to him.

Becket walked in and Dave told him that we were all doing an exercise and that Dave wanted him to pick out some uniform parts for some crew to wear. He asked Becket to describe the most hideous outfit that anyone would ever want to wear. With Beckett's consultation, the outfit ended up being:

1. Pink running shoes
2. White socks that went past the knee
3. A huge cowboy belt buckle
4. Bright green short shorts
5. A pirate shirt with four inch black buttons on the chest
6. Fluorescent yellow fanny pack, and to top it off
7. A red riding hood.

"That is hideous," Dave said and then thanked Becket for his help. As Becket left the room, Dave Miscavige turned to the CC Int team and said that this would be their uniform and that they had to wear it whenever they were in ANY public areas. He also specifically added that they could not EVER pick trash up with any sort of tool. It always had to be handled with their hands, same with ashtrays, they were to dig the butts out with their bare hands and no tools could ever be used except in the case of toilets or urinals where they could use a sponge or greenies, but no gloves or extended brushes.

Just when we thought it all was over and we could at least get off to our Conts, Dave asked that each group pick one person amongst themselves who everybody could agree was the worst of the pack. The most out ethics, most disliked, whatever. The least liked person from each group was singled out. By this time, how could it get any worse?

Dave said that each of these most disliked people would be writing the issue assigning one OTHER group to the Cont they were being sent to! And it would be signed COMMANDER. So Mark Ingber who was going to Canada, was writing the issue for the PAC group and it was going to be coming from COMMANDER MARK INGBER. This was being done for all the groups and everybody had an issue that was being written by someone who was also being offloaded, but just not to the same area! Each group had their issues written up by hand. Each group was then charged with getting the issues proofread, typed, copied and ready for distribution.

Once all this was done, Dave gave everybody a final pep talk. He asked if anyone had anything to say. No one did. He said that the buses would be ready to leave at 6:00 A.M. It was now 1:00. Each person would need to be ready to go and NO items would be going with them except for the clothes on their backs. Of course, any spouses had already secured for the night, as had any friends, family, co-workers or people that they wanted to talk to before leaving. Anyone who had not been in the meeting was unable to be contacted. The buses would be long gone BEFORE any of these people came in for post. All the phones had been ripped out of the room so that no calls could be made to other parts of the base where staff might be working late. All communication lines were cut. About thirty minutes after the meeting ended, there were a few people saying how this was the "last chance people would have to make things right in their S.O. careers" and that "if they made the Conts expand, they probably would be able to come back to the Int Base one day far, far in the future."

An hour later, the different groups had found their way back to their little space under a desk or in a chair and most people had gone to sleep for the night. Sobs and faint crying could be heard for hours throughout the room. If you were not crying yourself to sleep that night, someone else was doing the crying for you.

THE MORNING AFTER: The crew were rounded up and mustered. Change of plans. NO ONE WAS GOING ANYWHERE! Turns out it was going to cost a fortune to fly all these people all over the place and the logistics were not finalized as to how to ship everybody off to the different continents. Dave had called down late during the night and said that he was not willing to waste one single cent of Scientology's money dealing with the Int Base SPs. Some people might end up going later in the day, and some might end up going that night providing everything was properly worked out. The day went by painfully slow. No one knew who was doing the logistics workouts and no one was leaving the "SP Room". It was just more torture, everyone waiting, but nothing they could do.

Days went by and nothing ever happened. Dave Miscavige actually ended up leaving the Int base and going off somewhere for a legal case and the whole thing sort of faded away. Everybody just assumed that whenever the logistics got worked out, they would get shipped off to their Cont and until then they would make the best of it. Later we would find out that NO ONE HAD EVER WORKED OUT ANY FLIGHTS, COSTS, OR ANYTHING. It was all just one big pile of crap. Dave Miscavige never intended for anyone to leave, be offloaded to ANY Conts or wear ridiculous outfits while scrubbing urinals by hand. But he wanted us to all think that we were!

Suffer Well

I was working furiously to get several production targets done as ordered by Dave. I had been, like everyone else on the base, in woeful noncompliance to Dave's orders and had not gotten several unobtainable objectives completed in the allotted time.

Dave was putting in "too gruesomes" for all those who were in noncompliance with his orders. A "too gruesome" was a punishment that was so gruesome that a person would get the objective done for fear that the gruesome punishment would be enforced if they failed to do so. All of CMO Int had scrubbed the entire galley with toothbrushes for two weeks straight. They cleaned the floors, the walls, even the grease traps, all with tiny toothbrushes.

This was after digging ditches out at the berthing buildings job site. Dave just kept thinking up more and more jobs for them to do. I was even asked if there were any really nasty dirty jobs in Sets & Props that the CMO Int crew could do as a too gruesome punishment assignment.

One day when I was heading over to the castle, I saw a huge cloud of dust over to the Northwest of the Studio, in the direction of the aeration ponds. The aeration ponds were two huge football field-sized ponds that contained all of the sewage that was created on the property. Huge underground pumps moved the sewage from all over the property to the aeration ponds. There was a large fountain in the middle of a small adjacent pond that would aerate the sewage and after many months the solid waste would either evaporate into the air or settle at the bottom and the water would slowly seep back into the water table of the property.

As required by law, the solid waste was supposed to be removed from the ponds every so often. For this, the aeration ponds would be allowed to completely dry out in the hot desert sun and a backhoe or some sort of heavy equipment would come in and empty out the solid waste, after which the pond would then get filled back up with fresh water and the process would start all over again with new waste.

Well it looked like the new too gruesome had been found. All of the Int staff were now out in one of the newly dried aeration ponds and were emptying out all of the solid waste by hand. I could not believe it at first. But I was assured this was correct by some of my crew who had helped set up a few huge work light towers out there so they could work well into the night. I could not imagine how that could even be healthy. I am sure that OSHA (Occupational Safety and Health Administration) rules forbid such activity without some sort of breathing apparatus or masks or something.

The same day I noticed the huge dust cloud coming from that direction of the property, I was called to the executive offices. When I got there, the Commanding Officer explained to me that the Commodore's Messenger organization staff were out at the aeration ponds now and that several of the targets that were not completed by them relied on targets that I had not gotten done and that by request of Marc Yager, I, too, was to go out to the aerations ponds and clear them out.

Just when I thought that I would never truly believe what they were doing I would get to experience it firsthand. And, of course, I had my "good buddy," Marc Yager, to thank for it.

I was driven out to the pond by Security. Danny Dunagin, naturally, who else. I was teamed up with a girl from Int who was supposed to watch me and make sure I did not try to take off.

I arrived at the aeration pond. It was at least as big as a football field, maybe even bigger. It was at least twelve feet deep and the bottom two feet was the solid waste that needed to be removed. There were a hundred or so crew working there. All were in T-shirts and shorts or jeans. A few here and there had small white painter's masks on, but for the most part, people were unmasked and breathing the dust clouds that filled the air. Most crew were in the middle of the dry ponds picking up solid waste and filling small five gallon paint buckets that would then be passed out in a long line and dumped in piles outside the pond. The handling of the solid waste was what created the huge dust clouds. As you picked up the waste, it would crumble in your hands and make dust. Multiply that times a hundred people walking, handling and moving all that waste and that made a pretty big cloud. A giant cloud of dust made up of excrement was what I was breathing in. I tried to wear a mask, but with the temperatures being in the high 90s, the sweat just mixed with the dust and made mud around the mask. It seemed worse than just breathing the dust.

By dinner time, I had absolutely no appetite whatsoever. I spent the entire time allotted to grab a quick bite to blowing out my nose and coughing up crud that had made its way into my mouth over the past several hours. We went back into the pond and worked into the night. By the end of the night I had been completely covered with sweat and crap dirt. Every pore had been penetrated or covered and in between dry heaving and coughing full time, I was exhausted. At midnight we all made our way over to the garage where we were supposed to take showers. I hosed myself down while waiting in the line for a shower. There were only two or three showers and at least 40-50 guys and by the time I got into a shower, the water was freezing cold. We were allowed to sleep until 6:00 a.m., at which point we were awakened, given some trays of cold soggy eggs and sent back out to the ponds. This went on for two days. I was the only crew member from Gold there, everyone else was from CMO Int.

I guess CO CMO Int thought that I had learned my lesson and suffered enough. On my third day out at the ponds, I was brought back to the garage and ordered to get cleaned up. After an hour, I was brought back over to the CO Gold's Office and asked if I had had a change of heart. I don't even remember what I said. But the entire time I was talking, I thought of how I would one day escape this place and write about this experience.

That night when I got to wash up, I took a two-hour shower to try to get the stench off me. It did not work. I think it took a week for all of the crap to work its way out of my pores, nose, throat, and ears. Even my eyes would tear crap mud. It was the most disgusting, humiliating experience of my entire life. Yeah, I had suffered well enough.

Dangerous

By this time — it was now 2004 — there were at least four or five senior executives in Int who had been declared SPs. There were goldenrod issues posted up on the Int notice board saying, "Ray Mithoff is hereby declared a Suppressive Person."

Sue Koon, Marc Yager, Mark Ingber, Ray Mithoff and Guillaume Lesevre were all declared suppressive and had to work and stay in the same room together in CMO Int. It was referred to as the "SP Room."

They were not allowed to mix with the rest of the Int Base crew except when Dave called a meeting and their presence was required or requested. And even then, when an event would come up, they would write their speeches and attend and even speak at the event as if they were still the CO CMO Int or ED Int or whatever. It was surreal. You would have guys digging ditches and scooping up crap in the aeration pond and the next thing you know they would be in a tuxedo on stage at the Shrine yapping about the latest international expansion of Scientology.

As the months went by and the SP Room had more and more people assigned to it, the rest of the crew were instructed to get these guys to admit to all the crimes that they had committed against Scientology. At first these confessions would consist of a bunch of the Int Base executives sitting in a room together yelling at them to confess their crimes. Rarely would any of them actually come up with anything of any real significance, but after a while they started coming up with some really mind-blowing things.

One day when both Marc Yager and Guillaume Lesevre were on a roll, they started telling us stuff that was just plain crazy in terms of things that people were told happened back in the 1980s. In the 1980s, both Marc Yager, CO CMO Int, and Guillaume Lesevre, ED Int, were running all of Scientology internationally while getting advice from LRH and being told what to do by Dave Miscavige, who was COB ASI at the time. Well, Guillaume and Marc were false reporting and manipulating the international statistics to make it look like they were doing what they were being told and it was working. Through this entire period, they were regularly receiving huge production bonuses and large cash payments for the stellar statistics to the tune of tens of thousands of dollars. During these years, LRH even went so far as to write several Executive Directives about the international expansion occurring at the time and he created the International Birthday Game and all sorts of things, all based on the false information being fed to him by Guillaume and Marc. The entire time this was being done with the justification of them "not wanting to let LRH down." They had started a lie that could not be undone. It was for this reason that they started comparing statistics to well known landmarks and cooking up how things could be conveyed to make them sound better than they ever were.

Marc Yager was the undisputed king of this. He would take a stat like international student completions and turn it into the biggest expansion ever realized. Even though it was drastically down from the year before. He would take the figure of 12,000 student completions internationally this year and say something on the order that if you took all those courses and stacked them end to end it would reach all the way around the moon! Well, yeah sure they did. He would calculate that if each single piece of paper in the longest course pack they had was laid out it would be 3500 feet long, then you have that many packs and checksheets and you multiply it times 12,000 and you end up with a figure of miles that is more than the circumference of the moon. It still does not say that the previous year they had 15,000 completions. And it also does not take into account that everyone reporting in on that figure was padding the figures they reported and so you had people in some orgs finishing a two hour course and then never ever coming in again being counted as "Scientologists."

So, after Guillaume and Marc got on a roll, Marc confessed that with his falsely obtained riches, he went on to do even more despicable things. Someone even told me that when Scientology was running a campaign against *Time* magazine and Eli Lilly and driving their stock prices down, Marc Yager confessed that a few weeks before the campaign ended, he purchased a large number of shares in Lilly's stock, knowing that the price would be going back up!

Up to that point, many Int Base staff could not understand how both Guillaume and Marc had expensive sports cars while the rest of us struggled to be able to buy cigarettes each week. Well the answers started coming, and they were coming in spades.

We heard how the Key to Life and Life Orientation Courses were compiled completely wrong and how they were never supposed to be the way they were released. Ray Mithoff had misunderstood what LRH had laid out in the advices for the courses and he could not think with what LRH had intended the courses to be. This one was confirmed by Dave to be what actually happened. But now that they had been released and thousands of public had either done the courses or paid for them, they just let people keep doing them knowing that they were complete crap and an exercise in futility.

We got to hear about how the Scientology Lower Grades were revised and instead of a person having to do thirty commands for each Grade, the grades materials had been revised so that in order to complete each grade a person had to have a floating needle on 300 commands even if they were done after 30 commands. This alone increased the time it took people to complete the grades and slowed people down enormously on getting through their auditing. But people had to pay a lot more to get the auditing, so they left it that way and for years it has been a situation needing resolution. Of course this was all done under the direction of Dave Miscavige and he personally checked and approved all of this, but now that it was a problem, it was conveniently shunted off to someone else as their "overt."

We got to hear about how Ray Mithoff was the highest technically trained person on the planet and how, while he was responsible for insuring the technical accuracy and standardness of the course and auditing materials being issued, he was rubber stamping these items and in most cases not even bothering to read them at all.

Ray even approved a Dianetics How To Video that contained detailed technical aspects showing how Dianetics Auditing was to be delivered, which was to be released to the public at an event and be distributed in the hundreds of thousands. It turned out that he didn't even read the script or watch the video before he approved it.

This went on and on. Some staff in these meetings could not believe what they were hearing. The worst part was when COB came down and asked what they had coughed up and he was told. He was not surprised in the slightest. He had already known all this and was not impressed! He wanted to know what *else* these guys had been up to!

These were the top executives in all of Scientology and had been for decades and they were confessing crimes that would have gotten any other person in Scientology, well, declared an SP. Well they had been declared SPs and that was not changing them in the slightest.

The Int Base was rotten to the core. Dave Miscavige knew this. He had known about all of these crimes, yet these bogus courses were still being sold, the faulty auditing was still being charged for, the money was still being taken in by orgs all around the world. That was just his point. He was the only one trying to get these things fixed. Dave Miscavige was the only one trying to figure out how to convince the public who had already paid for these things that they should buy the new improved, revised version and go back and re-do the courses they had spent years doing and newly purchase the books they had bought and read many times before. And he was the only one convincing them to throw away the past several years of studies that had been done because those were the old "unverified by RTC" versions that he had released only five years prior. Dave Miscavige was the only person out of all of the people on the Int Base who was holding the line and enforcing what LRH had intended. Dave Miscavige was the only one curtailing the dangerous activities of International Management and forcing in a new era where people could go into an org that was posh and upscale and that cost a lot of money to make look nice.

Dave Miscavige was also the only one who already knew about all of these things as in most cases, he was the one that approved or directed they be re-released or produced in their current or previous forms.

Yeah, and Dave Miscavige was the only one that already knew all this and was NOT sitting in the SP hole at the Int Base.

Enjoy the Silence

The Int Base is a 500-acre property divided in half by Gilman Springs Road, or Highway 79 as we called it. Back in the old days if you wanted to go from one side of the property to the other, there were pedestrian gates that you would walk through, cross the highway and then go through the gate on the other side. This was fine for the occasional person going across. But when a meal was about to happen or just ending, you would have 600 people crossing the highway in one long stream. It was a bit dangerous, just like crossing the street with no traffic light.

In the early 1990s, the Soboba Indian tribe, whose reservation was several miles east of the base, decided they were going to make some money off of their little casino. Up until this time, they had a small building with a few gaming tables, slot machines and a steak restaurant. First, they worked on putting in a huge parking lot that could hold thousands of cars, and then they brought in the tents, three of them. Each of these huge white tents would hold an entire casino each.

There are two ways to get to the Soboba Indian Casino, You can drive from LA and come down Highway 60 East and then down Gilman Springs Road which takes you past the base, or you can come from the Palm Springs direction and go west on the Interstate 10 and take Lamb's Canyon to Gilman Springs Road, which again takes you past the base.

There was one other way you could go instead of using Gilman Springs Road, and that was to take Sanderson Street to the Ramona Expressway. This way might have been a little faster even, but was little known.

The traffic going by the base was getting heavier and heavier. It was actually becoming VERY busy.

The road was pretty crappy and not well taken care of, and for the most part, was unlit at night.

And there was also a matter of the security problems that the road presented. Staff could (and had) easily slip out any one of six pedestrian gates and be gone forever. There was no way to control people coming in or going out these gates and even though there were security cameras at every gate, at night it was hard to see and many people had blown by simply walking out the gates and into cars that had pulled up to rescue them.

Dave Miscavige directed and approved a new plan for the highway that would not only make it harder to get out, but harder for cars to drive by. They would build two tunnels under the road and connect the North and South sides of the property together to get rid of the pedestrian gates.

Then the road would be made smaller by putting in a median and curbs on both sides of the property lines. While construction was occurring, the alternate route was to be made popular and promoted as faster and easier. The idea was that this road construction would handle all of the problems the old road presented.

In fact, if Dave had actually had it his way, the road would be rezoned and made a private road and gates would have been put up on the highway at both ends, preventing ANY through traffic. But he would have to settle for his acceptable plan.

This plan was easily approved through the city planners. Most of the time, anything built or constructed at Gold would be scrutinized by the city planners to no end. They did not seem to like us and whenever we were briefed on any of the city related stuff by the External PR staff, it was always how "despite all odds and the SPs in the City Planning Office," they had managed to get a permit to build something.

For the road, though, the city whizzed everything through. Even though it was Dave's plan to reduce the traffic, which would not appeal to the city, construction work was to move forward.

During the initial construction, the road was all but closed to through traffic. The amount of cars going past the base was down to hundreds instead of tens of thousands. It looked like the plan was going to work. People had already started taking the alternate route; so much so that we had heard that the Ramona Expressway was starting to back up at rush hour. This had never happened before and was a good sign that the traffic was being successfully redirected.

After two years of construction, the road and tunnels were completed. It was one of the nicest roads in Hemet or San Jacinto. To keep the road noise down, the asphalt was made very smooth. New road lines were painted in and turnouts were made for all four security gates. The tunnels meant no more waiting for cars to be able to cross the road and no more pedestrian gates that allowed staff to leave when they wanted to.

It appeared that Dave's little plan had been successful. But a few short months later his plan would be foiled as it always was. A fairly large rainstorm had hit the area, and when I say the area, I do not mean Riverside, or Hemet or San Jacinto. No, I mean Gilman Hot Springs.

This was not like the August 1990 flood. That was a lot of water in a very short amount of time, maybe an hour or two. This storm went on for days. And while it was raining in San Jacinto, it was simply pouring down in Gilman Hot Springs. It was unnatural.

There was a lot of worry about the new tunnels and the new road. Would the storm undermine their integrity and cause them to collapse? Would the mountain slide down onto the new road? None of those things would happen. But what did happen would be worse.

Just like in the 1990 flood, the river that ran along the south side of the property ran high and threatened to break the levees which ran the entire distance of the property.

Teams of people were assigned to run dozers and backhoes to shore up the levee, no matter the cost. Several of us were "rovers". We were given walkie-talkies and rode our motorcycles around the property line assessing the damage and reporting back to "Station One" the status of the water line and any levee breaks.

After three days of being up all night and day riding my motorcycle around in the freezing rain, I could not do it any longer. I was sick, very sick. I had to go to isolation. When I got there, it was packed with other staff, most of who had been on the same rover duty as me. I slept for two days and when I awoke, I heard one of the craziest things I had heard in ages.

After the San Jacinto River went past our property, it went under Sanderson Street. Well it had gone *over* Sanderson Street and taken it down river. It was no longer there. I did not believe it and rode my bike down the road to see for myself.

Sure enough. The road was GONE. The asphalt literally dead-ended and there was now a twenty-foot drop where the road used to be. For someone from anywhere else in the US, this might have been a periodic occurrence. Not here in Riverside County. We got a few inches of rain the entire year! For a major road to be washed away was a big deal.

One of the older security guards who had been at the base forever told me that this road had been damaged many years back by a similar flood in 1980. It was at that exact moment that I realized why the city had fast tracked the road. They knew that their road was going to get killed at some point and without fixing up the road that went through the property, the trip into town or the casinos would be threatened.

Sure enough, as soon as Sanderson was gone, the traffic through the base was not only back up to previous levels, but it was now *all* traffic— heavy trucks, semi-trucks, cars—everything had to go through the property.

To add insult to injury, the turn outs were somehow confusing and people were using them as passing lanes! So people would be driving down the two lane highway road, and when they got to the property, they would gun it to pass other cars as the road would widen to four lanes!

To say Dave Miscavige was pissed was an understatement. Where he thought he had gotten the best of the locals, it was the other way around. We had spent millions putting a new road in, and as a result ALL traffic into Hemet or San Jacinto or the Indian Casino was now going past our property.

As for Sanderson Street, it was official; they were not going to risk it being washed away again. This time they would build a huge overpass bridge instead of a road and redo the interchange between Lamb's Canyon and Gilman Springs Road. It was planned to take 3 years at least!

This was a flap that would never end and many people would suffer now that it had gone as wrong as it did. Dave Miscavige would make sure that people suffered.

There were hundreds of pages of orders, meeting transcripts, plans, you name it, about how to handle the highway situation. Months and years would go by and the orders kept coming from Dave on what to do with the highway.

Every few weeks or months, we were briefed on the latest handling that was being done on the highway. None ever resulted in anything that would do what Dave Miscavige wanted. He wanted the road completely closed, no traffic. So anything that was done would never be what Dave wanted, so in the end, no matter what you did, it was going to be crapped on by Dave.

The people behind this flap were the PR Division of Golden Era. This consisted of Ken Hoden and Muriel Dufresne (pronounced Do-frane). They were the ones who were supposed to get the road closed or handled so that Dave did not have the problem of the highway on his lines.

In the year 2000, Dave had a new reason to complain about the highway: It was keeping him awake. Dave Miscavige lived in a building that was within 100 feet of the highway. He lived in the Lower Villa that was located directly east of the Star of California Clipper Ship. Apparently, the number of semi trucks using the highway was at an all time high and the peak time they drove by the base was around 6:00 A.M.

Dave Miscavige had been trying for years to have the highway traffic shut down. Now it would keep him up all night. He decided to share the experience. One day an order came down stating that Ken Hoden, Muriel Dufresne, Steve Willet and Jim Mortland (the latter two were Estates area executives) were to get up at 5:30 A.M. and stand out by the highway just below Dave's bedroom for a few hours. This was to go on until they handled the noise from the highway. Either by getting the speed limit changed, getting the road zoned as a county road, shutting it down, whatever it took, they were to sit out on the road EVERY SINGLE MORNING until it was resolved.

Months went by and, sure enough, there they were every morning standing out next to the highway.

Jim Mortland had it the worst. He was out there because he was the Estates Sec years prior. Well at the time he was working in the A/V systems area and would routinely be up very late at night working and would not even bother trying to go home since he would have to go out and stand on the highway in just a few hours anyway. He would catch a catnap at his desk for an hour or two and then get out on the highway.

All this so Dave Miscavige could enjoy the silence.

Never Let Me Down Again

T he May 9th event 2004 (anniversary of the original publication of *Dianetics*) was just completed and we all knew that we would be up all night every night for the next several weeks preparing for the June 6th events that commemorated the *Freewinds* Maiden Voyage anniversary.

Normally the June 6th event was the worst because it was actually a week of back-to-back nightly events. There were two-hour presentations each night for six nights in a row. On prior June 6th events we would have at least one 5-10 minute video for each night and then a ton of speeches on all sorts of subjects. Sometimes we would have multiple videos each night if COB wanted that and this year there was not much progress to report. Depending on what happened during the prior year we would have:

1. One night on the SBC's or Social Betterment Corporations: Applied Scholastics, the Way to Happiness and Criminon.
2. A night on the destruction of psychiatry.
3. A night devoted to Preservation of the Tech.
4. A management night on International Scientology Expansion.
5. An awards night that acknowledged various public Scientologists for their application of Scientology technology in the field of business, i.e., whoever donated the greatest amount of money that year.
6. An IAS event night showing what their funded programs had achieved throughout the previous year.

For those of us at Golden Era Productions, we would have to gather up all the past activities of the year and obtain photos or video footage of anything that could be made into something that could be talked about for each of the nightly events. This is the same as would be done for any other event that occurred throughout the year, except that for the June 6th event, we had to have tons of pictures and tons of data because the people who attended these events aboard the *Freewinds* were financing all Scientology enterprises. They had to be impressed in order to give more money.

Each day at Gold we would have meetings to go over what would be included in each night's event. These meetings were usually useless since everything that was planned would eventually be thrown out the window as soon as Dave saw the plan. Nevertheless we would spend every day gathering up the photos from around the world, writing speeches, shooting videos and putting together each night's event.

The staff working on putting an event together normally numbered around 300. People from the following areas contributed to events:

1. COB
2. COB's Office
3. RTC Execs
4. ED INT
5. CO CMO INT
6. LRH PPRO
7. ED ASI
8. CO IASA
9. CMO INT PR staff
10. IMPR Speechwriters
11. IMPR Scriptwriters
12. Cine Research Dept
13. Cine Scriptwriting Dept
14. Cine Props Dept
15. Cine Logistics Dept
16. Cine Make-up Dept
17. Cine Costumes Dept
18. Cine Sets Dept
19. Cine Camera Dept
20. Cine Lighting Dept
21. Cine Grips Dept
22. Cine Post Production Dept
23. Cine Video Shoot Crews Dept
24. Cine SFX Dept
25. Audio Mixing Dept

26. Audio Music Dept
27. A/V Manufacturing Dept
28. Shipping Dept

So these 300 people all knew that they would be getting 4-5 hours sleep, if that, for the next four weeks while these events were being prepared. Couple that with the fact that the first two weeks of work would most likely be wasted and that the last two weeks would be twice as stressful with even less sleep.

For all of the events put on for the fifteen years I was at Gold there were three main components that made up the event:

1. New releases
2. Speeches
3. Videos

If we were lucky, all three would somehow correlate to each other. So if we were talking about Applied Scholastics, we might have a video that showed a new school being opened and then maybe a new course having to do with Applied Scholastics. That would be the ideal arrangement.

Now when you have hundreds of people all working in different directions on different things and most of them not getting much done, it is unusual for the ideal event combination to occur very often. In most cases, the new releases drove the event. If a release was guaranteed to be done by the event, it was worked into the planning. The speeches and videos were drawn up based on the releases.

This worked fine if there were things that were being completed on a regular basis. Dave was the only one who could approve anything that got done at the Int Base, so not much got done. And when things did get done they might not actually have anything to do with the event that was coming up. For instance, if a new revised Dianetics "How to" video was completed in December, it would sit around and not be released at the New Years or March 13th events but would be "saved" for the May 9th event. Herein lies the problem with the Int Base—nothing was ever done on schedule and because of this, we got to stay up all night and day pulling stuff out of dark holes before an event to come up with something to talk about or show, when we really had nothing.

Then you had Dave Miscavige who had laid out a master plan of things to occur over several years and each new release was tied to an event. In 1990, a list was issued that contained 10 years worth of events. By 2000, all of the "new" products were to have been released and then all events thereafter would be devoted to focusing on the unchecked expansion that would be occurring worldwide.

By 2000, a small fraction of those items had been released, and by 2004, all of the items that had been released had to be redone or re-released due to being incorrect or needing upgrade in some way later on.

Things did not always go as planned at the Int Base; in fact, they never did.

But back to the event for the *Freewinds*. Most of the event crew stayed up for two whole weeks leading up to the events.

For most of the videos, Dave would sit in the editing bay and critique each cut and each sequence, in each and every video. Then he would head over to Music where he would listen to the music scores and have those revised or redone. Peter Schless could crank out a five-minute video score in a day or two. So doing ten videos in a month was no big deal. But when you have to do ten videos twice over in a month, it adds up. And in between the scores for each video, the music would still have to be recorded and mixed and laid back to the off line edit. And you have to be part of all of the attendant meetings about the videos and then also all of the meetings with COB on how the videos suck and have to be redone. All of this does not leave a lot of minutes left in the day to eat, sleep or be merry.

Now, event speeches would normally be written by the executives who would be delivering the speeches. This was a very short list of possibilities that would routinely be jumbled around right up until the actual night of the event. And depending on which event it was, and what was happening at the base, the people speaking could be doing so from a number of posts or titles. But the usual suspects were:

1. COB – Dave Miscavige
2. Mike Rinder
3. Marc Yager
4. Guillaume Lesevre
5. Danny Sherman

Most of these guys would have to write their own speech for the event and submit it to Dave Miscavige for approval. There were a few Catch 22s put in place by Dave though. No one could submit his own speech unless the others had been written and coordinated with. Something that Marc Yager wanted to talk about could not be in any of the other speeches and each person had to come up with enough stuff to talk about in his own speech so that it could stand on its own.

There was the added bonus that someone in the Management PR Office would have to propose a speech for Dave Miscavige and that his speech had to be much better than all the other speeches so as to put him on a pedestal far above the other speakers.

Last but not least, the speeches could not talk about the stuff that was in the videos, but could only have a short introduction to the video that went with the speech.

All of this had to be coupled with the fact that all of the speeches, videos, and releases were constantly changing and some might not be done in time for the event.

It seemed that Dave Miscavige would leave it up to the regular executives to get everything prepared for an event up until about three to four weeks before the actual event date. So, most people had been working flat out preparing everything and maybe had a bunch of stuff submitted to Dave for approval. A month before the event, like clockwork, he would review everything submitted and reject it as being the worst he had ever seen. Then he would hold several day and night long meetings explaining to all involved why and how it was the worst he had ever seen, and then complain about the fact that he would have to do it all himself again and make sure everything was done correctly.

After years and years of this, most of us were not even surprised by this; in fact, it was expected. As it drew closer and closer to an event, it would be like, "Is COB going to come down here and tell us what he wants to do?"

The *Freewinds* Anniversary week of events for 2004 would be no different than most other years. We would all stay up day and night and get all the stuff out at the very last second.

There was also the matter of preparing the *Freewinds* to be able to hold these events. The *Freewinds* normally operated at a financial loss year round, except for the one week at the June 6th event. The idea was that the money they made during that week put them back in the black for the year. This was their "Black Friday," so to speak, and it was for this reason that the *Freewinds* crew LOVED the Gold event crew. Also, when the Gold event crew were aboard, we made any work they normally did look like a walk in the park. Most Gold event crew were up day and night for the entire week and then after the week of events, we would spend two full days packing up our stuff and clearing out.

The *Freewinds* is a tiny cruise ship. It has very small crew quarters and we brought 50 crew members from Gold to put on the events. The ship holds a little over 350 passengers total. So, between the Gold and *Freewinds* crew that was about 100 people right there. That left only about 250 paying passengers that could fit. This meant that all the *Freewinds* crew would have to free up their beds so that the Gold event crew would have a place to sleep. Usually the *Freewinds* crew slept on the floor in the course rooms, restaurants or wherever they could find some open floor space during that week.

Then there was the matter of technical gear. For any given *Freewinds* event, we had at least seven high-end broadcast cameras that fed into the "production truck". At any other event during the year, an actual TV production truck would pull up to the Shrine Auditorium in LA or Ruth Eckerd Hall in Clearwater. The cameras would be set up and cables run into the truck. Well, there is no place on the *Freewinds* to put a huge semi truck trailer. So, a crew of people went to the *Freewinds* three weeks ahead of everyone else to load the gear onto the ship and build a TV production truck aboard.

About four weeks before the event, the TV production gear was rented in Burbank, CA. The sound and lighting equipment was rented from a place in Camarillo, CA. The sets and props made at Gold were loaded into shipping containers that met up with the other equipment at Long Beach harbor and all of this stuff was loaded onto container ships that headed over to Miami.

When the stuff reached Miami, it went through customs and was loaded into planes that flew to Curacao where the ship docked. When the gear arrived, it was loaded onto the ship in individual cases and then all the empty equipment cases were stored on the island. You can imagine that this was an expensive operation. A normal event that was produced in the United States cost around $400,000. That included a few days or maybe one full week of rentals. For the June 6th event, this stuff was being rented for a month at least! Granted, not as much money was spent on a hall or stage items, but $300,000 in rentals was a large expense for one week of events at the *Freewinds*.

So it was now two days after the *Freewinds* events had concluded for the year. Most of us at Gold were relieved that the week of events had gone well. All the gear had been removed from the *Freewinds* and was on its way back to Miami. Most of the crew were already on their way back or would be heading back now that the *Freewinds* and its facilities had been converted back to their normal operating routines.

We were eating lunch in the MCI dining room. Suddenly, several people throughout the room got up and rushed out. Great! Something is up! Anyone on COB's lines had a Nextel radio / phone. Most could only dial other Nextels on the Scientology network. No outside lines could be dialed, and if they could, they were monitored closely for "out-security calls." These Nextels issued group text messages whenever a flap occurred. Whenever people suddenly got up from a meal it was one of three things:

1. COB was pissed off and had called a meeting.
2. Someone had blown the Int Base.
3. Electrical power outage.

As the power was still on, chances were it was one or both of the first two. Sometimes someone blew the Base and then Dave found out about it and was outraged, so no matter what the deal was, we were most likely screwed.

Gold after lunch muster was held and it was a quick one. An announcement was made that anyone who was on the Cine event crew was to meet in the Cine Conference room for an urgent meeting. Well most of the event crew were either still at the *Freewinds* or on their way back to Gold, and those of us who were here were just getting used to sleeping six hours per night again and not in the mood for more event craziness just yet. We headed over to the conference room from the dining hall.

After we all filed in, the CO Gold, Lisa Schroer started to speak over the Conference room speakerphone. She was at the *Freewinds* still. She said that we had another event that had to be put on at the *Freewinds*!

"We are going to throw a birthday party for Mr. Cruise aboard the *Freewinds*!" she happily exclaimed.

What the hell did that have to do with us? Damn, we thought we were going to have to do a bunch of work for an event. That was close! Who gives a crap? Play some music, bake a cake and we are good. Happy Birthday, Tom!

"So this is what we need," she began. Most of us are ready for the cake and whatever else they needed and then we realized that this party would be like no other. She started listing what they needed, "I will list it out. Write this down. We will need to know the status of all these items in the next few hours:

1. All of the production truck gear needs to be gotten back.
2. All of the cameras and decks need to be set back up at the *Freewinds*.
3. All of the musicians' gear needs to be brought back.
4. All of the audio gear needs to be sent back.
5. All of the sets items need to be sent back.
6. The teleprompters need to be sent back out.
7. We need about 15 plasma flat screens sent out here.
8. Any event crew who were on their way back to Gold need to be sent back to the *Freewinds*.
9. Whatever gear is being rented, the rentals need to be extended for at least another week or two.
10. Cost is no matter; the costs will be taken care.
11. There is a sushi restaurant in Santa Monica that Mr. Cruise loves. That restaurant needs to be airlifted out to the *Freewinds*. The chefs, the sushi, the whole place needs to be set up at the *Freewinds*.
12. Every single movie that Mr. Cruise has been in needs to be located.
13. Get these movies to Video Editing.
14. An hour long video will be made from these movies and cut to music.
15. Also, the DVD authoring crew needs to get out here so that some DVDs can be made on the ship.
16. If we think of anything else we will let you guys know.

"Okay, so you guys have your marching orders, get it done! I will call back at the end of the night to get a report on where everything stands. All department heads better be on top of their items and be able to report up!" She hung up.

The looks in the room were like no one had ever seen. A birthday party for Mr. Cruise that would take place aboard the *Freewinds*? We throw a birthday party for L. Ron Hubbard and that costs $400,000. Now we are going to throw one for a public Scientologist that will rival that? Wow! The stuff that happened at the Int Base never ceased to amaze me. Oh, and the list of stuff they needed sent back was ALL of the stuff we sent in the first place. She might as well have said, "Send it all back." That would have been quicker and more accurate.

As the day went on and people were burning the phone lines to get their stuff sorted out, we began to find out what the party would entail:

1. There was going to be a big show in the Starlight Cabaret.
2. It would be a music show just for Tom Cruise.
3. All of the hit songs from each of his movies would be performed by the Golden Era Musicians.
4. There would be moving visuals playing behind the stage that were the best scenes from all his movies.
5. These would also be playing on tons of plasma flat screens throughout the Starlight Cabaret Lounge where all of this would be taking place.
6. When the whole show was over, a DVD would be made of the entire show and this would be presented to Mr. Cruise.

In other words, we were flying all this stuff back to the *Freewinds* for a giant butt kissing! We were going to play his songs and show his movies to him and then give him a DVD of us doing that!

As soon as we heard how the gig was going to go down, most of us came to the same conclusion. One word - Cheese. This was going to come off hokey as hell. It had all of the recipe ingredients for cheese. In fact, if you wanted to make some cheese, you could do so very easily with these people. Luckily, we were thousands of miles away and would not witness this cheese-fest first hand. And, since it was COB's idea, no matter how cheesy this thing turned out to be, Dave would love it and Tom would at least pretend to love it. I mean, Dave Miscavige once stated that *Battlefield*

Earth was by far the BEST movie he had EVER seen! Let this be a yard-stick for his taste and quality standards.

The Video Editing crew stayed up for two days cutting the background visuals for the songs. All the rental gear was turned around in Miami and sent back to the ship. The event crew were sent back to the *Freewinds*. The equipment that normally took at least a week to set up had to be set up all over again in just two days. The gear rental companies knew they had us in a tight spot and they told us that we would be paying more for the additional rental time since they had other customers scheduled for the gear that was supposed to be returned to them. We had to pay, there was no other option.

The sushi guys were set, and all other attendant accoutrements were on schedule to arrive for his highness, Lt. Pete "Maverick" Mitchell, Vampire Lestat, Jerry Maguire, Ethan Hunt, Cole Trickle, Charlie Babbitt, Brian Flanagan, or as we had to address him, Mr. Cruise.

We were told that several other key executives were also going to be there and supposedly if any of the upper level Scientologists wanted to stay and partake, they would have to pony up the cashola for the cheesola. Tommy Davis, Mr. Cruise's dedicated Scientology handler at the time, would be there. Dave Miscavige, this was his idea, of course he was going to be there. Dave Miscavige's wife/assistant Shelly would be there. And then ASI execs, IAS Execs and the *Freewinds* Execs could tag along so as to fill the seats in the small entertainment lounge.

Dave and Tom were just hanging out and their entourages were living it up on the private yacht that had been hired for a few weeks to follow the *Freewinds* around. They went aboard the *Freewinds* for dinner and then went over to the Starlight Cabaret Lounge.

Everything was set, the band, the crowd, and the videos.

Dave Miscavige was wearing a tight white t-shirt and black jeans. Tom Cruise was wearing jeans and a green button down shirt with the sleeves rolled up. As they walked in to the theme song from the 1986 movie *Top Gun*, Tom Cruise patted Dave on the back. Fighter jet footage from the movie played on the huge screen behind the lone guitarist on the stage. Everyone in the room was standing, clapping, and cheering. I mean, a guy just turned 42 years old, why not stand and clap for this to Top Gun music?

Tom hugged Dave and Dave's wife Shelly as the music continued to play. After three minutes of awkward standing and clapping went by, Dave motioned for Tom to sit down. Yes, Tom, there will be another hour of this coming up.

The musicians had been practicing the songs all week and the set list was ultimately dictated by what videos were edited to go with the songs. All songs had constant clips from Tom's movies playing whilst the band performed. In between each song there was a standing ovation. This went on for the whole set. The songs were:

1. "Top Gun Theme" performed by Golden Era Musicians with guitar solo from Chris Maio.
2. "Old Time Rock and Roll," from the 1983 film, *Risky Business*, where Tom Cruise becomes a pimp and gets roughed up by some other pimps. This was performed by Stacey Francis.
3. "Kokomo," from the 1988 film, *Cocktail*, which won the Worst Movie of the Year award and for which Tom Cruise was nominated for Worst Actor.
4. "Werewolves in London," the Warren Zevon song from the 1986 film, *The Color of Money* soundtrack, performed/butchered by Elena Rogero. There is no way to explain how bad this was; you had to see it to believe it.
5. "Mondo '77," from the 2001 film *Vanilla Sky*. This song has no lyrics so what appeared to be an interpretive dance was performed by three of the girls from Mad Hatter Studios. None of them dance professionally and this was well demonstrated in the video.
6. "You've Lost That Lovin' Feelin'," from *Top Gun* soundtrack, performed by Stacey Francis.
7. "Don't Worry, Be Happy," from the *Cocktail* soundtrack performed/butchered by Elena Rogero.
8. "Iko Iko," from the 1988 film, *Rain Man* soundtrack performed by Stacey Francis.
9. "Tutti Frutti," from *Cocktail* soundtrack performed by Stacey Francis.
10. "(Sittin' On) The Dock of the Bay," from *Top Gun*, performed/butchered by Elena Rogero.
11. "Take My Breath Away," [Love Theme from *Top Gun*] performed by Stacey Francis.

12. "Sympathy for the Devil," from *Interview with the Vampire* butchered/hacked to millions of little pieces by Elena Rogero.
13. "Playing With the Boys," from *Top Gun*, attempted by Stacey Francis, the song was so far out of her range that she broke into laughter throughout the song when she could not hit the notes.
14. "Mission Impossible" theme, done "Limp Bizkit" style by Chris Maio and the rest of the Golden Era Musicians.
15. "Old Time Rock and Roll" reprise where Tom Cruise got up and sang the song with Stacey Francis, sweaty pits, bad dancing and all.

When the show ended, there was a full minute of applause and a standing ovation.

Tom Cruise stood in front of the crowd and said the following:

"Whoa! ...(laughing)...Thank you! ...(laughing)...I'm just... I am not... I don't know where I am right now."

Crowd laughs.

"You know, you have to be there to understand this reality. Ya know how that is? This is incredible, this is just, I will never, this is just, how do I thank you?

"Thank you, thank you, thank you, thank you, thank you.

"This was the best, best birthday ever, ever, ever, ever, I mean EVER!"

It was over. It was by far the cheesiest performance ever recorded by seven broadcast quality cameras in the history of the world.

But would Dave be happy? There were screw-ups during the performance and these did not go unnoticed. But Tom Cruise was happy, that meant no matter what happened, Dave could not be that upset. Overall, the gig was a success and Tom Cruise was apparently happy.

The big day had come and gone. The show was put on. We were on pins and needles back at Gold. From all accounts on the ground, it seemed to have gone off okay.

Tom was happy and this would represent itself in many ways. Over the next few days, a lot of the musicians and a few other crew stayed at the *Freewinds* instead of immediately returning home to the Int Base.

Tom was trying to get a theme song nailed down for *Mission Impossible III*, which was in pre-production, and he wanted the Gold Musicians to help come up with some ideas for this. I mean, how could he have not come to this conclusion? Danny Elfman updated the theme in 1996 and it was a huge hit.

In 2000, the band Limp Bizkit totally reinvented it for *Mission Impossible II* and that movie was the most successful of the Mission Impossible franchise to date.

If the Gold Musicians could come up with a red-hot theme for the new movie, they would be stars forevermore. Just getting to work with Tom Cruise was considered a privilege. Here he was asking them for their help! But trying to get the Golden Era Musicians to come up with something that was even on the same level as the previous versions was a joke. They knew it and it only took so many hours before Tom would as well. After two days of back and forth with the musicians, Tom Cruise no longer needed their help. They came up with nothing.

In fact, in the process of trying to work out a new theme for the MI3 movie with the Gold Musicians, Tom Cruise was so unimpressed with what they proposed that their ideas were not even remotely considered.

Of course, the person who eventually worked out the new theme for the movie was Kanye West, whose Impossible theme went almost completely unnoticed and did not impress much either. In my opinion, Limp Bizkit knocked it out of the park and there will never be a version better than what they did.

Why, you may ask, were the Golden Era Musicians trying to come up with music theme ideas for Tom Cruise's movie? Good question.

In 2000, in a meeting with several Int Base Executives, Dave Miscavige explained to us that he and Tom Cruise were figuring out how we were going to get all of the Ideal Orgs purchased and built around the world. It was a no brainer. Scientology was not making nearly enough money to buy any new orgs, while Tom Cruise had already made enough money for him and his next ten generations of family to live in luxury. With Tom's newfound devotion he was now trying to work out how he could directly contribute to Scientology in a huge way.

Tom had now been producing movies, in addition to just starring in them. With his production company he was able to negotiate foregoing his acting fees while, instead, receiving a much bigger take of the box-office sales on the back end. This new arrangement was netting him a much larger payout on his huge movies. On *Mission Impossible II*, Tom's production company got 30 percent of Paramount's adjusted receipts for the film. On a film that made 546 million dollars worldwide, that is not chump change. If Tom could do one or two movies per year and make this kind of money, Scientology would be set. They would be able to buy hundreds of buildings, renovate them and drive the millions into the orgs needed to clear the planet.

In other words, and as Dave liked to put it, Tom Cruise was now going to fund Scientology's "war chest."

So, the Golden Era Musicians had one small part to play in this overall plan and they failed miserably. Either way, this was a huge blow to the musicians. They had just spent a week, up day and night, getting ready for the biggest concert they would ever perform. It went great and two days later they were back to being the scum of the earth in Dave's eyes.

This was enough to have them sent back to the Base in disgrace.

Corrupt

After being posted as the Producer Gold for a while, I had gotten used to what was needed from all areas. Even though I was supposed to be over all production areas of Golden Era Productions, I spent most of my time working in Manufacturing. The manufacturing area was a disaster and was about to have the biggest production demand in history placed upon it.

We had purchased a CD replicator and several printers that could produce the transcripts for the lectures and the covers for the plastic binders that held CDs. We had a mini plant in place for producing just about everything needed for CDs and DVDs.

COB had recently laid out that he wanted all of the "new" LRH books and lectures released by 2005. Now that all of the lectures were being reviewed and re-edited, all of Hubbard's books were also having the same done to them. For the first time in history, people were looking at all of these items as a whole and when this was done, discrepancies were found between lectures and books, and it appeared that earlier marketing actions had paired up the wrong lectures with the wrong books.

These prior releases were either approved or announced by Dave Miscavige himself. So now he would have to come up with a plan of how to re-release all of these items and sell them newly. His plan was to produce all of them and have them ready, and then when the time was right, release them. A new Mark VIII E-Meter that was being produced in Japan would also somehow tie into this.

We had an exact quantity for each lecture series in each of the 16 languages spoken where there were Scientology orgs around the world. I was asked for a plan on how we would produce all of the CDs in the time frame allotted.

For me to figure out how to produce this huge amount of CDs was not really rocket science. The machines were being run 24 hours per day, the machine could crank out a certain amount in a day and there were a certain amount of days that I had to produce the amount of CDs required.

No matter how I crunched the numbers or no matter how many times I cut down the average amount of weekly downtime on the machines, I still came up short. With the current amount of equipment it could not be done.

I spent hours on this before I finally went and saw Russ Bellin. Russ had been brought in by COB to figure out how to set up Gold's CD manufacturing line. Although Russ worked for CST, he did all of the research for Gold under the direction of COB. I am not sure how that worked corporately, but Russ knew what was done to work out the numbers and capacities of all machines in the area, so I showed him what I had worked out.

"You need more machines!" he concluded after looking over all of my workouts.

I knew he would say that. That was what I was trying to avoid. After being at the Int Base for several years, I knew the one wrong thing to tell COB was that you wanted more toys. He always nuked the person who asked for more equipment in order to make some target that he had laid out.

Nevertheless, Russ and I sat down and did all the calculations on what additional machines would be needed to make the targeted production quantities. It was not that many machines, but it would come with the hefty price tag of 2.5 million dollars!

I had to make the named quantities and if that meant buying more machines, I really had no other choice than to make that the plan and submit it. The meeting would be any day now and I had to have the plan ready when COB wanted it presented to him.

Later that week, the fateful meeting was called. COB wanted to meet with us in the CMO Int conference room. All the CMO Int Execs were there as well as Russ Bellin and his staff. When COB showed up, he was not in a good mood. I was sure that this would be a short meeting once I opened my mouth. It was. After I explained my plan to him, he went ballistic.

"I ask for production and you say you want to spend money!" Dave yelled. "What is it with these Gold guys? They always try and spend as much money as they can on anything and everything!"

Days later I was taken off post as the Producer Gold because of my plan. Of course someone who has such a destructive concept of production should not be over any areas that have to do with dissemination of Scientology materials. There is actually a policy where LRH says that people that are out-ethics or PTS should not be put on posts that involve dissemination.

Ironically, the department head over the CD manufacturing area would also be taken off post weeks later for a similar plan to mine. Who ended up replacing him? Of course it was me. COB came in to where I was working and told me that I should take the Director of A/V Manufacturing post and get the CDs made. He also said that he had a plan to get all the CDs made.

I took the post. So now I was the one directly responsible for making all of the CDs that I had failed miserably on planning out a month earlier.

In a meeting a few weeks later, COB unleashed his new plan of how we would be able to make all of the CDs needed by his impossible release date. I was sure that he was going to just extend the date and make it workable within the confines of the equipment we had already purchased and set up. I was so far off it was crazy.

His plan was to blow out a whole floor of the manufacturing building. Move all of our storage to a warehouse in Los Angeles. Make the second floor area the printing facility with banks of new printing machines that could print both color and black and white pages. We would also set up our own foil stamping equipment, laminating equipment, paper cutters, UV coating machines, hole punchers, binding equipment, additional CD replicators, you name it, anything you could imagine that would be needed, it was in this plan. Besides thinking that this plan could not be done for less than 15 million dollars, I found an immediate flaw, there were no elevators in the manufacturing building and it would be impossible to get printed items from upstairs to downstairs easily. Of course Dave Miscavige had thought of that. He said that a new elevator would be installed in the building!

His plan would cost upwards of 20 million dollars. And I was taken off post for my 2.5 million dollar plan!

A few weeks later Dave was doing an inspection in A/V Manufacturing. It was like every other inspection he did, he had his usual entourage of people and there were execs from RTC and CMO Int who were hovering as we walked through the different parts of the production line.

I think COB knew that I now thought he was full of crap and taking me off the Producer post was wrong, especially in light of the fact that his own plan was my original plan on steroids. But Dave was in a bad mood today and had obviously had a bad meeting before he showed up in my area. He was angry and asking questions and not even waiting for the answers. I knew he was in a bad mood and I knew that I should have played it safe, but I just couldn't.

"So Marc, you know you will be able to make the release dates now, right?" Dave asked snidely.

"Well, after we buy all that equipment, we will practically be able to make any dates laid out," I said, regretting the words as they came out. Although it was a perfectly normal answer, I knew Dave would interpret it as a dig. He did.

As the first fist hit my face I was unsure what was happening. After the second and third blows hit, there was no question. COB was punching me in the face! He literally leapt forward and was punching me over and over again. I was up against a sort of desk/counter area and I had lost my glasses after the first several hits. The frenzy had certainly caught me off guard. I did not go down though. The desk was supporting me and I used my hands to steady my balance and stand up straight.

Once I righted myself and Dave had stopped punching me, he took a step back. Although in pain and startled, I knew what would come next. It was my turn. I looked right into his eyes and started to advance towards him slowly.

"I am sorry, Marc, I should not have done that. I am sorry. Take a walk, man! Walk it off. Get yourself together!" Dave said frantically.

I was immediately grabbed by three people and shoved in the direction of the exit. I headed towards the door that led outside.

"Did you see that? He was actually going to hit me just then!" Dave said as I made my way out the door.

"You bet I was!" I said under my breath as I went through the door.

Several people were sent to console me and profusely apologize for Dave hitting me. Greg Wilhere was the first to show up. Greg told me that Dave personally wanted to make sure that I knew that he had lost it and he never should have hit me and that he was sorry for what had happened.

The next girl who came and found me told me that it had been an hour and asked if I was cool and would come back to the building. I agreed that I would, but if Dave ever even thought about touching me ever again, I would do whatever was needed to teach him a lesson.

"You really were going to hit him, weren't you?" she asked. "I could see it in your eyes."

"Yes, I was. If I weren't grabbed, I would probably be in the back of a police car by this time. I really was planning on hitting him. Hard. Someone has to stand up to this crap. Everyone knows that it is wrong. But no one ever does anything," I told her, still pissed that I was pulled away from him at the last second.

Well, after this, I did not last very much longer on the A/V Manufacturing Director post. I obviously disagreed with COB and that I tried to punch him out as well was not helping any. But I was not to be posted anywhere else but in Manufacturing, which I think was Dave's way of making sure that I saw what he was doing and it was his way of rubbing my nose in it.

Flexible

I had been flying below the radar for sometime in A/V Manufacturing. I was the UV Coating I/C. I would put UV coating on printed products used for labels and binder transcripts. I was about as low as one could get on the totem pole and I was completely content.

I did not have to attend any meetings with Dave Miscavige. I did not have to report up every five seconds about where I stood on all the orders I had from him. I did not have a worry in the world except how many papers I coated each day. As long as I did all that I was given to do, life was simple. Most parts of the printing line ahead of me could not produce more than one other guy and I could coat in one day, so it was a lower stress activity. I was still working over 100 hours per week, but not being yelled at during 80 of them.

I had lost an insane amount of weight since being on this post. I did not know for certain why. I think it was a combination of several things: not eating, standing all day at my machine, walking to and from my berthing each day, working with highly toxic UV chemicals and standing next to a very powerful bank of UV lights. I had not really noticed the weight loss until a lot of chubby people kept asking me what diet I was doing. Most of the women who had desk jobs could easily stack up the pounds if they did not watch it. The diet at the Int Base was so horrible; and with no time for exercise, it was just a losing battle.

There had been a flurry of activity happening lately. A new org in Spain was supposed to open in a few weeks and then right after that a new org in New York was being opened. These were both Ideal Orgs based on Dave's grand plan to re-do all orgs in the world.

Every time a new Ideal Org was opened, Gold would get our butts kicked to get the A/V systems installed. No matter how much was done on the org in terms of construction, if the systems were not installed ahead of time and set up perfectly, Dave Miscavige would wreak havoc on Gold.

It was a sure thing, you could bet on it; Spain and New York were on a collision course with an angry Dave Miscavige.

The A/V Systems area had two people in it and there was no way that the new systems for these orgs would be built without other people doing it for them. The only guy in the area who was any use was Trevor. He was the guy that built the systems but also the same guy who had to install them at the orgs. He was a good guy but being in two places at the same time was not his specialty. I felt sorry for him and wanted to do whatever I could, so I would occasionally sneak off and build a few cassette decks or film room computer systems whenever he needed it. I had to be very discreet and make sure that no one saw me while I was doing this stuff, though. It was not that I was not qualified to build the systems, I had been busted off post by Dave and since A/V systems was a subject that he was very vocal about, people wanted me to help without Dave seeing that I was helping.

Trevor was just about to take off to Spain to install a bunch of systems and I told him that I would help him from Gold if he needed it. Trevor was the kind of guy who would regularly reach his busting point, throw a hissy fit and then walk off angry. A few hours later he would show back up like nothing had happened. Where he went or what he did, I was not sure, but this would happen at least once or twice a month.

Well, Trevor was supposed to be leaving for Spain and he did not have what he needed to take with him. He threw one of his fits and disappeared. I tried to wrap up as much as I knew he needed and pack it up for shipment out to Spain.

I went back down to A/V Manufacturing and did some more UV coating. The next day Trevor came down and saw me. He thanked me for what I had done and gave me a list of the stuff he still needed for Spain and some stuff that he would need for New York.

"You know, someone should be in New York right now installing the systems they need there," I told Trevor.

"I know. I have been saying that for the last month but there is 'no one' to send," Trevor conceded apathetically. "It will flap and then I will pass out 'told you so' tickets."

"Okay, man, have fun," I said facetiously.

I managed to build everything on Trevor's wish list for both Spain and New York in the next couple of days and ship them out to both locations.

As I was getting back to work in UV coating one day, I was approached by the Manufacturing Sec, a girl named Caroline. She was in way over her head on this post. I doubted she would last more than another year or so. She explained to me that a mission needed to go to New York org to install all of the new A/V systems. I explained to her that I had already built all of the components they needed and shipped them out earlier that week.

"I know that, Marc, I'm telling you because YOU are going to go install the New York AV systems," she said.

The truth was that I loved working on systems. It one the one thing that I did at the Int Base that I actually truly loved and had fun while doing it. That is why I think I was never allowed to do that as my post. I just had too much fun and no one could stand that. For my last ten years at the Int Base, I had always gravitated back to working on A/V systems and someone would always take me off it. I was still, no matter what anybody said, the most qualified to work on systems and knew more technically than anybody else by far. But as of late I had given up on trying to work on it more than a few hours here and there. I did it more to help out and keep my chops up on the subject.

"You really think that is a good idea?" I asked. "I mean, I was born on the weekend, but not last weekend."

"I know. No one thinks this is a good idea. It is our only option to get the systems done and ready before COB arrives in New York after Spain is opened," she said.

"Well, whose idea was it to send me?"

"Marc Yager is the one that approved it," she answered.

"I am so not going." I walked back over to my UV coating machine. This conversation was over.

Marc Yager had been behind every bad thing that had ever happened to me. The IAS Tapes in 1993, the QC Gold fiasco in Clearwater, the A/V Manufacturing proposal and then the Systems blow up the year before. This guy was bad news. If I had learned my lesson, it was that any time I had been involved with something this guy had worked out, it would end up bad. I could already think this one through and see what he had planned. I would go to New York, the systems would flap with COB and Marc Yager would hang the whole flap right around my neck and that would be the end of me. I think it was well known that I did not have a high opinion of Marc Yager and he and I had clashed before on a number of occasions.

No way, I was not going to do it. No matter how much I loved working on A/V systems, this was just a trap.

"If you refuse to do this, Marc Yager is going to use that against you when it flaps in the end," Caroline said to me.

It was a familiar position to be in at the Int base. Screwed if you do, screwed if you don't. I had been here before and knew what would happen.

"Well, I guess I am flexible. When do I leave?" I asked Caroline.

"Tomorrow morning," she answered. "You should go up to CMO Int and get briefed by them on exactly what is needed."

"Okay," I said. This sucked. It was a total set up.

I arrived in CMO Int. They were expecting me. I was told about all the stuff that had been happening in New York and where they stood on what they were supposed to have installed. The org was not even done being renovated. The renovations usually had to be completed before the systems could be installed and tested. This was the normal routine with these new orgs. They would drag the renovations on until the last possible second and then everything else would have to be done practically overnight in order to be ready by the time COB rolled in to inspect the place.

The only difference about this New York org was that with the time left, I did not see how it could possibly be done by the time the org was supposed to open. It was physically impossible. I told the CMO Int guys this. They knew this already.

"That is why it was decided to send you, Marc. If anyone could get this done, it was you. We have no other options," the girl from CMO Int said.

"Who is going to go with me?" I asked.

"Gerald Duncan," she replied.

Gerald Duncan was the Director of Inspections & Reports Gold. He knew nothing about systems. In fact if you could pick the one person who knew the least about systems, Gerald Duncan was probably the person you would pick.

I did not even have to ask why Gerald was being sent. Gerald often went to events to watch over people and make sure they did not blow. And if someone needed to be escorted back to Gold from an event and needed to be watched on the plane on the way back, Gerald was the guy. Gerald used to be a security guard. He was basically a Sea Org police officer. When someone blew from the Int Base, Gerald would routinely be involved with tracking them down and bringing them back. In my case, he would go with me so I would not even have a chance to blow at any point during my trip to New York.

In order to have a proper Sea Org mission, you had to have at least two people. A Mission I/C and a 2nd were the minimum required to send out a mission. I would be the Mission I/C and Gerald would be my Mission 2nd. What a complete joke. This had been planned down to the last detail of how I would be escorted back to the base after this became the biggest flap Gold had seen in years.

I packed enough stuff from Systems Gold to build everything I would need plus anything I could think of that I might run into while there. I had approximately two weeks to install over $400,000 worth of A/V systems in New York. I had never been to this installation site and the renovations happening there were not going to be done for another week or two at least.

I also packed a few other things that I might need in case I had to make a break for it while there. I had a laptop that I always used that had Internet access if I needed it. I also had my Nextel phone and I knew I could probably orchestrate an escape on the fly depending on the situation.

Gerald and I rode down to the airport together. He explained to me that he would do what he could to help, but that he was really just coming to make sure I did not take off. I could care less about him. He would be absolutely no use to me whatsoever. I did enjoy the thought that I would be pulling probably at least ten all-nighters over the next two weeks, and poor ol' Gerald was going to have to keep up with me if he was to be my full time watchdog. He would never make it. I knew that. Here was a guy that did nothing more than enforce arbitrary penalties and pass out life sentences handed down from COB. He never made anything. He did not actually work; he was a pencil pusher with a badge.

When we showed up in New York it was worse than I thought. The place was at least 3 weeks away from being completed on renovations alone. COB was arriving in 18 days. I probably needed at least a week or so after the renovations were completed before I could finish the installations.

The girl in charge of the renovations was from the Int Landlord Office, I knew her really well. Her name was Alex. I had planned out at least fifty individual Ideal Orgs with her and where all the film rooms and systems would be located. She was a bit of a wild card in terms of what she did. Even though she was from Int Landlord Office, she was almost never there. She was always out in some org overseeing renovations.

Alex showed me around and told me that she had been asking for someone from systems for weeks. There were a lot of systems that could be installed in the few areas that were completed. I planned to have those done in the next week. I set up shop in one of the course rooms. I built all of my systems in there and installed each one as I finished it and as renovations were completed.

After the first all-nighter, Gerald said he would be going to sleep and that I needed to check in with him if I went anywhere. I had not even been over to where we were supposed to be sleeping yet! The next night I went over there. The room was in the CLO EUS berthing building. The room was slightly bigger than the bunk bed that had been installed. If you were not in the bed, and someone opened the door you would have to get into the bed in order for them to get in the door. The room was small. I would not be there much so did not really care. I dumped a few of my clothes there and took a shower.

Gerald was taking advantage of not being at the Base and not having to report up to anyone. He was getting a good night's sleep. Having full 30-minute meal breaks for breakfast, lunch and dinner and having nice leisurely strolls back and forth between the CLO and the New York Org every meal. I thought about how his mood would change once COB arrived. When all the Gold event crew arrived and Dave started telling everyone around how they were out-ethics scumbags, Gerald was not only going to be watching little ol' me, he was going to have fifty or more potential staff that would be blowing, sent back to Gold, you name it. I hoped he was storing up some of that sleep he had been getting because he was going to need it in a week or so.

After about a week I had completed the installations in the rooms that had been renovated. Each day I would hear about how it was going in Spain and how COB was freaking out over how behind the systems were there. It was supposedly the biggest flap in Spain and the only reason COB was not getting rid of people was that Tom Cruise was there and Dave was having to pal around with him instead of assigning people to the Rehabilitation Project Force.

The renovations were truly a disaster in New York Org and I kept reporting this back to CMO Int. If they did not quickly send some reinforcements, there was no way the renos would be done, much less the systems. It was just about to start going past the point of no return.

That week more people showed up. Tom Devocht showed up and started tackling the issues with the renovations. After being there only a few days, he found out, or figured out, that Alex, the girl running the whole show, was sleeping with one of the guys from the org who was also doing the renos. She was shipped off as soon as this was found out.

The next excitement was that the Spain event had been completed and a few of the Gold event crew were being sent directly from Spain to New York to help with the systems and get them installed before Dave showed up a few days later.

When the Gold crew arrived the next day, they recounted the horror stories from Spain with regards to the systems there. It was a disaster no doubt, but I tried to explain to them that New York was not going to be better and in fact, based on the progress of the still ongoing renovations, I could almost guarantee it would be worse. As Trevor walked around the org he could not believe his eyes. It was worse than Spain and he had already been up going on two weeks straight. The only sleep he'd had in the last two weeks was on the plane flight over.

I showed him all the stuff that I had installed or pre-built ready to be installed. By myself, I had already done everything that could be done. But if they finished the renovations any time soon, there was at least another week or so of work needed even if you had ten people doing it.

We got to work getting things ready to install. We did pre-wiring and anything that we thought would speed up installing the systems. All the digital film rooms had yet to be built. Once the rooms themselves were finished, we would have to install screens, speakers, projectors, remote control touch panels, computers and all wiring between all of these things. There were at least six different digital film theatres to install plus a full auditorium with speakers and full equipment rack as well. Then there were about fifty cassette decks and CD players that were needed on several floors, a dozen or so flat screens around the org and about 16 video display systems in the reception area.

The last of the event crew were about to leave Spain and wanted a report on where things stood in New York with regards to the systems.

Whoever was relaying the information mentioned my name in some way, and that is when all hell broke loose. Henning Bendorf was the Art Director. He was not only the one who had designed all of the event and film sets for the last five years, but he was also the one designing all of the Ideal Orgs. He was one of Dave's favorite people in Gold. Henning could not believe that I, of all people, was anywhere near New York Org systems. He actually told Gerald that if Dave even knew I was there, those who had sent me would be taken off post and sent to the Rehabilitation Project Force. Apparently, I was the most out-ethics person in Gold and Henning told Gerald that if I was still in New York when he got there, that he would get on a plane to Gold and not show up for the opening event at all. As soon as Henning hung up after talking to Gerald, he called CMO Int and told them that they were crazy for sending me and demanded that I be recalled immediately. He gave them the same spiel about how upset Dave would be and since he had been with Dave in Spain for the last two weeks, who would know better.

An hour later, Gerald came and told me to make sure that I was ready to go by 3:00 P.M. the next day. I was going back to Gold. Trevor begged Gerald to let me stay. I worked as much as I could through the night. I even managed to install a bunch more items as renovations were completed. There was just no stopping it.

As I was installing one last item around noon the next day, I saw Amber O'Sullivan. Amber was going around to all of the places Dave might go and making sure that he had cigarettes, water and all the things he liked in any conference room or space that he might use while here in New York. Amber was not only one of COB's personal stewards; she was my wife's cousin. Amber was also from the UK and had red hair just like my wife. Amber asked me what I was doing here and could not believe that I was here installing systems. I told her I just stopped by to help out and was on my way out very shortly.

I went and got my belongings from the room where I had been staying and said goodbye to Trevor who was actually crying as I left the New York Org. I felt for him, but this was purely a political move and I had no say at all in what was happening. I had to leave and no one could stop it. Everyone there was told not to even bring up my name as it might upset Dave. As far as everyone was concerned, I had never been there.

I was to go to the airport by myself. Gerald had his hands full in New York and he was sure to be even busier once COB arrived. I was told that if for any reason I did not make it back to Gold, the dogs would be cut loose to hunt me down.

Henning was arriving on a 1:00 P.M. flight. Dave was supposedly getting in a few hours later. I was leaving at 3:00 P.M. and I think that as I was taking off, Dave's flight was landing. I knew this would somehow bite me in the butt.

I arrived back to Gold late that night. I had a nonstop flight and was picked up at the airport by Int Base staff as soon as I arrived. When I woke up the next day, I went back to the UV coating area like nothing had happened. Everyone else pretended I was never gone. It was like a big secret. No one spoke of it at all.

At lunch muster that day we started to hear about the fallout from New York. COB had arrived and nothing was ready to show him. He had even rejected some of the renovations that had been done and was telling them to redesign and build new things before the Opening event that coming weekend.

A few mornings later when I came in to post, I got a call from Gerald in New York. He asked if I had heard from Trevor. I hadn't but he was in New York so there was no reason I would have.

"We can't find him here in New York," Gerald said.

It was poetic on so many levels. When I go to New York, I get personally escorted and watched so I don't blow. The guy who watches me is Gerald. Then after I leave, the guy who shows up to replace me goes missing right under Gerald's nose. And who does he call? Gerald calls me to find out where Trevor might be.

Trevor was a young kid. He was in his early twenties. Both his parents were in Scientology, his brothers and sisters were in Scientology. He had aunts and uncles and grandparents all in Scientology. He would never leave knowing that he would be disconnected from all of them in one fell swoop. He like I had nowhere to go and knew nothing else. While blowing from the Sea Org seemed like a possible alternative to the constant torture, with no money, no job and no outside real world connections, the logistics of doing so were daunting.

"He is probably sleeping somewhere," I told Gerald, knowing Trevor all too well. "He overloads and has to get some sleep before he can chill

271

out. I guarantee you he is sleeping under a desk or behind a pile of boxes somewhere."

"Yeah, that is what Matt Price said." Gerald hung up.

Wow, this was getting really bad. Now they had people disappearing from the org while COB was still there. Later that night, I heard that they found Trevor sleeping between some partitions in the auditorium. He had slept for 14 hours straight. When he woke up he had no idea where he was or what had happened. Gerald had combed the entirety of Times Square for four hours looking for him. Like that is where Trevor would go if he blew and even if he did, like Gerald would find him amongst all those people anyway!

Over the next week, I heard more and more tidbits of disasters occurring in New York. At this point it was not about what could go wrong, it was about what couldn't go wrong.

The New York Ideal Org Opening event was held as originally planned, but the renovations were still not done and the A/V systems were still being installed. A few of the rooms that they readied for the Open House after the event still had wet paint on the walls! Rooms that were not completed were locked and not shown. Teams had been up every night since the opening and even the org staff had still not been able to completely move all of the stuff from the temporary org location that was being used while the new place was being renovated.

It had all culminated with COB meeting with anyone involved in the systems for New York. Lisa Schroer, Fed Tisi, Matt Price and Trevor Sargeant were all given $200 in cash by COB and told to pack their stuff and "get out." They had been offloaded from the Sea Org by COB right there in New York!

This came as a shock to the guys at the Int Base. That had never happened before. Usually guys were dragged back and tortured here at the Base. But never had this been done at a remote org and never so swiftly and directly. After we were briefed on this at muster, Caroline came and saw me and told me that it was me that should be walking the streets of New York and not those guys. I knew it was only temporary. I told her that they would be back on the systems by morning; Dave would never let them leave at this point. It was clearly one of his little games that he liked to play with people. Make them think he did not want them, then have them beg to come back when they should be running for the hills. This was right out of his playbook.

Sure enough, the next morning we were all assured that nobody was actually offloaded and that they were all back installing the systems.

After about two more weeks of work, all of the systems in New York Org were installed and most of the event crew members were returning, as well as Dave and his staff. I knew that there might be a slight chance that someone had spilled the beans about me being there and that I might still have to face the music if COB found out about this. I expected it would come out sooner or later, I just did not know when.

The day Trevor got back to the Base, I went and saw him. He recounted the horrors that had occurred. He could not believe that I had managed to escape just in the nick of time. He assured me that no one in New York had said a peep about me having been there. Everyone was so scared that it would ignite more flames from COB so no one dared even bring it up or try to throw me under the bus for everything being screwed up. He told me he could not imagine what would have happened if I had not gone down and done the work that I did.

He told me the whole story about COB giving them all $200. He said that he and Matt Price had left with their stuff and went to Times Square and got some authentic New York pizza with the money and were just hanging out until Gerald Duncan found them and brought them back! I asked Trevor about his little sleep vacation and told him that they had even called back and asked me if I had heard from him. We laughed about this and he said that he was going to sleep for a few days and that he would let me know where.

The next day I was at my workstation doing my thing and the Mfg Sec came running in and told me that COB and COB Asst were outside and wanted to talk to me. This was it. I could not have expected to escape this fate forever. I walked outside.

Dave Miscavige was sitting on his motorcycle that was still parked on the road and Shelly was walking towards me as I exited the building. He was about thirty feet away and the bike was still running.

"COB says you should be the A/V Systems Director, Marc," Shelly said. "He said that if you were in New York getting the systems done, that this whole fiasco would have never happened."

"Yes, Sir," I said.

"Good." She turned around and walked away.

I nodded to COB and he nodded back. Shelly got on the back of his bike and they drove off. I smiled. I walked back into the building and told Caroline that Dave just made me the A/V Systems Dir. I also told her what he said about New York and that it would have been better if I was there. It was actually perfect for me. Now, nobody could ever tell him that I was there in New York as it would appear that they were trying to tell him that he was wrong by saying that if I were there it would not have happened. I was off the hook and I was now finally doing what I liked after being here at the Int Base for almost fifteen years.

Happiest Girl

Late one night, I had to go over to the Cine Castle and get some computer parts that I had lent Darius Wilhere a few weeks earlier. He was still the Pre-Production Director in Cine and was always playing around with some computer stuff. Since I was back in systems, I had all kinds of that stuff.

I went up to his office, which was my old office above the research and assembly area. He was not there. The girls in Research & Assembly told me that he had been spending all his time up in the Talent area. As I had previously been posted as the Pre Production Director, these were my old stomping grounds.

Talent was around the West side of the Castle above the Costumes and Make-up Departments. I could hear Darius cutting some audition videos as I walked in.

He was sitting at the desk in the back of talent where there was an Apple G4 with Final Cut Pro Editing installed on it. The Talent Dept used this system to cut together audition tapes that were done in LA at the Talent Office located in Celebrity Centre. Marie Bystrom, the Talent Chief, would put ads on Internet Casting sites, video the auditions and send them up to Gold where they would be submitted for final approval to the Director and then on to Dave if it was for an important video or film.

Darius took his headphones off as I walked in.

"Hey, man, what's up?" Darius said.

"Oh, you know, same ol' same ol'," I answered, pawing through the tapes he had laying around the desk.

"What submission are you doing?" I asked him, seeing he had Mini DV tapes stacked everywhere.

"Some project for RTC," Darius said.

"This many tapes?" I ask, motioning to the piles on the desk.

"Yeah, well first, we auditioned every single up and coming Scientology actress we could get our hands on in LA. We have seen all of those and now we are reviewing *any* Scientologist actresses whether they are working or not."

"Wow, what qualifications do they need for the part?" I asked, thinking this seemed like the most bizarre casting submission I had heard of yet.

"Well that is just it," Darius said, obviously frustrated with the entire thing, "We have no idea what it is for. It seems like it is for some kind of Tom Cruise movie but we don't have any description or lines for them to read. We just ask them a bunch of questions about Tom and have them explain what they are doing in Scientology and where they are on the Bridge. That's it. And a hundred girls later, here I am, still cutting these together."

"How do you know if the girls you are sending up are right or wrong?" I asked.

"We don't. The submissions just go up to RTC, and they don't come back," Darius said. "We just keep sending them up assuming that when they get one they like, we'll get told to stop sending up new ones."

"Wow, how did you get roped into this?" I asked.

"My dad. He is apparently going to New York to interview some other actresses as well," Darius said.

"Wow, maybe it is for Mission Impossible: 3," I told Darius.

"I doubt it," Darius said. "Some of these girls would not make it as background extras in MI:3, much less any speaking part."

"Well, as much as I would love to sit here with you and cut footage of these girls together, I need to get those drives I lent you a few weeks ago," I told him, looking around for my drives.

"I still need them for a bit longer," Darius replied. "With so many of these girls auditioned, I have like 300 gigs worth of auditions on these drives that I don't want to have to re-digitize."

"Okay, well as soon as the plug gets pulled on your little project, bring the drives back over." I tell him as I head out. "Have fun, dude!"

I went back over to Systems before securing for the night, grabbed a few things and headed home. It was around 1:00 A.M. and my wife had mentioned that she might be home early so I might even see her tonight if I was lucky.

My wife worked with Greg Wilhere in RTC, so I figured I could maybe find out what movie they were auditioning all these girls for. I knew she would know about it. There were only so many people up there and they all talked amongst each other about this sort of stuff.

When she got home a little while later I asked her. "Hey, what movie is Cine doing all those auditions for RTC on?"

"What auditions?" she answered.

"Oh come on, there is no way you could not know what I am talking about. Darius probably had at least fifty submissions up in RTC on this thing. You would have probably been buried by the envelopes sent up by him alone." I told her.

"Oh, *that* project," she answered.

"I knew you knew," I said. "You so suck at lying." I laughed.

"You have to promise not to tell anybody about this," She told me, which is what anything she told me about what went on in RTC was prefaced with.

"Shelly told me that COB has been getting calls from Tom about getting him a girlfriend," my wife continued, "since now he obviously can't have a girlfriend who is not a Scientologist. COB told Shelly that he wanted her to sort this out and get him a girlfriend. So Greg has been going through all of these girls that Cine has been auditioning and trying to find one that Tom might like. They are trying to screen which ones might have potential baggage attached to them that could flap later on if Tom actually ends up going out with one of them. And of course COB has to like her as well."

As we all know, Tom Cruise was married to Nicole Kidman for close to ten years. Well, Nicole was only a Scientologist very briefly, after which she wanted none of it. Next, he was with Penelope Cruz, and his attempts to convert her from her prior religious beliefs were unsuccessful. So this was building up a history of being a problem for Tom, and now Dave was going to solve it for him and find him the perfect Scientologist partner.

"So it has nothing to do with any movie? I knew it. I knew it. Oh my god, if Darius only knew. He has been slaving away over in Cine cutting these tapes and it is not even for a movie. What a scam," I told her.

"Well, that's between Greg and him. Greg's the one that got him involved. I don't even think they will end up using any of the girls on those tapes," she said.

"Why?" I asked.

"Well, Greg just got some brand new suits and is supposed to be flying off to New York to meet a few girls," she said.

"Wow." I was speechless.

"COB's Celebrity Pimp Service. How may I help you?" I could hear the receptionist now.

(At the time I did not know which women got picked and which ones were auditioned by Tom himself, but since then I have heard of at least one woman who spent time with Tom but did not end up staying with him. I omitted her name out of respect for her. If there were others or not, I guess only Greg, Dave and Tom, and any other women "test driven" will know for sure.)

Personal Jesus

Auditors Day's 2004 had just been completed and the IAS event was next up to be produced at the Int Base. This IAS event was going to be huge. Dave Miscavige had finally decided that Tom Cruise would get a Freedom Medal at this event. This was a big deal as Tom Cruise had done more than any other celebrity Scientologist. Not only had he given more money, but he was just a bigger star than any other celebrities who were in Scientology.

Whenever someone was awarded an IAS Freedom Medal, they traditionally had a video produced that told their story and what they did to earn the medal. Every year, there were at least two or three winners and video teams would go out and shoot the videos and then these were edited, the music scored, recorded and mixed, etc.

Larry Jacobs, Video Team Director, was assigned to the Tom Cruise video. The idea was that we already knew the story of what Tom Cruise did and we were going to just video a bunch of people who knew Tom, interview them and cut those interviews together. Larry spent a few weeks doing interviews with every single celebrity Scientologist in LA.

The interviews were all cut together and it was a bunch of Scientologists talking about how much they loved Tom Cruise. It was a complete puff piece and when Dave Miscavige saw it, he hated it. We did not have a lot of time to make these videos and a few weeks had been wasted on this one so far. Back to the drawing board. Larry Jacobs was taken off the project and was surely going to get in big trouble for this.

The day after Larry was taken off the video, I was contacted by Security Gold. They brought me a laptop that they needed me to get working. I plugged the laptop in and turned it on. It worked fine. I told them that it was fine. They wanted me to get into it.

"It just needs to be logged into and you can get whatever you want," I told them.

"We don't know the password," I was told.

"Well, whose is it? They will surely know the password."

"It is Larry Jacob's laptop and he is not available to ask," the security guard answered.

"Well, I can't help you then," I said.

Larry had obviously blown and they were trying to get onto the laptop to find out any clues as to where he had gone.

With Larry Jacobs now blown and probably on his was to being declared or RPFed, anyone working on the video was on pins and needles.

The next batch of interviews done was of non-Scientologists who knew Tom. Everyone from Steven Spielberg to Will Smith was interviewed. Again the video was a complete wipe out. Now we had all of these people talking about how Tom Cruise was a really nice guy. Being a nice guy does not get you an IAS Freedom Medal award. Dave hated the new interviews and we were out of time. There were only a few weeks left until the event and a video had to be done.

No matter what anyone came up with, Dave hated it. In the end, Dave's conclusion was that nobody at the Int Base really knew Tom Cruise or what he had done. None of us were hanging out with him in Telluride, Colorado. None of us were regularly going down to his house in Los Angeles. None of us were going to big time celebrity birthday parties with the likes of Oprah and Will Smith. None of us were going high-speed motorcycle riding or to the car races with Tom Cruise. None of us, except one David Miscavige. Dave and Tom were not only buddies, but they talked all the time. Dave would routinely name drop about who he had met with Tom the week before or about who he talked to at the latest movie premiere. Dave was showing us *Last Samurai* trailers that had not yet had music added to them. Dave and Tom might as well have had the same circle, they were that close.

Dave Miscavige ended up dictating the entire Tom Cruise video project. Dave's idea was that no one could talk about Tom Cruise better than Tom Cruise himself. A list of questions was drawn up and Tom would be shot on video and, more than anything, Tom would say whatever he wanted to say and from the footage, a video would be cut together that would tell the story of Tom Cruise the Scientologist.

When the tapes came in, the footage was transcribed and all the transcripts were reviewed by Dave himself. He would cut up portions of the transcripts and piece these together to make a script. The music that Dave decided on was the Mission Impossible II movie theme. The video would start out with a VO and some graphics of Tom Cruise. Then we would use footage of a lot of other videos that had anything to do with Tom or anything he had ever done, Ground Zero in New York, CCHR, Interviews with Larry King, movie premieres, you name it, the footage had to be tracked down so it could be used in his video. Everything from supermarket magazines to newspaper articles was sent in from Tom's PR people. We shot it all five different ways, pan across, zoom in, zoom out, static, you name it, we shot it and gave Dave Miscavige six ways from Sunday to edit it.

Dave sat in the video edit bay for over a week straight, day and night, tweaking every single frame of this video until it was perfect. This was going to be his baby. He worked out what was used and exactly how one shot transitioned to the next, what interview bits from Tom were used, everything. There was nothing about this video that was not seen by Dave Miscavige at least ten times.

The music had to be perfect; the shots used had to all be perfect. No stone was left unturned. Dave was not only making a video that would be about Tom Cruise, but Tom himself would have to be blown away when he saw it.

The funny part was that in the end when the video was done, it was as if Dave Miscavige had put on a Tom Cruise mask. The way Tom talked and acted was as if he were a clone of Dave Miscavige. People who know Dave well and don't know Tom Cruise could tell you, in 2004 Tom Cruise started acting like Dave Miscavige. Now all Tom Cruise needed was to get an acting role as some foul-mouthed executive that beats his staff and he would be set.

Dave Miscavige thought he was the Tom Cruise of the Int Base. Dave once met Bill Clinton. When Dave was telling the story to some of us, someone commented, "You met the President of the United States?" Dave Miscavige answered, "No, he met me!" That was Dave Miscavige in a nutshell.

Dave made the entire Int Base watch his Tom Cruise video several times and told us that this was how a video got done and when someone really wanted to get a product, it could be done.

A special Freedom Medal of Valor was designed and made for this event. It was just like all the other freedom medals that had been given out over the years except it was a bit bigger and was encrusted with diamonds and instead of being gold plated it was white gold or platinum or some such thing.

When the event finally came around and everyone went off to UK where it was held, we all knew that Tom Cruise would be there. It was even leaked that Tom Cruise might be there so that more Scientologists would attend the event in a remote part of East Grinstead, England.

Oddly enough there was not that much concern for Tom Cruise at the actual live event other than making sure he had a seat in the front row. The event video cameramen were instructed to keep the cameras off Tom for the entire event while he was in the crowd. He was sitting next to a girl that he was going out with who was not EVER to be on camera during the event. Even so, she still ended up on camera when he got up from his seat to accept his medal and when he sat back down.

At the event that night Dave Miscavige did a whole intro to the Tom Cruise video, even saying that Tom Cruise was the most dedicated Scientologist he knew. When he said that, the Int Base staff knew that was the case because Dave had already told us that if he could, he would have made Tom Cruise the Inspector General RTC, the post second only to COB RTC in Scientology.

Dave Miscavige later said that his Tom Cruise video was one of the most important videos that had ever been produced. He had no idea how true that was.

Christmas Island

t was late 2004.

I was now the A/V Systems Director Gold. My job was to design and install all the audio/visual systems for Scientology internationally. This consisted of everything from high definition film theaters to introductory video displays. In any single org location, there could be more than 30 different types of systems to install.

Over the past ten years, everything had turned into something audio/visual. No one at the Int Base was knowledgeable in enough different fields to be able to comprehend how any of these systems could be designed, much less produced and installed.

After fifteen years at Golden Era Productions, I had worked in pre-production, shoot production, post-production, manufacturing and had done system installations in orgs all over the world. I had more cumulative experience than anyone at the Base.

Anyone who had anywhere near the systems experience that I had, was blown or long gone.

Russ Bellin, the CO CST, was the only person who could boast to having this much experience with newer more modern types of systems. But Russ Bellin had recently been given the task of designing a few A/V systems and had failed. I got those same systems designed and approved by Dave Miscavige.

I was told by Lisa Schroer, the CO Gold, that Dave Miscavige wanted to have a meeting with me on systems later in the day. I headed over to the Cine Conference room in the Lower Lodges.

Dave showed up as did several other people from CMO Int and CST. Most of the people in the room had attended at least 50 meetings on the subject of systems. Nothing had been getting done on systems for years. I was actually the first person to get any new systems approved in over ten years. In addition to this, there had been more than five different A/V

Systems Directors in the last few years and each one of them had been assigned to the Rehabilitation Project Force. So each time a new person went on post, everything would start from scratch.

Dave did his usual recap of everything that had occurred on systems in the last few years and where we stood. This was needed because people changed posts so often that you could have more than half the people in the room with no idea what had happened or what Dave had asked for in the last five meetings on the subject. Well, I had just gotten several Audio Visual systems for the orgs approved by Dave Miscavige and he brought this up as a good thing.

Then he told me what he wanted now. He wanted every single system for every single org designed, built and submitted to him for approval. Once approved, he wanted them built for all orgs. This was huge. One org alone had over $300,000 worth of systems in it. Building all of the systems for all orgs would easily be a 100 million dollar project. I had already mapped out most of these systems and this was known. But I had not formally proposed any of them. Several of them were fairly simple in design and simply needed to be funded in order to be built and proposed. That was it. It was huge, but it was clear cut and straightforward.

After the meeting, the CO Gold met with me to go over what I was going to do. I had already done most of the design work and just needed to build and program the systems and do the overall proposal.

By the end of the week I had a proposal ready for Int Finance that included what I needed to buy in order to get the proposal done. It was all of the equipment components for the individual systems and all of the ancillary items that would be needed to fabricate each system.

While that proposal was up, I streamlined how the new breed of systems would be produced. Until I started working on them, there had been a hodgepodge of different types of systems and formats being used. You had 16 mm film, 35 mm film, xenon based, tungsten based, cassettes, CDs, DVDs, VHS, etc. No system had any basic structure that was similar to any other system.

A few years earlier, another Gold staff member and I had designed and come up with a Hi-Def Film projection system that was computer based. We had an HD playback computer that was custom programmed and employed a revolutionary playback system, which was not only completely hard disk based, but was completely secure. Dave had a huge concern about the security of the media, and any system designed would have to be completely secure so that even if stolen, its built-in security features would render the media useless.

Well, we had designed this film system and it was completely computer based and driven by many different methods of remote control.

After designing the HD film rooms, they were being installed in all of the new orgs. I had overseen the installation in over 20 film rooms and each one was a huge hit.

Shortly thereafter, Russ Bellin had completely bombed on designing a personal film system called a "Reg System." The Reg (Registrar) system was something that an org Reg could sit someone in front of and play a film that would sell them on the service that the person was supposed to do next. It took all the guesswork out of selling new services and as long as there was a film for the service, the person could watch it and then pay for the service.

Russ Bellin had hired the same outside professional designers that had designed the new Mark VIII Ultra E-Meter. The designs were then made into styrofoam prototypes and built into wood cabinets. They looked like Wal-Mart A/V system cabinets with a bizarre style to them. They sucked. Dave Miscavige rejected them out of hand.

I worked out a design that looked like a candy red sports car that had been turned into a huge TV with speakers. It was completely self-contained and looked cool. It sounded awesome. It was a 3.1 speaker system, years ahead of its time. It was also computer based.

The third and final system that would cement my place in Golden Era A/V systems history would be the Bookstore system. Dave Miscavige had laid out what he wanted in a system for the bookstores in every org.

Russ Bellin attempted to produce this and came up short. His designs were still reminiscent of his ugly Reg system designs. That gave me an idea.

I designed and built a Bookstore system that looked like it was from the same family of systems as my Reg System. This new bookstore system would also be computer based.

So, as with all of the other systems that I had designed and gotten approved by Dave Miscavige, I would make all the systems computer based. This would greatly simplify the entire process of designing and building systems and give us a stable base as well as an upgrade path for everything that was being installed. All of the menus and screens to control the systems would be Flash based, and since I had someone who could do all of that programming, we were set.

I could do all programming and designs in house and the only things that I would need to purchase for my proposal would be the computers, screens, speakers and fabrication materials.

After a few days, I had not heard back on my finance proposal. I went to CMO Int and saw Marc Yager. Marc was still a declared SP. He was being addressed by Dave Miscavige in dispatches as INT BASE SP MARC YAGER or just INT BASE SPs if the dispatch was to more than a few of the SPs.

Well, at this point not only was he an SP, but he was the single point of approval on all International Finance items. He was the one approving all the weekly Financial Planning disbursements and if you wanted any money for anything, he had to approve it.

Well, when I went and met with him, he said that in order for him to approve any finances for systems, I would have to have approval on them by COB! I could tell he was trying to screw me over. He was there when Dave told me what he wanted. He knew that I could not get the systems approved without the money and that COB would not approve the systems without the prototypes being submitted.

He made it very clear, unless I had a dispatch from COB specifically stating that I was to get funding from Int Finance, that I would not get any, period. He told me that my only other option was to get the money from Gold FP. That was the equivalent of saying, "you are never going to get the money, ever." Gold FP could barely pay for food for the crew much less computers and crap for upcoming projects. I was screwed.

This was typical of the Int Base. People trying to stop others from getting something done just to spite them. I was doing well. I was getting stuff done, I was producing high quality systems that were being installed all over the world. I had produced over 700 HD film systems, over 350 Reg systems, totaling millions of dollars, and now Marc Yager was going to shut me down on a $30,000 finance proposal for prototypes? Not a chance.

It took me a few hours to figure out a plan. I had no idea that this plan would ultimately change my life forever.

There was a huge warehouse in LA, called the Bandini warehouse, that was a shared storage and production facility used by both Golden Era and Bridge Publications. So much room had been taken up by the new E-Meters being stored there, that a lot of older stuff was being cleared out and thrown away.

I had received a list a few weeks earlier of all of the old systems items that were located in the warehouse, with information on what was being thrown out and what was being sold.

One of the items on the list being thrown out was several pallets of 20-year-old 16 mm projectors still in the original boxes. There were stacks and stacks of these being chucked into dumpsters. I wrote down to the warehouse manager and asked him to have them sent up to me at Gold and that I would get rid of them at my end.

I looked on Ebay and found there were several of these projectors being sold for over $500. And the ones being sold were old used ones that had been damaged or had parts missing. The ones I had were still in the original packaging and had been unopened for the most part.

I had an Ebay account and a Paypal account that I used on occasion for personal purchases.

I did a new proposal on how I was going to get the money I needed. I was going to sell off all of the crap that had been accumulated in systems stocks over the last 20 years. I estimated that I could sell off $50,000 worth of old equipment and unneeded items that would never be used on the new AV systems, and that were otherwise already being thrown away.

My division head, all Gold Division heads, top executives and finance staff had approved the proposal. In order to sell any org equipment, one had to have the authorization from all of these people. So, there it was, I had the approval in writing. I started selling the items right away.

Within the first week, I had made $3,000. I had pallets arriving daily from the warehouse in LA. I was selling the items faster than I could get them up to the Int Base. After a few weeks, I had made $15,000. All the while, I was still getting my systems designed, programmed and was assembling my overall proposal to Dave Miscavige.

After a few weeks, one of COB's Office staff came down to see me and we decided that with what I had put together, I could submit my proposal. The systems that I had actually built, I could have ready to demonstrate, and any others I could just show pictures of how the system would look and what items it would consist of. This worked for me.

In a few days I completed the submission and sent it up. As with all submissions to COB, they had to go through about five other people before they could be presented to him. The routing on my submission was the following:

TO: COB RTC
via: CO CST
via: CO CMO INT
via: CO GOLD
via: MFG SEC GOLD
FROM: A/V SYSTEMS DIRECTOR GOLD

The submission went back and forth with the Manufacturing Sec several times to fix points that might be interpreted wrong or lead to someone having to do more work than they wanted to.

Then it bounced around between the CO Gold and CO CMO INT several times and parked with CO CMO INT while event stuff was being worked on.

Being the end of the year, Christmas was coming up. At Christmas time, when you were at Gold, you could usually count on getting some sort of year-end bonus. Every year, it would get smaller, but still, each year, you would look forward to the small chance that this year's bonus would be awesome. Well that year, I think it was $35. That was less than one dollar a week as an end of the year bonus. Awesome.

In addition to that, because the crew had to buy a group gift for COB and COB Asst, $10 was taken out of each person's pay for the two weeks before Christmas for the gifts. Dave would usually get a $10,000 handmade suit from High Society Custom Tailor in Beverly Hills and Shelly, his wife and personal assistant, would get some sort of clothing item worth more than I made all year long. This did not only happen at Christmas. This same sort of thing happened on Dave and Shelly's birthdays as well. I was there for 15 years and each birthday and Christmas they got a gift that was easily worth more than a few thousand dollars. Also this was not something that only Gold did; Gold was actually considered the cheapskate of all orgs! Because we had so many people, we could get away with just giving a few bucks. And if you did *not* give, you were "disaffected or had Black PR on Dave". RTC staff would sometimes pony up $100 each for their org's present. RTC, IAS, CST, ASI, CMO INT, CMO GOLD CMO PAC, CMO CW, CMO EU, CMO EUS, CMO SHIP, CMO ANZO, FLAG, and other orgs all did this. In 2004, ASI gave Dave a brand new BMW 645Ci for Christmas! If Dave Miscavige did not get over $50,000 dollars worth of gifts each birthday and Christmas, I would be surprised.

Well, I decided that this was crap and that I would get something for Dave and Shelly from my wife and I, and that the $40 auto deduction would not apply to me. When I picked up my pay those weeks, I told the payroll officer that I was getting them my own gift and was not to have my pay deducted.

The week before Christmas Day, we got two hours to do our Christmas shopping at Wal-Mart. The buses were filled with people in shifts and everybody went to Wal-Mart, bought what they needed, climbed back on the buses and came back.

Each year the Christmas shopping time had gotten shorter and shorter, but this was insane. I considered a gift from Wal-Mart an insult and I certainly was not going to purchase gifts for Dave and Shelly from Wal-Mart.

Since I had an Ebay account, I decided to get something that was unique and would be cool. I bought Dave a Depeche Mode album, which is what I usually gave him each birthday and Christmas anyway. I found an original printing of a book that L Ron Hubbard's uncle, Elbert Hubbard, wrote called *A Message to Garcia*. The book is referenced in a few policies. There were a few different ones on Ebay that I could get, all fairly cheap, so I bought all of them. When I got them in, the best one was printed in the early 1900's and was the original leatherbound booklet in mint condition. I had a little wood box and wrapped some velvet around some foam and put the booklet inside.

When Christmas eventually came, we did not get the day off. Since the New Year's event speeches and videos were so behind, everybody had to work all day on Christmas, even if they had nothing to do with the event production. Because it would be unfair to have only the event crew miss Christmas, the theory was that the fair thing to do was to have everyone miss Christmas! Sure, that's totally fair!

So we worked all day, during which most people ended up sitting in their offices complaining about how much it sucked that we were working on Christmas Day. But at least we got to have a 45-minute Christmas dinner instead of the normal 15-30 minute dinner break!

The only good thing about that Christmas for my wife and I was our gifts to Dave and Shelly – they were a huge hit. About a week after Christmas, my wife was told that the gift that we gave them was the most "On Source" gift they had gotten from anyone in the world! I was actually getting serious kudos from a lot of people for being so clever. I thought that I was doing pretty well. Even though Christmas totally sucked, maybe, just maybe, things were looking up.

I could not have been more correct.

The New Year's event this year had been scheduled to occur mid-week on December 28th, so that the event could be produced on DVD and sent out to the orgs thus allowing them to have their events on New Year's Eve.

Because I was in the Systems Department now, I had little to do with the live event. This was a huge relief for me. Normally I would have been working day and night myself, but that was not the case this year. I actually sat in the audience at the Shrine Auditorium in Los Angeles.

One of the biggest parts of the New Year's event was always the FSM awards. The FSM (Field Staff Member) awards were given to the public Scientologists that recruited the most new people into Scientology during the prior year. Heber Jentzsch was handing out the FSM awards. I remembered this because ED Int, Guillaume Lesevre, had given them out every year since their inception. This was the first year Guillaume would not be handing them out and it was a huge deal.

Months before, Guillaume had severely pissed off Dave Miscavige and had been on heavy manual labor at the berthing buildings for months. It was not unusual that most of the regular event speakers would be in severe trouble right before an event, and would end up doing the event anyway. But Marc Yager and Guillaume had really been working their hardest to get on Dave's bad side and Dave had them off his lines a lot – Dave's "out of sight, out of mind" theory. Marc Yager was at least still doing some post functions and approving and disapproving people's submissions, but Guillaume was doing hard labor. Not only was he outside most of the day, but he was lean and gaunt. That is one of the things about working at Gold—there were not a lot of fat people around. For people who were put on "heavy MEST work," as it was always referred to, they were just plain skin and bones. I think when it came down to whether Guillaume was going to do the New Year's event, he looked too bad to even walk out on stage. He looked like a cancer patient. His face was thin and he was starting to look much older than he was. He seemed beaten down like a dog. No amount of make-up could hide these features. Also, since he was being punished by Dave, there was always the slight chance that Guillaume would screw up something at the event just to spite Dave. No chances could be taken. Heber was brought in to announce the awards.

Since Guillaume was out, this was Dave's chance to kick out some more people as well. Normally the other speakers were Mike Rinder, Marc Yager and sometimes Ray Mithoff if Dave was really desperate. So all of those guys were now out. Dave Miscavige brought in Claire Edwards from Scientology Missions International, Rena Weinberg from the Association for Better Living and Education and Don Drader from the World Institute of Scientology Enterprises.

Between Heber and the new guys, it seemed that all new people were now putting on the events, except for Dave Miscavige, of course.

Claire Edwards came from a long-time Scientology family. Both her father and brother were once declared SPs. Her father, David Gaiman, worked for years to get undeclared and her brother, Neil Gaiman, became a noted bestselling author and was undeclared and apologized to for the mistake in declaring him an "SP" in the first place.

The event started at around 7:00 P.M. and was over by 9:00 P.M. My wife, Claire, and I met up with her parents, brother and two sisters. My wife had been down in LA before the event with another CMO Int staff member and had one of the organization vehicles. Since we were down in LA at the event, we managed to sneak off to Claire's parents' house for the rest of the night. As long as we were back at the base on post the next morning at 8:30 A.M. we were fine. We went over to their house to exchange gifts and catch up with them. Even though we lived less than two hours away, we usually saw them around Christmas or New Years and that was the only time we could visit them all year.

When we arrived at their house in La Crescenta, we exchanged gifts and played around with the kids. Now, Claire's step-dad, Hugh, is not the most talkative person in the world. In the 12 years that Claire and I had been married, I estimate that her stepdad and I had spoken to each other for a total of 60 minutes. That night, Hugh talked to me for probably two hours straight. Apparently, he was in major trouble over something that had happened a few months earlier.

Hugh was the Executive Director of the Beverly Hills Scientology Mission. He had been doing that for over a decade. He had been a Scientology auditor for his entire career. As the head of the mission, he would routinely fly off to places all over the US and audit high paying clients for the mission. The Beverly Hills Mission had a unique ability to draw in very wealthy people to deliver to. Some of these people, however, were only in Beverly Hills doing business and lived out of state. In most cases, the orgs or missions in the person's own area were low quality dumps and these people wanted nothing to do with them. This is how Hugh ended up flying out to where they lived and auditing them there. This had been the way the Beverly Hills Mission had ALWAYS functioned and there were never any questions about this. Until now.

Well, with the advent of Dave Miscavige's Ideal Org Program, no org or mission was allowed to deliver services to any person that was not in their immediate "sphere of influence." If you drew a circle around the Beverly Hills Mission and their nearest competing org or mission, and then made those circles larger until they touched each other, you would have established the sphere of influence of each of those organizations.

So this meant that any person who did not live within the sphere of the Beverly Hills Mission could not receive any services from them.

To add insult to injury, the way all orgs or missions were to get new people into the org and onto services was now only through E-Meter stress test tables! That was it. Dave Miscavige had piloted this technique at New York Org and had established this as the best way to get new people into the org. Based on his isolated test, he cancelled all other forms of getting new people in and made this the ONLY way that any org or mission could get new people in.

Well, in Beverly Hills you didn't find many high-class operations busting out the crappy folding table and chairs and setting up shop on Rodeo Drive next to Gucci, handing out flyers and asking the filthy rich to get a stress test! But Dave Miscavige had spoken. This was now the ONLY way orgs or missions could operate. According to Hugh, the mission had tried this and failed miserably. They had, over a period of years, perfected an exact way to generate business and keep the mission producing. The new method with the stress test tables simply did not work for them. Based on this, they carried on doing business as usual and ignored the new rules.

Months earlier Dave Miscavige told a story about something that had happened in New York. At the time it meant nothing to me and I thought it was just another story that Dave liked to tell to show that he was the boss. He had been in New York right after the new Ideal Org opened and the place was a ghost town. He demanded that the org be filled with people and could not believe that it was not packed already. Whilst he was going around the org and trying to find where all the people had gone, he happened to run into a guy from a WISE group. David Singer was a chiropractor that had a consulting business. He would consult chiropractors on how to expand their practices and then when they did better and wanted more information, they would end up getting into Scientology.

Well David Singer was walking through New York Org and ran into Dave Miscavige. Dave Miscavige did not like David Singer. According to Dave Miscavige, he approached David Singer and leaned in close so as to whisper to him, and said, "I am going to find out what you're up to," and then walked away. Miscavige then sent some of his RTC staff to track down Singer and put him on the E-Meter to be interrogated.

Apparently, David Singer was planning on doing one of his consulting seminars to a bunch of doctors at the new auditorium in the New York Org. The seminar had nothing to do with the New York Org, it just happened to be a nice place that he could gather up a bunch of people and do a seminar and because he brought new people into Scientology, the org would let him do this for free. He was not even necessarily planning to get people onto service at the org. He had just arranged that a lot of East Coast chiropractors would meet up there.

When Dave found this out, he was furious. Here he was working to make new Ideal Orgs and guys like David Singer were sabotaging his efforts and using the orgs for their own profit. Dave then ordered that anyone involved with this activity be Comm Eved, with the option of being declared an SP if warranted.

So what did this have to do with Hugh Whitt, Executive Director Beverly Hills Mission? Well upon "investigation" it turned out that David

Singer Enterprises, Hollander Consultants and the Beverly Hills Mission had an arrangement that these prominent doctors and professionals were being sent to do their services with the Beverly Hills Mission. As a result, the Beverly Hills Mission was one of the most productive missions in the world. It was routinely winning awards for doing so and this REALLY pissed off Dave Miscavige. They were doing well and had not been doing one thing that he had worked out. In fact they were doing the exact opposite and it was working well for them.

Hugh did not know any of this about Dave Miscavige in New York and why all this was happening. He only knew that somehow, out of nowhere, the mission was being investigated for getting clients from WISE groups and that Vanessa Stoller, the owner of the mission, was being Comm Eved and that he was going to be Comm Eved and possibly declared an SP.

He was trying to get through his OT Level 7 at Flag and this would make it nearly impossible for him to do so. If he ended up being declared, he would not be able to see his children and wife, would have to get another job and probably start his life over from scratch. If Vanessa Stoller was declared, that would surely end up closing the mission and he would have to get a new job anyway. Things looked bleak.

He told me how RTC had done inspections of the mission several times over the years and they knew exactly how the mission operated. They even had a Keeping Scientology Working Award from RTC! It all meant nothing now.

Hugh had talked to me more that night than the entire time I had known him. He was devastated. I remember thinking to myself at the time, that here was an example of the most dedicated public Scientologist around. The guy had been auditing people his entire life, he was at the mission all the time, and gave up most of his personal freedoms to do Scientology. Even with all of that, it meant nothing. He just happened to be in the wrong place at the wrong time when Dave Miscavige was upset.

I could not tell him what I knew and why he was being put through this. I simply told him that I knew some other information that might be related to this and that this was a lot bigger than he knew. If I said anything more and it was found out about, I would surely be declared an SP myself.

After Hugh and I talked, I went back into the living room and played with the kids a bit more. They were staying up late that night so they could spend a few hours with us. A little after 3:30 A.M., Claire and I left to head back to the Base.

As we drove back, Claire slept in the passenger seat and I just sat there in the driver's seat. The radio was turned off. I sat there with only the sound of the road accompanying my thoughts. I could not help but think about Hugh and his family. How could this be happening? How could Hugh, of all people, be in trouble? I was angry, but I could not think of anything to do that would help him. If I even brought up the subject, it would be investigated how I even heard about the Beverly Hills Mission's involvement in this. If I said anything at the Int Base it might get him in even more trouble.

When we got back and Claire woke up, I talked to her a bit about it. I told her what Hugh and I had talked about and that he was about to get royally screwed. She had no ideas about what to do either.

It was now around 5:00 A.M. We decided to watch a DVD before going back to post in the morning. We watched *I, Robot* with Will Smith and went back to post.

That day I could not help but think about my conversation with Hugh some more. It was really bugging me. It had struck a chord and I was not able to just "forget about it."

New Year's Eve came.

In the Sea Org, there was a holiday that historically took place around Christmas time and this was the Beer and Cheese party. Besides Sea Org day, this was really the only Sea Org party that might possibly take place all year. Well, of course, this years' Beer and Cheese party was postponed and would be combined with our New Year's Eve Party.

The Beer and Cheese party was, as expected, amazing. It was only missing three things – beer, cheese and party. Everyone was called down to the dining hall at 11:50 P.M. There were a few tables that had Ritz crackers and some orange sodas on them. Jenny Devocht from CMO Int said that we all needed to get every one of the event items done and that we could have a good New Years if that happened. We then counted down the New Year and gave three cheers to LRH. We were dismissed and most people went back to post, wondering if we would even get the next day off. Not likely.

Any Second Now

When I showed up to post on New Year's day, I was lucky enough to have a dispatch from COB's Office on my desk. It was from COB's Communicator.

It was actually not written to me, but was written to HCO Gold. I was simply cc'd on it since it had to do with me. It said that "COB had not gotten my systems submission and if I was not working on that, what was I working on?"

Essentially, the dispatch implied that I must be up to "no good" and HCO Gold was to find out what this was. By the time I finished reading it, Gerald Duncan had already showed up at my office. Gerald had been in HCO his entire time at Gold. Before that he was the Security Chief at the HGB. That's where I first met him. His radio handle was "Panther." I think that was because he was a tall black guy.

I sat down in his tiny office. He told me that he was going to give me an ethics interview on the E-Meter. He asked me a bunch of questions about what out-ethics I was involved in. Nothing came up. My needle was floating and Gerald was stumped. This went on until lunchtime. We took a break so I could get something to eat.

I knew how this was going to go down. When you get a dispatch from COB's office asking for some guy's crimes, you HAVE to write back with the crimes. It does not matter if there aren't any there to report on. That would be the equivalent of saying, "Sorry, Sir, you are wrong!" Noncompliance with the order could get someone in even hotter water. This was not going to end until they found the "Sherman Tank" — Scientologese for massive sabotage or crime — I was hiding.

After lunch, I was told to go back to post and Gerald would let me know when I was needed next.

That evening after dinner, Gerald came back and grabbed me. We went to his office and he took another stab at getting me to cough up the crimes, but this time, he offered suggestions:

"Sex crimes?
"Out-ethics?
"Out-admin?
"Out-tech?
"Off policy?
"Misunderstood words?
"Stealing?
"Doing other things than post?
"Visiting porn sites?"

The list went on forever. He got nothing out of me. My needle was floating and I was content to sit there forever on this one.

I explained to him again that I had already done the submission, that it was submitted days ago and was sitting on Marc Yager's desk. Gerald was not interested in this. He had to come up with a crime and there would be major consequences when this finally came out. Not only was I on the spot, but so was Gerald. This was Sec Checking 101. If he could not get me to cough up my crimes, than as far as anyone above him was concerned, he was no use to them in HCO.

At the end of the night, I went back to my area. My senior, the Manufacturing Sec, asked me what came up.

"Nothing," I told her. "The submission is with CO CMO Int. I don't understand why he is not being investigated. He has been sitting on the thing for over a week. "

"Well, he rejected it back to you today," she told me.

"Of course he did!" I said. "He ain't going to be the one holding the hot potato now, is he?"

Brilliant.

As I walked back into my office, I saw the submission sitting on my desk. He had some teeny tiny "wording" reject that could not have taken a week to send back to me.

Right as I sat down to handle the reject point, Gerald walked in and told me that I "needed to get some sleep so I could be sessionable for tomorrow."

"Really?" I said. "Are you kidding me, Gerald? The submission is right here. Why can't you guys just say that the submission was completed a week ago, sat with CO CMO INT and is now back up on its way to him? What is so complicated about this? Is it possible for you guys not to be robots and just write what the actual facts are?"

"I will see you in the morning," Gerald said as he walked out.

The next morning when I showed up in HCO, Chris Guider was there waiting for me. Chris Guider was the Rehabilitation Project Force In-Charge at the Ranch for years. He was the guy someone would be sent to if Gerald or the Master at Arms, Jenny, could not handle it. They did not even bother trying to have Jenny take a crack at me. Time was running out and they had to get an answer up to COB's Communicator.

I spent the entire day on the E-Meter with Chris. Nothing came up.

While I was on the meter with Chris, HCO people had been going through all of my office files and out at my berthing looking for anything that would give them a clue as to what my out-ethics situation was.

The next morning I had been on the meter for a few minutes with Chris when Gerald knocked on the door. Gerald and Chris talked for a few minutes outside the interview office and Chris came back in, obviously with some sort of new info that was going to break this thing wide open.

Chris sat back down and placed a piece of paper on the table next to the E-Meter. It was an invoice for a projector lens that I had sold on eBay for $300.

"Yeah?" I said.

"What is this?" Chris asked. "It was found in your office."

"It's an invoice for a projector lens that I sold," I told him. "So what?"

"Well, why are you selling $300 of org equipment on Ebay?" Chris asked as though he had found the goods and this whole charade could now end.

"I have a CSW approved by all Gold executives to get rid of all of the systems dead stock so I can fund the new systems R&D being done," I said, all the while maintaining my cool.

"Well, apparently this did not get invoiced by Treasury, so where is the money?" he said.

"It's in my Paypal account. That is what Treasury and I had worked out as they don't have any credit cards that they wanted to link to a Paypal account. So I used my own, and after I sell stuff, I transfer the money to them so they can transfer it into the Systems account."

"So you have $300 in your personal account?" Chris asked.

Oh, I get it now. This was the Sherman Tank. "Marc Headley had $300 of org money in his own personal account and had not given it to Treasury!" This was going to be rich. They were surely going to freak out when I dropped the bomb on them.

"No," I said, knowing the effect that would be created as the words hit Chris's ears, "I don't have $300 in my personal account, I have several thousand dollars in my personal account!"

"I see," Chris said. He got up and walked out of the office.

A few minutes later he showed up with Gerald and they wanted to come up with me to my office. Gerald wanted the logins and passwords to my Paypal account, my bank accounts, he wanted all my bank cards and any other cards I had to anything, They wanted my social security number, and security info answers, they wanted everything I had on anything.

People started showing up in my office as we were going through the online info. Treasury personnel, HCO people, the MFG Sec.

The Manufacturing Sec began attacking me verbally. "You never told me that the money was going into your personal account! You said that you were selling this stuff on Ebay!"

"Yeah, in my CSW it specifically stated that the money would go into an Ebay account and that the money would come in to Paypal!" knowing that I might as well be speaking Greek. About ten people at the Int Base had any clue how the internet worked, and she was not one of them.

"Well, no one who approved your CSW knew that was the case! The CSW approval is rescinded," she yelled back at me.

Wow, it did not take long for her to throw me under the bus.

"We are going to do an audit of all of these accounts. We are going to find out how much money you have embezzled here!" Gerald said. "Go back down to HCO and stay there until we let you know to do otherwise."

I sat in the small yellow office for hours. Every so often some person would come in and ask what some charges were on some account and then leave.

Around 8:00 p.m. that night, Gerald came in and saw me. He had stacks and stacks of papers and figures highlighted.

"So here it is, Marc. All the evidence of the money you have embezzled from the org," he said as he placed the papers on the desk.

I looked through the figures. All the account charges for what I sold on Ebay were on there. The Paypal fees were on there. They added up to around a few hundred bucks. I was unimpressed.

"I don't think so. I would have to go through these and double-check these figures. I seriously doubt that any money has been 'embezzled' from the org," I told him.

"Go ahead. Look through them and mark anything that you don't think is a personal expense," Gerald answered back.

I could tell by the way he answered, that this was not going to go away. He would be the hero and would be the one that busted Marc Headley.

After a few minutes, I had gotten rid of a ton of expenses that were related to the equipment and had narrowed down any personal purchases from the Paypal account down to a list of about $100. Funny enough, the $100 worth of charges were for the gifts Claire and I had gotten for Dave, Shelly and a few other people we worked with!

I went to Gerald's office and showed him the list.

"So here it is," I said.

He looked it over and said, "So?"

"So, I will give you the difference and we can all go back to work," I told him, reaching for my wallet.

"No, I don't think so, Marc. This is serious business. LRH says that those involved in financial irregularities can join the walking dead. You are in serious trouble here," Gerald said solemnly.

So that was how it was going to be. They did not seem to mind me spending hundreds of dollars over the years on uniforms or things that they were supposed to be providing. They did not mind all the money I spent on gas for the entire shoot crew when we were out on location with no gas money from the org. They did not mind billing me for damaged materials or expendables used while on post. It was okay to mix my money with their money and for me to pay for their stuff. But they seem to get all fussy when their money was mixed with mine. Even after I offered to pay back any monies "allegedly" improperly spent and this was denied? I knew it. This was not about me; this was about politics and HCO answering their stupid dispatch.

"You can go back up to your area and pack up your things," Gerald said.

I went back up to my office. The Manufacturing Sec met me there and told me that I was being taken off post. But first I needed to fix a few points on the systems submission to COB! Unbelievable. Really? I thought to myself. Half of me wanted to tell her to go fly a kite, but the other half of me had a plan.

I fixed all the points on the submission. It was going up to COB's Office and now everybody was totally cool with it getting passed on and getting to COB by the end of the night. Of course, now that someone can go to the RPF everyone was happy.

The Manufacturing Sec and HCO were actually rewriting the submission so that it was coming from the Manufacturing Sec and at the beginning of the submission there would just be a little note about how I was off post and the submission was going to come from the Manufacturing Sec while I was being dealt with in ethics.

While we were waiting to see if there were any points from COB's office on the submission, I was to pack up all of my stuff in the office. Perfect. I can get all my stuff together and it won't even look like I am planning to get the hell out of here!

For several months I had been listening to a little AM radio that I had whilst I built computer systems and cloned hard drives. The only station that I could get was an AM station in LA called KFI AM 640. I would listen to these two DJs called John & Ken. John & Ken challenged the status quo and had something to say on many different subjects. I did not pay too much attention to what they were talking about, most of it seemed completely foreign to me, but I was thoroughly entertained with their bad attitudes and not accepting what they were told as fact. I likened myself to them and realized that I had been told many things as fact and I was slowly realizing that they were ALL LIES. Add to this the fact that I had seen a few episodes of Late Night with Conan O'Brien and he constantly dissed Scientology. Between Conan O'Brien, the KFI DJs, and 15 years of a miserable existence, I had decided that it was all crap and that getting out of here was my best bet at having a happy existence.

Can I even get out of here? If I do leave, I will certainly be declared. My wife, Claire, will divorce me for sure. I will never see my family ever again. How will I get a job? What job can I even do? Will I end up being a bum on the street begging for money? How can I even get off the property without security seeing me? I will most likely be restricted to the base anyway and won't be able to leave.

Screw it. I am blowing. I will have to figure out a way. Once I am gone, I will worry about where I go and what I end up doing. Until I break out of here, there is no use in trying to figure all that out. The chances of me making it out of here are slim anyway.

I spent a few hours gathering up any valuable personal documents I had.

I had my driver's license still and HCO had not taken that. I had no bank cards. I downloaded a few items I needed from the Int Base computer network and got all my stuff into a few boxes.

Around 3:00 A.M. the Mfg Sec comes in and says, "The systems submission was passed on to COB. You can go home. Be sessionable because you need to get more sec checking. But you are going to the Rehabilitation Project Force tomorrow if Gerald has his way."

"Yes, Sir," I say as I walk out with my boxes of stuff, never intending to see her again.

I stop by Treasury and see if anyone is around. The Director of Income, Scheri, is there. She opens the door and asks me what I want.

"I need to see if I have any back weeks of pay here so that I can come up with enough money to straighten out this silly mess," I tell her, knowing full well that the money will be counted on her income stat and that it is Wednesday.

"Let me check," she says.

With New Year's and Christmas I had not made it by to Treasury to pick up a few weeks here and there and hoped at least one or two weeks' pay were there.

"Sure enough, you have a few weeks here," Scheri says. "Your sister has a few weeks of pay here as well. I will give them to you and you can give them to her when you see her."

"Great idea," I say. "Jackpot" is what I think. This woman is working overtime for me here.

Between everything she gives me, I receive about $250.

I head over to CMO Int to see if I can talk to Claire. She is not around. One of the people who works with her says that she is in an interview with Tanja Lewis. Tanja's husband, Stefan, had been kicked off the Base in 1999 and eventually left the Sea Org and now Tanja has been trying to leave to be with him, after being separated from him for years. Tanja was in RTC and was Dave's personal secretary for 13 years. There is no way they are ever going to let her leave and be with Stefan.

My wife's purse is sitting under her desk. I grab it and take out whatever cash she has. She has $80 and I snatch it up and shove it into my pocket. I make my way out of CMO INT and realize I still need some more cash.

Right then it comes to me, Roanne Horwich, LRH's granddaughter lives in a small building right nearby; she will lend me some money if I ask.

I bang on her door. Even though it is around 3:30 A.M., she answers. I explain my plight to her about how I need to come up with some cash to sort out the whole embezzlement thing and she writes me a check for $250 on the spot. She was loaded and I was a good friend.

"Thanks, Roanne! You are awesome," I say as I leave. I make my way back over to the manufacturing building on the other side of the property.

I grab my boxes of stuff and start walking home. As I get near the gate that leads from the Gs to the Sublet houses, I see an RTC staff member making her way through the gate. She is one of the RTC sec checkers. Perfect. I start walking faster and meet up with her there. This way if Security sees me on their cameras, they will note that I am with an RTC sec checker and will not question where I am going.

I get through the gate and nobody shows up. I walk with the RTC staff member until we get to her house. I tell her goodbye and make it to my house, which is just a few houses further down the road.

Hopefully security doesn't get suspicious and come to pick me up. They have cameras on top of a lot of the houses on Sublet Road and if there is any kind of activity they will see it and send a guard down to check it out.

I get inside my room. There are four other people living in this two bedroom house besides my wife and I. Somehow I have to pack up what I need and not wake anybody else. I end up having to get a suitcase out of the garage and this makes a ton of noise. Nobody seems to wake up.

I spend a few hours getting my stuff together and wait around for Claire to show up. As I lay there and wait, I start wondering what she will say about me deciding to leave. Will she go along with it? Will she turn me in? Do I even tell her? Maybe she already heard about what happened?

If she comes with me, she will never see her family again. If she turns me in, I will end up on the Rehabilitation Project Force in Los Angeles and will never see her again anyway, so that would get me the same result. Well, we'll see what happens when she gets home.

It is 8:45 A.M. and there is someone banging on the door. I get up realizing that I fell asleep and that my wife never came home. I answer the door. It is Karsten Matthias from Security.

"Why are you late?" he says in his German accent.

"I was told to be sessionable," I tell him.

He gets on his radio and tells the main booth what I said. I cannot hear the reply as he has an earpiece on.

"You don't have to be sessionable and you need to come in now," he says.

I tell him okay but that I have to shower and then I will be right in. He leaves, not suspecting anything, I hope.

Okay, I have to work fast. I bail on the shower. I get dressed and load my bike with my stuff. I have two duffle bags and a small suitcase. The gas tank is full. The bike has been sitting for awhile so hopefully it starts up okay. I have never heard of anyone blowing the Int Base by walking into town. My bike is a dual sport motorcycle, so it is like a dirt bike, but is street and highway legal. Top speed is about 70 mph. I have gotten it up to that speed once or twice. It is not exactly the most reliable form of high-speed transportation but it should work fine to get me out of here on this very significant day.

I decide that I will first head to the U-Haul place to get a truck and then once I have my bike in the truck I can call my dad and drive to Kansas City.

I get on the bike, I put my helmet on and hit the electric starter. She starts right up. This is it, I am actually going to do this. I am leaving my life behind and starting over.

I pull out of the driveway onto Sublet Road and head towards San Jacinto…

Nothing's Impossible

ow that I have been run off the road by the Gold Security SUV, attempted to be recovered by at least two other Golden Era staff in vehicles (that I knew of) and very politely escorted into San Jacinto by the Riverside County Sheriff's department, the morning is tuning out to be pretty jam packed.

The ceremonial motorcade of two police cars keep me moving and I eventually arrive to the U-Haul station in town never having broken 10 mph due to the condition of my bike after the fall. I get off my bike and thank the sheriffs so as to acknowledge that I no longer need their assistance.

"I don't think so, pal. On the way here they sent at least three vehicles after you," one of them says. "We'll just hang around until you actually get into a truck with your stuff."

"Thanks, I really appreciate it," I say.

I head inside. I am thinking I can get the $29.99 special daily rental deal for two or three days and that will give me enough time to get to Kansas City to see my dad. I can put the bike into the truck and I will be set. Should I call him? I still have my Nextel radio/phone but I do not dare turn it on. They have GPS on them and I know from my sister who was over all phone communications that they can track you in a second as long as you have the phone turned on.

The place is empty except for the lone employee at the counter.

"How can I help you?" the guy says as I walk up to the counter.

"I need your smallest truck for 3 days," I tell him.

"Where are you headed?" he asks and starts typing info into the computer.

"Kansas City."

He types in a few more things and then he is satisfied that he has all the info correct.

"Okay, our smallest truck is going to run you around $1500 for that trip. I just need a credit card and we will get you all ready to go," he says.

"$1500? How could it possibly be that much? I thought it was $29.99 per day! I only need it for three days!" I argue, realizing that my loosely laid plan is falling apart rather quickly.

"That is for local rentals, man. If you are taking the truck a long distance, we charge by the mile, not by the day," he says. "I'm sorry, but that's what I got."

This is a disaster. What do I do? I should probably call my dad and find out if he is even there and what he thinks I should do. I don't even know if he will want me to come and stay with him and his wife. Maybe I really should call him. I might not even be able to go there anyway. Maybe he can send me some money. Maybe I can get a job somewhere in Hemet for a while and save up. Maybe I can sell my bike. I decide that calling will be best and then I'll go from there based on what comes up in the call.

Luckily, my dad has had the same phone number for 10 years. I know it by heart. He was like that; the ten years he lived in LA he had the same phone number the entire time. He moved to Kansas City but he had a 1-800 number so that my sister and I could call him toll free whenever we had the chance. Although we called very infrequently, I still remember the number. Good thing for me.

If I use my Nextel, not only will they be able to find me, but they will know I am going to see my dad.

"Can I use your phone?" I ask the U-Haul guy. "It's a 1-800 number."

"Sure, man. Go ahead." He takes the phone and moves it so I can dial. I dial the number. Please pick up. Please pick up. Please be there.

"Hello," the voice answers.

"Dad?" I say.

"Yeah. What's up?" he asks.

"I left dad. I couldn't take it anymore," I tell him.

"Okay. Where are you?"

"I am at the U-Haul place in Hemet."

"What happened? What's going on?" he asks.

"I just could not take it anymore and had to get the hell out of there."

"Where's Claire?" he asks. "Is she with you?"

"No she is not with me. I had to leave her there. I don't know what to do. I was going to try to drive out to where you are, but they want like $1500 at the U-Haul to give me a truck that I can take there."

"Why do you need a truck?" he asks.

"I have my motorcycle."

"Okay, let me see what we can do."

"Can you send me $1500?"

"No, but we might be able to figure something else out. How much money do you have?"

"Not much. Maybe a few hundred."

"Okay, do you have a place where I can call you back?"

"I'll give you the number here at U-Haul. I will just hang out here until you call back." I give him the number.

"Okay, I'll call you right back."

I hang up. Well, at least he is playing ball. I might have a chance to get out of here.

The guy at the counter has been eyeing the two sheriffs' cars right outside that showed up with me. "Are they with you?" he asks as he motions towards the cops outside.

"Yeah, actually, they are," I say. "I think I can tell them that I am fine now."

I go back outside to talk to the cops.

"I am waiting for a call, but it looks like I will be fine. I am going to get a truck in just a bit and get out of here," I tell them.

"Like we said before, once you get in a truck, we will take off. Those people seemed pretty determined to get you back over to Golden Era. We can stay here for a bit more," the officer says.

"Okay."

It's not really doing me any harm, I guess. I mean I did have two Riverside County Sheriffs helping me, looks like I would get one chance to utilize the tiny amount of taxes I had been paying for the last fifteen years. I doubt the Golden Era guys are going to pull into U-Haul of all places. They were probably not sure where I would go. Having the bike actually adds a unique aspect to the blow drill. Most of the time people blew on foot or caught a cab or bus. Security would then check the local bus or train stations or airports. How could I get on a bus, train or plane with a motorcycle?

I head back inside. Just as I enter, the phone rings.

"It's for you, man," the guy at the counter says.

"Dad?" I say, as he hands me the receiver.

"Okay, so this is what we can do," my dad says. "We can get you a ticket from LAX to Kansas City that leaves in a few hours."

"Okay, what about my bike?" I ask.

"We know somebody that lives in Sherman Oaks who will keep your bike for you," my dad answers. "At least for now until we figure out how this is all going to work out. She can also take you to the airport."

"Okay," I say. "I will just rent a truck here and bring the bike to Sherman Oaks and then get a ride to the airport."

"Okay. We are going to send an email to the girl in Sherman Oaks with your picture."

"Cool. I will call you once I get to Sherman Oaks. Thanks, dad. I really appreciate it."

"I knew this day would come sooner or later. I'm glad you called."

"Thanks. I'll call you in a couple of hours." I hang up.

"Okay, so I need a truck to get from here to Sherman Oaks," I say to the guy behind the counter.

"That we can do," he says as he changes a few things in the computer.

For around $50, I get the keys to a small U-Haul truck and head outside. The sun is now out and the rain has stopped. The cops are standing next to their vehicles and can see that I have keys to a truck.

"Let's get you loaded up," one of them says.

I open the back of the tiny truck and pull out the metal ramp on the back. I drive the bike into the back, with the help of the cops, and throw my bags inside. We tie the bike down with some rope that is in the back of the truck from the last renter.

"Thanks a lot. You guys saved me today. You really have no idea," I tell them shaking their hands.

"Actually, I think we do. You take care and do not stop until you get where you are going," the main cop tells me.

They get into their cars and drive off.

The Love Thieves

I climb into the U-Haul truck. I have a few last things to take care of before I leave town. I need to get some money from the bank and I need to call Claire. I try to think of the best way to do both these without being caught and dragged back. Then it comes to me. Not two blocks away are the San Jacinto Police station as well as my bank. I head to the bank first. I cash the check from Roanne. That gives me an extra $250. Then I head over to the Hemet police station. There is a pay phone right outside. I decide to call the Base from this payphone. If they track the call, it will lead them straight to the police station. Then what would they do? I call the 1-800 number. 1-800 I-WANT-HELP. That really is the number. That number rings in the main guard booth so I know I can get through to my wife because they will have her on standby somewhere waiting for my call. Matt Butler answers the phone.

"Hey, Matt. Can you put me through to my wife?" I say.

"Where are you?" Matt asks me.

"If you don't put me through to my wife right now I am going to hang up on you and never call back. I know you don't want that, so put me through now."

"Okay. Hold on," Matt says, knowing that I would hang up on him in a second. Hell, this was the guy who was in the truck that ran me off the road not an hour earlier. He knows I am in no mood to mess around.

"Marc?" my wife says through the phone.

"Hey, baby. I'm sorry about all this. I tried to get a hold of you last night but you never came home."

"What's happening? Where are you? Security told me you called the police! What's going on?" I can hear the concern in her voice.

"Well they lied! I never called the police and they know that. Someone called the police when Danny ran me off the road on my bike. They are lying to you. I never called anyone. The cops insisted on escorting me into town. I had to leave. They said I was going to go to the RPF. I knew that meant I would never see you again. I could not bear to have that happen. We would both be miserable forever. This is the best thing. I am going to disappear and I will always love you no matter what. I just cannot deal with the torture of not being able to be with you ever again and have that constant reminder always around me. I need to start over in another place far away from you.

"You and I both know that I have crossed the line and we will never be together ever again. I really wanted to see you for one last time last night, but you never came home and I knew that I would never have another chance to blow so I had to do it. I really do love you and I have thought about this long and hard and did not think that you would come with me anyway, as you would have to leave your whole family behind. I knew you would never do that."

"Marc, we can handle this. You don't have to leave." She was pleading.

"I love you always forever Claire." I hung up the phone.

I get back in the truck and start driving to LA. I cry the whole way there. I don't think I have ever cried as long as I did that day. Two hours straight. Between the crying and talking to myself, I was a wreck. I have just left my wife after thirteen years of marriage. She is the only reason I had stayed there on a number of occasions. If I had not married her, I figure that I would have left at least 4 or 5 times earlier when things got rough. She was awesome. No matter how many times I had gotten in trouble, she always stood by me and supported me. She is one of those people who is liked by everyone. I did not know one person who did not like my wife. Even people who hated me still liked her, even though she was married to me. I think about all this and cry some more. She is the best thing that ever happened to me and now she is gone forever.

I get to Sherman Oaks and call my dad back. He gives me the address of the girl he knows. She lives right off Ventura Blvd, close to where I had stopped. Her name is Stephanie Blake. She is evidently a high school friend of my dad's current wife. I take a few minutes to get myself together. I have been crying so long my face is wet with tears, my eyes are red and I look like I have just been beaten.

I drive a few blocks to the address I got from my dad. I lock the truck and ring the buzzer of an apartment.

"Marc?" a female voice asks.

"Yeah."

"I will be right down."

A good-looking woman in her late 30's comes down. She has on sweat pants and looks as if she has just come from the gym. She tells me that we can put the motorcycle in the parking structure. I take it out of the truck and park it in a spot she points out. She asks me if I want to come upstairs where she has my itinerary and flight info. She is very nice. She does not ask me any questions about what is happening. She is just there to help and whatever she has been told was enough.

We find the nearest place I can take the U-Haul truck to return it and when my flight leaves. We do not have a lot of time.

Stephanie has some posters in her apartment from plays or productions that she has been in. She is an actress or performer of some sort. She gives me something to drink while we figure out exactly how we will return the truck and get me to the airport. I profusely thank her for helping me and taking time out of her day to deal with my drama.

The U-Haul place is in Agoura Hills, the exact opposite direction of the airport. But it is the closest place that will take back a truck from another U-Haul place. I have no idea there is so much involved in renting a truck. Well, I might as well have been locked up in a cave for most of the past fifteen years, so how the hell would I know anything about what takes place in the real world. I drive the truck and Stephanie follows and picks me up at the U-Haul place and from there we will go to LAX. We have about three hours before my flight is supposed to leave.

As soon as I get back in the truck and on the road again, all I can think about is my wife. And the crying starts again. Then it hit me. I have been so upset over the loss of my wife and now I realize that I have also lost my sister, my brother and my mother. I am never going to be able to talk to them again for sure.

My mom is in the Sea Org at Flag so there is no way I will see or talk to her again. My sister is still at Gold so that is a no brainer. They are not going to let me talk to her again. And my half-brother lives in Clearwater with my mom's ex-boyfriend. There are five people in my life that I love with everything I have or am a direct relation to. I have lost four of them that morning. I try to tell myself that this is still the best option and that it will all work out, but part of me is still considering going back. By the time I arrive at the U-Haul place in Agoura Hills, another 30 minutes has gone by. I am cutting it close. I still have to get to the airport and through the check in, security and to the gate to make my flight to Kansas City.

We leave the U-Haul place and head to the airport. Stephanie drives like a Formula 1 driver in her little BMW to the airport. We make it there in time. I still have at least an hour before my flight leaves. I grab my stuff and thank Stephanie again for all she has done. I tell her that I will try to get my bike soon. She tells me not to worry about it and that it is no problem. She says goodbye and drives off. She is a huge contrast to what I have been told people are like. At the Int Base, the general public is portrayed as drug addled criminals and corporate cubicle drones bent on having a house, two cars, two kids and a dog. Here is the nicest person I have met in ages, nicer than any Int Base Staff member and she does not know me at all. She just dropped everything she was doing and spent four hours driving me around and giving me a place to park my bike for an indeterminate amount of time.

I make my way into the airport. I still have to be on the lookout for people trying to get me back to the Base. I no longer have the services of the cops protecting me. I do realize that if there is any trouble, getting the cops involved seems to make them back off rather easily. There must be some threat the cops present that they are not willing to deal with.

I get to the ticket counter and give them my e-ticket number.

"Oh, I am sorry but your flight has been cancelled, Sir," the lady says pleasantly.

Brilliant. Just my luck. I rush over here and now I am stuck. The problem is in Denver. They are snowed in and my flight has to go through there. The next flight is the following morning. I would be staying in LA another night. Another night I could be apprehended by the Int Base "blow drill" currently taking place.

I get a voucher for a hotel and head over to the Airport Hilton. Even with the voucher, I have to pay tax and some other fees. It ends up being "only about $50," as the guy at the counter puts it. That is about 1/5th my net worth at that point.

I head up to the room and realize that I am starving. I have not eaten all day. That, combined with the intense stress of the day's activities, I really need to get a bite to eat.

I sit down for a meal in the hotel restaurant. The food is so good that it is actually a pleasure to eat. It is delicious and fulfills my hunger. Too bad that fifteen years at Gold has indoctrinated me to eat a meal in under five minutes flat. For most of my years at Gold, we had 15-minute meal breaks. That included travel time to the dining hall. You had to get to the dining hall, get your food, sit down, eat it, clear your plate and get outside for a cigarette, all in under 15 minutes. Taking more than five minutes to eat was sure to use up your remaining time to do any of those other things, so gulping your meals was more a necessity than an acquired skill.

So here I am at a decent restaurant in a hotel, and my entire plate of food is gone before the waitress can come back and ask how everything was. She gives me a shocked look when she comes over and takes away the empty plate. I have eaten an entire beef dip sandwich, fries and a bowl of soup in no more than three minutes. I have also polished off the full glass of coke and am chomping on the last few cubes of the ice as she approaches my table.

"Was everything to your liking?" She asks awkwardly.

"Oh yes, thank you. Can I get the check?" I say, hoping that is the right thing to say.

I can only imagine what she thinks as she walks away. National speed eating champion? Starvation survivor? Pretty close, just your average Scientology Int Base Staff Member recently escaped!

I go up to the room, take a shower and get ready for bed. I take about twice as long in the shower as I was used to and let the water run the entire time. Wow, a ten-minute shower, I am really living it up now. I turn the TV on and lie on the bed. As I lay there I cannot help but think about my wife and family. I cannot help it. I cry myself to sleep that night. I think I have finally gotten it out of my system, though. When I get on the plane in the morning I realize that I have not lost these loved ones, they have been stolen from me.

New Life

I arrive in Kansas City in the afternoon. I had a layover in Denver and decide that I will call the Base from a pay phone there and tell them not to look for me. My rationale is that they will trace the number to Denver and look for me there. Since I won't be there, that will burn some time and keep them off my trail for a while.

I go to a public payphone in the airport and dial the 1-800 I WANT HELP line. I know that rings directly to the Main Security Booth, so I will get a guard that will know about me leaving. Matt Butler answers the phone.

"Hey Matt, this is Marc. I am no longer in California and don't bother coming after me, I am never ever coming back and nothing you say or do can change that." I hang up before he even utters a single word back. Good. They will trace the call via phone records and figure out that I am in Denver. I have family in Denver so it would likely lead them to believe that is my final destination. This will work out even better. I doubt any of my cousins in Denver would be very helpful in tracking me down nor would they even think about talking to some goons from the Int Base.

After watching over my shoulder full time and expecting any minute for someone to pop out behind a pillar and grab me, I finally get on the next plane to Kansas City without incident.

My dad is there at the KC airport when I exit the baggage claim area. I had not seen him in awhile so it is good to just see him.

We drive back to the suburb where my dad lives. It is about forty minutes from the airport. There is snow on the ground and the roads have been cleared but the drive is slow and cautious.

My dad is normally not in town and works out of state on computer service contract jobs for IBM. I was lucky that I caught him because usually he would have been up in Nebraska where he had been working on a project for several months.

When we get back to his house, I explain to him what had been happening, not getting sleep, all the drama about leaving and that I was probably going to be declared a suppressive person and that my sister would most likely be calling him to find out if I had contacted him.

I tell him that if he lets on that he is helping me, this will mess up his chances of ever talking to his daughter again. We agree that he will keep it quiet, and play along with "helping to find Marc, in the event he tries to call".

Sure enough, my sister calls that night. My dad tells her that he has not heard from me and that if he does he would call her. That night I again sleep for what seems like forever. I think it is more like 14 hours. I sleep long and hard. When I wake up the next day, I have a very unusual feeling. I had forgotten what it is like to feel rested. I have not slept more than 5 or 6 hours a night in YEARS. It is like I was in a coma. Not having to get up, take a five-minute shower and eat a five-minute meal is a shock to my system.

At lunch I display my speed eating capabilities and my dad asks if I am still able to chew food and not just inhale it. I think he wonders if I am deranged. I can actually see the genuine look of concern on his face. I have not ever stopped to think about it, but that is exactly what I have been doing all these years, inhaling food. I would begin feeding the next fork load in while the last one was being swallowed whole. I had perfected my eating habits down to a time/motion study. No motions were wasted and the food was consumed in the most efficient manner possible. Fifteen years of very short or no meals will do that to a person.

I am going to have to work on slowing this eating thing down if I am to fit in. God forbid I should end up at a restaurant again anytime soon. I am still a bit embarrassed from my incident at the hotel.

After lunch I am ready to work. What will I do? My dad is a technician for IBM but also has a side job where he fixes computers locally for people that he knows and makes a few extra bucks on the side. He has some of these computers at the house, and I offer to fix them. He takes a few minutes to show me the basic things to check for and what to do.

By the end of that night, I have fixed the computers I could, and watched two movies. Yes, I said *movies*. I have missed 15 years of movies. I can't believe how many movies have been released in 15 years that do not have Tom Cruise or John Travolta in them. I do not count them all, but there are a lot. I have missed them all and it will take me months to catch up. Lucky for me, my dad has quite the DVD collection and I will be able to knock out a hundred or so without even leaving the house.

That is my new life, fixing computers and watching movies. Slowly but surely I begin getting more computer jobs. I charge around $50/hour and am doing a computer or two a day and usually working a couple of hours on each computer. I am making more in one hour than I was making in a week at Gold!

After a few days, I decide to turn my Nextel phone back on so I can delete the Int Base phone numbers and then sell it on eBay. No sooner than I turn it on, Claire calls. I answer.

"Marc! Are you there?" she asks.

"Yeah, I am here." I answer. "I am sure that Security or someone from RTC is listening so I am not going to say anything to give away my location."

"Where are you?" she cries.

"Don't worry about that. I am fine. Why are you calling me? You know I am never coming back, right?" I say coldly.

"I want you to come back." she says. "COB wants you to come back! He said that if you came back that you would not be in trouble. You did not do anything wrong. It was the guys that took you off post that screwed up. All the guys involved are in big trouble for pissing you off and letting you leave. COB talked to Jenny Devocht and told her that she was to get you back by any means necessary. The whole thing was a giant screw up. He could not believe that you had sold those projectors and that they were throwing them away and somehow you were selling them for tons of money. He said you are going to get all the people you need, the money you need, everything. He has ordered that the Systems department be manned up right away and that anything you need, you get."

"Claire, you dream," I start in. "That is exactly why I am not coming back. If Dave Miscavige has ordered all that, it is a sure sign that it will *never* get done. That in fact guarantees it won't ever get done. Go ahead, think about all the hundreds and hundreds of things he has ordered to get done. That is why nothing ever gets done. Tomorrow he will order another area manned up with people and that will cross order Systems getting manned up! It is the same story. Dave orders it, it does not get done, people get sent to the Rehabilitation Project Force for not doing it and now we have even less people around to get all of Dave's orders done. You know I cannot believe that I ever stayed there that long. After a few days of sleeping and proper food, I feel like I have come out of a trance. You would have to experience it to understand what I am talking about. I have literally woken up! Everything is so clear to me now. I was unable to leave that place for fifteen years and the only thing holding me there was that I was told that if I left, all these bad things would happen to me, I would not be able to get a job, I would be a bum, I would end up on the street, I would get mugged, you name it. Well I left. And what happened, I have been sleeping and eating. I am working and making more in one hour than I was making in a week. Yeah it is really terrible on the outside!"

"Well, what about us?" Claire is crying now. "You have to come back. Everyone is saying that Systems will be manned up in the next week. They already have people lined up to go in there and it is really going to happen this time!"

"You know I love you more than anything else, but that is part of the trap." As the words are coming out of my mouth I am realizing more and more how this has kept me there all these years. "If you and I had never met, I would have left years ago. I only stayed because I loved you and would never do anything to hurt you and just wanted us to be together forever and be happy. We were never together and when we were, it was for minutes at a time. I could not take it any longer. I was not there for me and I was not happy in any way whatsoever. You were not happy either. You will see, Systems is NOT going to be manned up. Nothing that Dave says is going to get done, and I won't be gotten back. If they were going to get me back, they would have done so already. I have been watching this TV show, they say if you don't find the people in the first 48 hours, it ain't going to happen. 48 Hours. Don't the security guys at the base have that same rule? If they don't recover the person in the first two days after they blow, they don't come back. Now I know why. It takes a few days for the spell of that place to wear off. After two proper nights of sleep and two days of proper nourishing food, that's it, they cannot lie to you anymore." Now I start to get emotional.

"I don't know what I am gonna do. I want you to come back. I love you so much," Claire cries.

"Well, I will never come back to that prison. Ever. Never. Never Ever. Never. Never. Not gonna happen! I am just not going to do it. I have tasted real freedom and once you taste that, you can never go back to that place and be a prisoner again. No matter what. I am sorry. Do not call this number again. I am selling the phone so you will not be able to reach me anyway. I have to do this, Claire. For both of us. I am sorry. Like I said. I will love you always and forever. You know that. Bye." I hang up.

I know if I do not hang up that the crying will just get worse and worse. I am already outside in the snow talking on the phone and crying my eyes out. I have to take a few minutes before I can go back inside. I have just hung up on the best thing that ever happened to me in the worst place I had ever been. The contrasts between the two are enormous, but neither cancelled the other out. I have been married to Claire for thirteen years. That is a long time to know someone and be in love. As much emotional torture as I endured while at the Int Base, Claire almost made it tolerable. Almost was not enough anymore. As much as I love Claire, we could never have the family we wanted or be truly happy in that hellhole. I really believe that. I am not sure how I will ever love another after Claire, but no matter what, I know that I will have to suck it up and stick it out.

I cry myself to sleep that night thinking about all the times Claire and I had together.

I have been working and doing my thing for a few weeks now. I have sold off my Nextel phone and have no connection with the Int Base. They do not know where I am and they have no way to contact me. My sister has stopped calling my dad and as far as I can tell, they have given up on finding me. Good. I am just starting to get over the whole thing and becoming accustomed to a normal life on the outside.

I am getting to know my way around town and am getting new computer clients on a regular basis. I even have some businesses that are going to have me come out once a month and service all the computers they have at their facilities.

Granted, I do not have much to cover in terms of food and rent since I am depending on my dad for that, but I know that if I keep going, I will be able to live on my own with no problem whatsoever.

One day I get an email from an address I do not recognize. It is Claire's sister, Becky! The message reads:

"I have a new phone number. Call me at 6:00 A.M. tomorrow! I love you! Claire"

Somehow Claire has managed to remember my old hotmail address that I had. I had rarely used it at the base as that was strictly prohibited, but somehow she remembered it and has managed to get her sister to send me that message! If she is now going below the radar to contact me, I know that there is a chance that she is not being listened in on or directed by RTC or Security to do so.

I cannot sleep that night. I call at 6:00 A.M. LA time. I block my number from showing in case it is a trap from RTC or Security Gold. She answers.

"Marc?" Claire says.

"Yeah?" I ask.

"I want to come with you!"

"What? How are you going to do that? You know that if you come out here, they are going to declare you an SP and you will never be able to see your family again." I tell her this while my mind is racing, imagining what could happen if she did get out of there.

"I know that, but maybe that does not have to happen," she says. "After I last spoke to you, they switched out my phone so you would not have the number.

The phone has been sitting in the main booth in case you call it. Did you call it?" she asks.

"No, I told you I got rid of my other phone and deleted all the numbers in it." If they tried calling me on my old phone, they probably got some 12-year-old kid in Indiana who got the phone for his birthday from his dad! I sold it to some guy on Ebay that was looking for a gift for his kid." I tell her, laughing at the thought of someone from RTC talking to some kid about where I was and who he got the phone from.

I am pretty sure that they are not going to let someone who worked in RTC for almost a decade under Dave Miscavige walk out of there and not make a fuss about it. I know that springing her out of there will be tricky as hell.

"Well," Claire continues, "I am coming. I have decided that I am not going to be able to stay here without you." Her voice seems steady and she is not crying.

Maybe she really is serious. This could be it. Maybe I will get Claire out and then we really can be happy and start our lives over again.

"How many people are in Systems now, huh?" I ask, already knowing the answer.

"Okay, you were right. No one has been put in the systems area since you left. It has gotten even worse here over the past few weeks. I have not been home once since you left three weeks ago. All of CMO INT is restricted to the base and has to sleep under their desks. It has been crazy. I am leaving and I want to be there with you."

"Be where?" I ask.

"In Kansas City where your dad lives," she says. "I know that is where you are. I even told Security that is where you were and told them that COB said to get you back and if that is where you were, then why didn't they send someone to get you? They have not done anything. There have been other flaps since you left and no one is even thinking about it anymore," Claire is really starting to make me think about busting her out of there.

"Well, maybe you can leave during cleaning time on Sunday morning," I say.

"No you don't get it, we can't leave! No one is even going home at all for anything. We are all restricted to the base. No one is allowed to leave for any reason at all." As she says this, I realize getting her out will be harder than I had realized.

"Well, you know how just about every person has ever blown, what's the best way to get out of there?" I ask, thinking about the people I knew that had blown.

"I think the Jan Simms method will work the best," she says

"What is the Jan Simms method?" I ask, wondering who the hell Jan Simms was. "Wasn't that the chick that was in RTC back in the 1990s?"

"Yeah. She blew after Dave broke his leg in 1992. She had a doctor's appointment that she had to go to and never came back," Claire says.

"Can you get a doctor's appointment?" I ask.

"I already have one to renew my prescription for contacts. I can't do anything without being able to see. There is no way they can tell me not to go get new contacts. I will get them in a few days at Wal-Mart in town."

"You know they are going to be watching you like a hawk," I warn. "The spouses almost always end up trying to blow after the first one leaves."

"Yeah, I have already had a lot of RTC staff come up and tell me not to worry, that Dave ordered that you be gotten back and to keep going and it will all get worked out. Meanwhile, nothing was done to get you back."

"When is your appointment? We have to work this out," I say, now convinced that I can get her out.

"It is 10:15 on Monday morning."

"Dave will be gone for four days at the Fort Harrison anniversary event in Clearwater, so that will hopefully make it just a little bit easier for me to make it to the appointment."

"Good. So what you do is call a cab for that exact time and have it wait for you at Wal-Mart. Get it under another name. Have it take you to the Riverside Greyhound bus station. I will get you a ticket for whatever bus that leaves there, as close to that time as possible no matter where it is going. That will get you moving fast so that they cannot find you. You will have at least an hour or so head start before they discover you have made a break for it. Don't call the cab until the night before so that if they are watching your phone traffic, they will not see it until the next day after you are gone.

"When you get to the bus station, call me from a pay phone and I will tell you your ticket info so you can get on the bus. I will have already paid for your ticket and it will be waiting there for you."

"Okay. Why don't I just call you on my Nextel?" she asks.

"No you cannot use the Nextel! They will use the GPS in it to track you. I have seen my sister do this in HCO. You turn it on and they can find you no matter where you are. They will see that you are at the Greyhound station. They will send someone there and they will find you in a matter of minutes. Meanwhile, they will call the bus station and pretend to be your sick mother and ask which bus you got on. Trust me. These guys do this enough to know all of the tricks for tracking people down. Also, if you call me on the Nextel, not only will they know where you are, but they will know where you are going. Do not use that Nextel at all once you get into the cab."

"Okay. So how will I know where to go?" she asks.

"I already found a bus online that leaves around 12:45 P.M. It is only going to take you around twenty minutes to get there from Wal-Mart. You will have a few minutes to call me, get your ticket and get on the bus. It is going to Barstow. When you get to Barstow, call me from a payphone and I will give you your ticket to Kansas City and I will pick you up there. As long as you can get to Barstow okay, you will be fine. We can get you the rest of the way. Barstow is north and even if they do figure out that is where you are going; you will be heading a totally different direction once you get there."

"Okay, so I am going to do this," Claire says. "I have to go, I think someone is coming."

"Okay, call me when you get to the bus station! I love you!" I say before she hangs up.

Wow, is this really happening? I think to myself. I think it is. If she gets out of there, we are going to have to figure out what she can do. We might be able to actually have some kids! Wow, this is going to be great! I try not to get my hopes up too much as she could get caught and then they would lock her up for good. It would be years before she was ever allowed off the property again, if ever. I have seen that happen enough times to know that for a fact. The wife or husband leaves and then the other one gets caught trying to leave. They make the person a dishwasher for the next ten years and restrict them to the base forever. That is probably what happened to Annie Tidman. She was married to Pat Broeker and was restricted to the Ranch and then the Int Base for years. Wow, I hope that does not happen to Claire!

The next two days are murder. Before this, all I was trying to do was forget and now there might be a chance that Claire and I could be together and then, no matter the consequences, we could start over and have a life. All I can think about were the chances she would get caught. Was there something else that we were not taking into account? Would she get interrogated before she tried to blow the base? Would she get caught calling the cab? It was torture just not knowing.

Route 66

The day arrives. It is just about 2:00 P.M. my time. I am expecting her call any second. 12:20 P.M. her time comes and goes. Nothing yet. Then the phone rings. It is her calling on the damn Nextel!

"Why are you calling on the Nextel?" I yell into the phone, instantly concerned, knowing that this will allow Security to trace her.

"I didn't know what else to do. None of the pay phones here take any coins! They only take calling cards and I have no idea what a calling card is or even where to get one. The bus is leaving in a few minutes so I had to do something! I called so I can get my ticket number! Do you have it?" she explains.

"Yes, I do." I give her the number. "So how the hell did you get out of there?"

"Well, everything was good up until the morning I left. I was expecting that Jocelyn from the Medical Office would drop me off as she usually does. Then at the last minute I was told that I would be escorted instead and that Christi Mullins would be driving me there, would be with me during the appointment and would then bring me back."

"Oh, crap, how did you manage to get away then?" I was amazed that my wife was this good at being "out-ethics".

"Well, when we pulled up to the Wal-Mart, I could see the cab waiting at the other entrance. I told Christi that I would run in while she found a parking spot."

"Good thinking!"

"Yeah, huh? Anyway, I went in one entrance, ran across the store, went out the other exit and got right into the cab that was waiting."

"Oh, my god, baby, you did it!" I am so happy. "So, did they follow you, what happened with Christi?"

"Well, after a few minutes she called me and asked where I was. I told her that I had to go to the bathroom and that I would be out in a few minutes. Then I turned my phone off."

'Okay, so they definitely know that you have blown by now and will be watching to see where you call. Damn! Well, whatever, get on the bus and get to Barstow. Turn your phone off and hopefully they don't figure it out so quickly. At least you are out. Do you have anything with you?"

"Just the clothes that I am wearing and my purse which has a few small things crammed into it. I wore three layers of clothes but any more would have looked too suspicious. So that is all I have."

"Do you have any money?" I ask.

"Not much - $200."

"Okay. Well, save what you have for food for the trip. Sleep as much as you can on the bus," I tell her, almost not even believing that this is happening.

"I love you, baby," she says.

"I love you too." I hang up.

It is happening! I run in and tell my dad.

"She got out!" I tell him.

"She did?"

"Yes! She is on her way to Barstow!" I am so excited that I get on the computer to see when the bus will get to Barstow. People bad mouth Greyhound, but they keep a pretty tight schedule. The bus schedules are literally down to the minute on arrivals and departures. I have mapped out the entire trip and know every time that she would be in every single city. I will be able to track her the whole way to Kansas City.

The trip to Barstow is not that long. I have the entire itinerary printed out starting in Barstow and am going to make sure that she makes it through every stop. I even know the route she will be taking, too. It is almost like I know it by heart, but backwards. She is going to be traveling on Route 66!

Location	Arrives	Departs
BARSTOW, CA		03:55pm
LAS VEGAS, NV	6:30pm	

Location	Arrives	Departs
LAS VEGAS, NV	**Transfer**	08:15pm
HENDERSON, NV	08:35pm	08:35pm
KINGMAN, AZ	11:00pm	11:20pm
FLAGSTAFF, AZ	01:45am	
FLAGSTAFF, AZ	**Transfer**	02:45am
HOLBROOK, AZ	04:25am	04:25am
RS GALLUP BURGER KIN, NM	06:50am	07:10am
GALLUP, NM	07:15am	07:20am
GRANTS, NM	08:30am	08:30am
ALBUQUERQUE, NM	10:00am	11:10am
TUCUMCARI, NM	02:00pm	02:30pm
AMARILLO, TX	05:20pm	06:50pm
ELK CITY, OK	09:20pm	09:40pm
EL RENO, OK	11:05pm	11:05pm
OKLAHOMA CITY, OK	11:40pm	
OKLAHOMA CITY, OK	**Transfer**	12:01am
WICHITA, KS	02:45am	03:00am
KANSAS CITY, MO	06:05am	

She would be arriving in Barstow in about two hours. I get everything ready to track her the whole way.

At 4:45 P.M. my time, the phone rings. It is an unknown number.

"Claire?"

"Yeah. I am here in Barstow."

"Awesome. Okay you have a bit of a layover there. The bus is supposed to leave around 3:50 P.M. your time."

"Okay, I am going to get something to eat and get my tickets and get on the bus," she tells me.

"It is going to take you two days to get here. You know that, right?" I want to make sure she knows that because taking a bus that far has got to be the longest way to get across the states. But for the price, what are you gonna do? Also, the airports will be crawling with people trying to track her down.

"Call me when you get to Vegas. I will be waiting for your call," I tell her.

"Okay, I will call you as soon as I get there. I love you."

"I love you, baby. This will all work out okay," I say, hoping that it will. We both hang up.

This is going to cause my entire head of hair to turn grey. The suspense between bus stations is excruciating, knowing that at any point, they could try and capture her and bring her back to the Int Base.

It is around 8:30 my time. Claire should be arriving in Las Vegas any minute now. Five minutes goes by and no call from Claire. Another ten minutes goes by and nothing. Then the phone rings. It is not Claire. The caller ID on my cell says "Greg Wilhere." Not good! He knows my new number? They tracked that Nextel call! I answer.

"Hello, Greg." I say, realizing he knows Claire has blown and is most likely coming out to see me.

"Hey, Marc. So I am here with Claire in Las Vegas," Greg says.

My stomach literally drops out. Damn! Damn! Damn! They caught her! And they sent Greg Wilhere of all people! I cannot believe it. They must have figured out where she was going and that she would have to go through Las Vegas to get out to me. Sneaky bastards are sneaky.

"We are heading back to the base and I just wanted to let you know, so you were not expecting her at your end. She is not coming out to see you," Greg says coolly.

"Put her on the phone, Greg! Let me talk to her!" I yell into the phone.

"Why? So you can tell her to leave and be with you? No way, Marc. I'm not stupid. You are just going to talk her into getting on the next bus and convince her to leave. That is not going to happen."

"Why do you have to get involved in this? It is her decision if she wants to leave or not. You would rather her be miserable and stay than to leave and both of us be happy?" I plead.

"Well that's just it, Marc, you will not be happy. You will end up working at Burger King or end up just being another bum on the streets. You will never be happy after what you have done. You have forfeited your entire eternity by doing what you have done. You caused this mess, Marc." Greg says, all the while knowing that I just want him to put Claire on the phone.

"You are breaking us up by doing this, Greg. You don't care that you are breaking up a marriage and disconnecting us from each other," I tell him, getting more and more infuriated.

"This is the greatest good for the greatest number of dynamics, Marc. You are the one that is disconnecting from Claire by leaving. You could have returned and none of this would have happened," Greg continues, "We will get Claire back to the Base and we will make sure that she is okay and she will be fine without you."

I hang up.

Words cannot express how furious I am. I totally screwed up. I should have planned it better. Now that I had imagined her here with me, I cannot think of what I will do without her. Knowing that she wanted to leave and be with me will haunt me forever now. It was one thing when I thought that she would not leave, and that she would be able to continue to live at the Int Base and be happy. Now I know she wanted to leave and would be restricted to the Int Base for the rest of time and never get to visit her family anyway.

I go inside and tell my dad that they caught her and that she is now not coming. The grief overcomes me and I feel destroyed. I do not know how I am going to deal with this.

I am so angry and desperate that I seriously consider getting on a plane and flying back to the base to get Claire. Maybe I can call the police and get them to help me get her out. Maybe the FBI will help me. I spend the next hour looking on the internet at anything and everything I can find regarding prison camps, POWs, Ross Perot breaking some guys out of some place in Vietnam, I read all sorts of stuff. Then my phone rings. It's Claire on her Nextel!

"Claire?" I say, half expecting Greg Wilhere to laugh derisively into the other end of the phone.

"Yeah, I am on the bus!" Claire says.

"What the hell happened? Greg Wilhere called me and said he was taking you back to the base!" I am so happy to hear her voice again I can't contain myself.

"Yeah, well they tried. Greg Wilhere and Sharon Johnston friggin' showed up at the bus station in Las Vegas!" Claire says with anger in her voice.

"Yeah, I wait until everybody gets off the bus," she continues, "and figure that I will just get something to eat because I have not eaten all day. As I am stepping off the bus, out pops Greg. He tried to get me to go with them to get something to eat. He tells me how I will never see my family again if I leave and how I will be declared an SP and ruin my whole life. I went into the bus station and sat down right in the middle of the floor. I told them that if they even tried to touch me that I would scream and to leave me alone. I sat there for an hour and a half, and as soon as the bus started boarding, I got on. The bus just left Vegas and that is why I am calling you now. I figured they already used the Nextel to find me, and they know where I am, so it did not matter if I called you on it or not."

"Oh my god!" I scream. "I thought they had you. Greg was telling me that you were going back with them and that there was nothing I could do. Oh my god, okay, so you are actually on the bus and it is on its way to Henderson?" I ask her, still not sure if she is safe from Greg.

"Yes. I am coming no matter what. I will not go back, no matter what they say," she reassures me.

"Wow! That was close! Man, I was really freaking out at this end. I was screaming and yelling into the phone and just really freaking out!"

"Okay, baby, so I will call you at each point. Don't worry about them, they are not going to chase you cross-country. I think that you are good to go now." I am hoping that she is going to hold up the rest of the way and not change her mind.

For the next two days, we talk at every stop along the way—Arizona, New Mexico, Texas, Oklahoma and finally, Kansas City.

I am there at the bus station at 5:30 A.M. I am so excited that I had not slept a wink that night. I stay up the entire time she is traveling. Even if I manage to fall asleep, I have my alarm set for the next stop and am ready for her call.

The bus arrives at a little past 6:00 A.M. I will never forget this moment: Claire steps off the bus and walks towards me. She is as beautiful as ever, her long red hair, blue eyes and perfect smile. I run to her and we hug for what seems like forever. I have my wife back! We have each other back.

This is one of the greatest moments of my entire life. This single embrace has more emotion wrapped up in it than any other, happiness, grief, love, you name it. We are starting our lives over from scratch and have nothing, but we have each other now. We have been locked up for over a decade and now we are not only free, but we're free together!

- The End -

Dedication

Conan O'Brien and all the crew at the former *Late Night* show, for dissing celebrity Scientologists on your show and blowing the cover on the entire 1984 Orwellian bull I was being fed at the Int Base. In some weird sort of roundabout way, your comedy actually might have saved my life. Keep the jokes coming!

John & Ken on KFI AM 640 in Los Angeles for being who you are and slowly "deprogramming" me daily over a two year time period. You guys opened my eyes to what was happening all around me.

To the musical group **Depeche Mode** for spreading the news around the world. Somehow, in some unexplainable way, your music kept me going. Also, because I always had your next album and subsequent plethora of remixes to look forward to over the years, so I stuck around. Your music kept me going – period. Oh, your music is also now strictly prohibited at the Int Base. Sorry about that.

And of course, to the group of people who patrol the internet and keep it safe for all of us mere mortals. You know who you are, and of course, I do not. Some day we will meet up and I will give you some caek.

And finally, to all those who lost faith that they would see a family member again, to those that thought they would never be able to start their lives over again, and to all those that thought they would never be happy again. Keep your hopes up, people do get out, people do still love you and no matter what you have been told, as long as you have faith in your friends and family, it will all work out in the end.

Until next time…

BFG

Special Thanks

Bernie Headley, my father. Without you, I would not have been able to get out. I know you had to make a sacrifice to do this and I will do all I can to get Stephanie back into our lives.

Gen Whitt, for sending us that cash after we left. Without it, we would have ended up back at the Int Base due to running out of money.

Hugh Whitt, for telling me your horror stories at the Beverly Hills Mission and proving to me that it was not only Int Base staff who were being abused by Dave Miscavige.

Kirsten, Robbie and Becky Whitt, for giving us a good reason to get the hell out of there and live our lives in hopes that you would be black-listed just by association and never allowed to join the Sea Org yourselves.

Stephanie Blake for letting me park my motorcycle at your place and for driving me to the airport on my big escape day. Helping a complete stranger in need and dropping everything you were doing that day saved many people's lives. Also, you did not ask any questions and drove like a mad woman to get me to the airport on time. You rock!

To my mother, **Trudy Hensley**, sister, **Stephanie Headley** and brother, **Maxwell J. Kingsbury**. Your choosing not to speak to me since I left Scientology has hardened my resolve to get the word out and to continue to speak out until the one day when you pick up the phone and give me a call and find out the real story. You are the reason for this crusade and will continue to be long after we have been reunited.

Riverside County Sheriff's Department – For helping me escape on that fateful day in January 2005. Without your help I would have been bagged, tagged and brought back to the Int Base within minutes.

The **anonymous 911 caller** who called the cops on that fateful day in January 2005. I owe you big time. Also for proving that sometimes being anonymous and doing the right thing can have huge consequences that ripple outward and change everything as we know it.

More books by Marc Morgan Headley

Since escaping in 2005, both Marc and his wife Claire have been heavily "fair gamed" by Scientology and many attempts have been made to keep them from speaking out in regards to their experiences at the Int Base.

Months after they initially left, both Marc and Claire received written confirmation that they had been declared "Suppressive Persons" by Scientology and their only contact was the International Scientology Justice Chief located in Hollywood, California.

As of the printing of this book, neither Marc nor Claire has spoken to any of their family members that are involved in Scientology for over 4 years. While Marc's sister has been confirmed to have been moved to a remote Scientology facility in Canada no contact has been had with her at all.

Subsequent events may become the subject of an upcoming book or books.

Meanwhile, Marc continues to write on a regular basis regardless of whether or not any of it will be published.

Additional copies of this book can be ordered at www.blownforgood.com.

Glossary and Index

Glossary

ABLE Int – **A**ssociation for **B**etter **L**iving and **E**ducation. The Association for Better Living and Education International, a California non-profit corporation, which controls and directs the "continental" ABLE offices and directs four other non-profit corporations Narconon International, Applied Scholastics International, Criminon International and the Way To Happiness Foundation International. These are all organizations that propagate Scientology's anti-drug, morality and literacy programs.

AC – **A**dvisory **C**ouncil. Every Scientology organization has an Advisory Council which is comprised of the heads of each of their organization's major divisions.

Academy Levels – The Academy Levels are the training courses offered to teach a person the basic procedures of Scientology auditing.

AOLA – **A**dvanced **O**rganization of **L**os **A**ngeles. Advanced Organizations are called that because they deliver the upper OT Levels of Scientology, up to OT V.

AOSH EU – **A**dvanced **O**rganization & **S**aint **H**ill of **Eu**rope. An organization called a Saint Hill refers to the fact that they deliver the Saint Hill Special Briefing Course, one of the more advanced levels of auditor training (referred to as a Class VI).

AOSH UK - **A**dvanced **O**rganization & **S**aint **H**ill of **U**nited **K**ingdom.

Apple School – A school located in Los Feliz, California during the 1970's through early 1980's that used some of the study technology devised by L. Ron Hubbard. The school administration refused to cooperate with demands that they pay licensing fees and follow the strict rules of Scientology and the heads of the school were declared Suppressive Persons and all Scientologists with kids going to the school were directed to take them out of the school.

Applied Scholastics – Applied Scholastics is the organization that owns the copyrights to the secularized materials of L. Ron Hubbard that deal with studying. In order to use this "study technology" in schools, it must first be approved by Applied Scholastics and properly licensed.

ASHO – **A**merican **S**aint **H**ill **O**rganization located in Los Angeles. Pronounced Ash-Ho.

ASI – Authored Services Incorporated. This is the organization to whom L. Ron Hubbard signed over all of his literary works. ASI is paid royalties for all of the books and materials that are sold by Scientology.

A/V – Audio Visual.

AVC – Authorization Verification and Correction. This is the Sea Organization unit which approves any and all locally written issues or directives concerning Scientology or its management. AVC International was located in Religious Technology Center until 2004 when Dave Miscavige transferred the unit and all of its functions and staff into CMO International.

Backflash – Backflash is when a Sea Org member or Scientologist gives an unnecessary response to an order. Anything besides "Yes Sir" is effectively defined as Backflash. In the Sea Org, backflash is strictly prohibited.

BI - Bad Indicators. Anything non optimum is considered a BI.

Battle Plan or BP – This is a daily to do list compiled. It is firm policy in all Scientology organizations that every single staff member write up a battleplan every single day.

Berthing – This is where the Sea Org members of Scientology organizations are housed. In most instances this is dorm like housing with multiple staff staying in bunk beds or cramped quarters.

Berthing Buildings – These are the buildings that were erected at the Scientology Int Base to house all of the staff working there. Each one of the buildings is named after a Scottish family and each building has its own family crest and it is called the "_____(family name) Hall".

Black PR – **B**lack **P**ropaganda (also commonly referred to as BPR). Any person who engages in criticizing or questioning Scientology, its staff, members or principles is said to have Black PR. Conversely, any so called "critics" are usually silenced or intimidated by digging up any and all Black PR (occasionally real but more often imagined) and spreading this to "Dead Agent" the person — i.e. try to render their opinion meaningless so they will no longer be listened to.

Blow – This is any unauthorized departure from any Scientology organization.

Blow Drill – Similar to a fire drill, a blow drill is called when someone leaves the Int Base without authorization. This could be from someone escaping over the perimeter fence or found to be missing at one of the regular musters or roll calls that are held throughout the day to account for all staff. Several staff are dispatched to bus stations, airports, local hotels, etc. to locate the person. Major airline flight records are searched for tickets being purchased under the staff member's name and the person is generally hunted down until "recovered" or they have been declared officially blown and not able to be found. Blow drills have taken anywhere from 3 hours to 3 weeks, and involves anywhere from 20 to 50 staff. Mostly this depends on how and why the person blew and what the risk is to let them leave versus their necessity to be gotten back to the property.

Blown – Anyone who has left a scientology organization without proper authorization is considered "Blown."

The Bridge – This is the progressive steps one is required to take to further his or her knowledge in Scientology. Also called the Bridge to Total Freedom. It includes both training and processing (or auditing).

Bridge Publications – This is the Los Angeles based publications organization that produces all of the printed materials of Scientology in the United States. All of the employees of Bridge Publications are Sea Org members.

BTB – Board Technical Bulletin. These are technical issues that were written in the 1970's through 1980's. While some of these were written by L Ron Hubbard, most were written by others based on directions from L. Ron Hubbard. In the 1990's Dave Miscavige had nearly all BTB's cancelled.

Building 36 – Building 36 is the brand new state of the art Manufacturing building that was built in the early 1990s for Golden Era Productions that houses production facilities for HEM (Hubbard E-Meter Manufacturing) and both 16 mm and Cassette Tape Production. Building 36 also houses the Executive, HCO, Dissemination, Treasury, and Port Captain Division offices of Golden Era Productions.

BV – Bonnie View or Beautiful View – This is LRH's house that sits at the highest elevation of the Int Base property and has a beautiful view of the property. The house was built from the ground up based on LRH advices. The entire house has different furnishings for each season that are routinely swapped out. Furniture, drapes, beds sheets etc. are all custom designed to match each season of the year.

CAN – Canada.

Canteen – Most Sea Organizations have a canteen which serves as the commissary or single location where snacks and personal hygiene supplies can be purchased. According to L. Ron Hubbard policy, canteens are supposed to operate at a profit to fund upgrades to the local facilities.

Car School – At Sea Org bases where staff are required to drive vehicles as part of their functions, a course is required to be completed before one can drive a car. This is regardless of already having a license or how many years of experience one has driving a car. In order to drive any sort of motorized vehicle, Car school is required. If a Sea Org member gets a traffic citation of any kind, the appropriate section of the course must be restudied. If multiple traffic citations are collected or the Sea Org member gets into an accident of any kind, their privilege to drive is revoked and they are taken "off the road" and not allowed to drive anymore. One staff member at the Int base who got into an accident was not allowed to drive again until she had retrained on Car School and reached the level of OT 3 (as ordered by Dave Miscavige).

Case Gain – In order to progress up auditing levels, one must make gains on their "case". People that are SPs (**S**uppressive **P**erson) or PTS (**P**otential **T**rouble **S**ource) cannot make case gain. If a person does well after auditing or has personal wins he is said to have made case gain.

CC – **Celebrity Center**. There are several celebrity centers located all around the world. These centers are specifically for the recruitment and training of local celebrities into Scientology.

CC Int – This is Celebrity Centre International and is located in Hollywood, California. It is located in a historic building that was purchased by Scientology in the 1970's.

Checkout – This is a required step in Scientology training where a student quizzes another student on the materials they have studied. If the person does not pass the quiz, they are required to restudy the materials and find out what they did not understand and get another quiz until they pass.

Chinese School – This is a memorization technique which involves a group of people chanting a specific phrase or paragraph of written material over and over off of a huge board or paper scroll until they can read it back verbatim without the use of the written aid.

CIC – Control Information Center. This is the department in CMO units which has all of the pertinent information regarding its subordinate organizations that it's responsible for. They have statistics graphed weekly for all the lower organizations as well as maps and binders containing any and all facts about the organizations and their operations.

Complex – This is the large hospital complex that was purchased by Scientology in the 1970's. The buildings were all painted blue and this is where several Los Angeles based organizations are located. Bridge Publications, AOLA, ASHO and LA DAY, CLO WUS, CMO PAC, INCOMM, PBC, are all located at "The Complex". This area is sometimes referred to as "Big Blue" or "PAC".

Comm Ev – Committee of Evidence. This is a disciplinary or justice procedure that takes place within Scientology. It consists of a minimum of four staff members, named at random – a Chairman, a Secretary and two members whose duty it is to interview, review evidence and determine if a staff member is guilty or not guilty of listed Scientology crimes they are being accused of.

Conditions – These are states of existence that have been laid out by L. Ron Hubbard. In order to progress into better states of Existence, one must follow the exact steps of a "formula" and once completed, one should rise up into the next condition.

Class V Org – This is a local Scientology organization that is staffed by local Scientologists. They can only deliver Scientology auditing and training materials up to Class V (generally known as Clears), thus they are called Class V Orgs. In order to get further training and auditing, local Scientologists must go to their continental Advanced Organization or the Flag Land Base, which is where they will go on to the OT Levels.

Clearance Unit – This is the CMO unit in Los Angeles that handles the "clearance" of individuals that are slated to work at the Int Base or any other high level Scientology organizations that require a special security clearance. ASI, CMO INT, CMO Gold, CST, Exec Strata, GOLD, INCOMM and RTC all require special extensive security clearances and get approved by RTC before a staff member is even allowed to travel to them for placement.

Cleaning Station – Each and every Sea Org or staff member is required to clean a specific portion of the organization they are employed at daily. This is their "cleaning station".

CLO – Continental Liaison Office. This is the local Sea Org unit that is responsible for reporting up on and managing the Scientology organizations in its continent. These units are located in Canada (CAN), Eastern United States (EUS), Western United States (WUS), Europe (EU), United Kingdom (UK), Africa (AF), Australia, New Zealand and Oceania (ANZO), Latin America (LATAM), and more recently the Commonwealth of Independent States in Russia (CIS).

CMO – This is the Commodore's Messenger Organization. This is an organization that was formed specifically by and for L. Ron Hubbard to manage all of the operations of the Sea Org and Organizations all over the world. After the Sea Organization was formed in the 70s, Hubbard referred to himself as Commodore. And staff recruited into the CMO, were said to be his messengers. Thus the name. They oversee the execution of any and all programs and expansion plans written by L. Ron Hubbard and enforce compliance to these. CMO International or CMO INT located at the Int Base in Gilman Hot Springs, California, runs all of the individual units around the world. There are CMO units located in Canada (CAN), Clearwater (CW), Eastern United States (EUS), Golden Era Productions (GOLD), Hollywood (IXU), Western United States (PAC), Europe (EU), United Kingdom (UK), Africa (AF), Australia, New Zealand and Oceania (ANZO), *Freewinds* (SHIP) Latin America (LATAM), and more recently the Commonwealth of Independent States in Russia (CIS).

CMU – Central Marketing Unit. This is the marketing unit located at the Int Base that provides all of the central promotion and advertising for Scientology around the world.

COB RTC – Chairman of the Board, Religious Technology Center. Currently this position is held by Dave Miscavige. He took over this position in 1986, shortly after the death of L. Ron Hubbard.

CO CMO INT – Commanding Officer Commodore's Messenger Org International. This post has been held by many people over the past 20 years but mainly by Marc Yager. Both Marc Yager and Dave Miscavige started in the CMO together in the 1970's and eventually worked together shooting Scientology Technical Training films for L. Ron Hubbard and then occupied the two top management positions in Scientology Internationally.

CO GOLD – Commanding Officer Golden Era Productions.

Course – A series of theoretical and practical study steps that one does in Scientology on a given subject. Also within Scientology, when one regularly attends daily classes, this is commonly referred to as being "on course".

Criminon – This is the organization that uses materials written by L. Ron Hubbard to attempt to rehabilitate convicted criminals.

Cross Order – In Scientology this is when a senior gives an order that either disagrees or crosses another senior order or policy that has already been laid out.

C/S – Case Supervisor. This is the staff member that reviews a person's auditing and determines the next step they must do. Whatever the C/S directs, the auditor (person who delivers Scientology auditing to its members) must follow exactly.

CSI – Church of Scientology International. **CSI** includes four of the five organizations housed at the Int Base in Gilman Hot Springs – CMO Int, Exec Strata, CMO Gold and Gold.

CST – Church of Spiritual Technology. Also called "Archives". This is the Sea Organization that is responsible for archiving all of L. Ron Hubbard's materials on special archival materials that can withstand a nuclear war so that they will be available to future races on Earth.

CSW – Completed Staff Work. This is a regularly used request form used in all Scientology organizations that requires an employee to list out the situation, data and solution to the thing that they are trying to do. In order to purchase something, take a day off, visit one's dying Grandmother or even request the smallest of items not commonly required by one's post functions requires getting a CSW approved by one's seniors and sometimes many other senior staff members.

CTO – Continental Training Organization. These are the local Sea Org training facilities that are located wherever there is a CLO.

CW – Clearwater. Location of the Flag Land Base.

D/CO I – Deputy Commanding Officer for Internal. This is a post that is usually located only in Sea Org Units. This post usually deals with internal issues such as personnel and local flaps that require internal organization handlings. This includes running the "internal" divisions of the organization – Executive, HCO, Dissemination and Treasury.

Declared – When someone is deemed a Suppressive Person, most Scientologists refer to this person as being "declared". This is from the fact that when a person is considered a Suppressive Person, a written issue on goldenrod paper usually comes out and is posted on all public notice boards that is called a "SUPPRESSIVE PERSON DECLARE". Thousands and thousands of people have been declared SP's by Scientology. When someone is declared a Suppressive Person, no Scientologists (family, friends or otherwise) are allowed to have any contact with them of any kind or form. The only way to be "undeclared" is to follow a lengthy program that includes and mandates getting back "in good" as a Scientologist, and often involves paying large sums of money to Scientology.

Delphi – This is a Scientology run school that has several locations around the United States. The school not only uses Scientology materials in the teachings of its students, but in most cases the teachers and administrative staff are Scientologists and the entire school is managed with L. Ron Hubbard administrative technology as well.

Del Sol – One of the buildings on the Int Base in Gilman Hot Springs, California. This is where the Commodores' Messenger Org International, WDC (Watch Dog Committee) and Executive Strata International and were located. Del Sol used to be the main hotel unit for the Gilman Hot Springs Resort. It has since been converted into the staff auditing facility for the Int Base.

Dept Head – Department Head. In both Sea Org and Scientology organizations, each leader of a Department is called the Dept Head. Each organization in Scientology generally has seven divisions. Each division consists of three departments. The Department heads report to their direct senior, the Division Head.

Div Head - In both Sea Org and Scientology organizations, each leader of a Division is called the Div Head. The Div Heads report to their direct senior, the Executive Secs who in turn report to the Commanding Officer (or head) of their organization.

Drug Rundown – A Scientology auditing procedure that is meant to handle a person's past use of drugs.

Eagle – This is a security lookout location that is cut into the side of the mountain that overlooks the Int Base in Gilman Hot Springs, California. Not only can the entire Int Base property be viewed from this location, but also, any and all roads leading to or away from the property in all directions. Since the property was first purchased, security guards were posted at this location all day and all night to keep watch over the property and ensure that anyone coming or going was kept track of. High powered binoculars and firearms were on hand at this location. More recently high powered, remote controlled, infrared cameras have been installed at Eagle to watch over the Int Base from this location.

EC - Executive Council. This is the Executive Secretaries from an organization – who are to meet daily and discuss production of their organization. EC is run by the Commanding Officer (head) of the organization.

ED INT – Executive Director International. This is the head of the Executive Strata International, the Scientology organization responsible for providing bright ideas to Scientology organizations all over the world. This post has been held by Guillaume Lesevre since 1982.

E-Meter – Electro-psychometer. An E-meter is a device that is made by Golden Era Productions and is used in Scientology counseling (also referred to as auditing or processing). Only an E-Meter produced and approved by Scientology can be used in counseling. As part of counseling policies put in place by L. Ron Hubbard, every single counselor in Scientology is required to have two E-meters on hand at any time so that if one breaks, a spare can be used. As of 2009 approximately 30,000 E-Meters had been produced for all of Scientology internationally.

EPF – **E**states **P**roject **F**orce. This is the indoctrination procedure that all new Sea Org recruits are put through to ensure that they will be able to perform up to standard within the Sea Org. A new recruit is not considered to have arrived in the Sea Org until they have completed and passed this program. A strict schedule of heavy labor and training courses are done over a period of weeks. It is very similar to a boot camp or military or armed forces entry training program.

ESI – **E**xecutive **S**trata **I**nternational. The Scientology organization responsible for providing bright ideas for Scientology organizations all over the world. ESI is composed of International Executives (Exec Ints) responsible for all of the areas that L. Ron Hubbard attributed to expansion. These are: Establishment Exec Int (EEI), Books Exec Int (BEI), Marketing Exec Int (MEI), Materials Exec Int (MATEI), Division Six International Exec Int (DSIEI), Gross Income Exec Int (GIEI), Fields Exec Int (FEI), Services Exec Int (SEI), Quality Exec Int (QEI), Audio Visual Exec Int (AVEI) and Call-In Exec Int (CIEI). The post of Manufacturing Exec Int was added to this list by Miscavige. In 2007, there was no one on any of these posts.

Estates – This is the division in all Sea Org units that is responsible for the upkeep and renovation of buildings and facilities.

Estates Sec – The Division head over Estates.

Ethics Officer – This is the staff member within a Scientology organization that is responsible for ensuring that both staff and members are following the ethics and justice procedures laid out by L. Ron Hubbard.

External Facing – Any post in a Scientology organization that has to deal with people outside of the organization – generally considered to be a production area of the organization as opposed to internal.

FBO – **F**lag **B**anking **O**fficer. This is the Chief Financial Officer in any Scientology Organization.

F&E – This was where the **F**ilm & **E**quipment branch of CMO Gold was housed. F&E was the CMO personnel responsible for maintaining LRH's wealth of personal photography equipment and all of his photos, including having them ready and in perfect order for use at any time. They also oversaw any CMO programs being run in the Cine Division of Gold. F&E later became a department in the Cine

Division.

Fitness Board – This is a procedure where Sea Org members are judged to be either fit or unfit for the Sea Org and given recommendations as to what they need to do to become fit, if deemed unqualified.

Flag – Originally this was used to describe the ship that LRH used within the fleet of Sea Org vessels that were operating in the 1970's, when the Sea Organization was first established. Later on when the Sea Org moved to land, Flag was relocated to Daytona Beach and then later to Clearwater, Florida, where it remains today.

Flag Orders – These are the Sea Org policy written by LRH or the International Officer's Board. They cover everything from how to wear and clean a Sea Org uniform to how to remove Suppressive Persons from Scientology Organizations.

FLB – Flag Land Base. This refers to the plethora of properties owned by Scientology in Clearwater Florida.

FPRD – False Purpose RunDown. This is a counseling procedure that takes place in Scientology where a person's crimes are thought to be from evil or false purposes that were implanted by psychiatrists many lifetimes ago. At the Int Base, any staff member that questions Dave Miscavige or vocally speaks out against him is said to have Black PR, Overts and Evil Purposes on Dave and FPRD style auditing is a regular handling used for this.

Freewinds – The Sea Org cruise ship that is used to deliver the highest level of Scientology auditing currently released (OT VIII). The *Freewinds* holds approximately 360 passengers and crew. The *Freewinds* regularly frequents the islands of Aruba, Bonaire and Curacao in the Netherlands Antilles.

Garage – At the Int Base, the garage used to be a public gas station that was converted into the maintenance facility for the entire property. Motor Pool Gold is located here as well as the entire Estates Division - which includes Grounds, Electrical, Construction, Engineering & Building Maintenance Departments. Cine's Set & Props Departments took up the west half of the building, until the Cine Castle was built in the late 90s. It also houses the International Landlord Office.

GAT – Golden Age of Tech. This is generally referred to as the new training technology that was developed and instituted in all organizations by COB RTC, Dave Miscavige in 1996. GAT requires that all students learn Scientology materials verbatim and pass a series of quizzes and does an extensive amount of pre-scripted drills for each training level that they train on. As of this writing, Scientology training statistics internationally have been continually down trending since the release of the Golden Age of Tech.

G.O. – The Guardians Office. Established in 1966, this organization was the legal and public relations arm of Scientology. After several of its staff were convicted and sent to prison for carrying out what is said to have been the largest infiltration of the United State Government, the GO was renamed the Office of Special Affairs (OSA) and largely carries out the same functions today that the old GO did. Even some of the former GO staff are still employed by the new OSA.

Golden Era Productions – Also called Gold, this is the Audio Visual headquarters for Scientology located at the Int Base in Gilman Hot Springs, California. All of the sales and training films, videos and audio lectures for Scientology internationally are produced here.

Gold Musicians – The group of musicians that produce all of the music for the soundtracks for Scientology films, videos and materials. This same musical group often performs live at Scientology conventions held throughout each year.

Golf Course – This was the public golf course that was located to the east of the main Golden Era property. It was closed to business in 2008.

Graduation – In some Scientology organizations, each week anyone who completed a training or counseling step in Scientology is announced and is expected to give a speech promoting the level to others at a local group gathering called Graduation.

Greens Keeper House or GK: This house was used for crew berthing. It used to belong to the Greens keeper that maintained the property in Gilman Hot Springs, California for Old Man Gilman and his family. (This building was later demolished).

G Units or G's – These are houses that were converted to luxury accommodations for VIP guests that stay at the Int Base. This is where Tom Cruise stayed while coming to the property in the 1990's.

Cine Gym – At the Int Base, this is the building where the Cine Division had their shooting stage, until the Cine Castle was built in the late 90s. Originally called the gym because the activities of the base were originally confidential to even the local residents, so the permit to build the studio was applied for under the guise of a "Basketball Gym". Any and all references to the building were to be as the "Gym". The Gym also housed the Make-Up, Costumes, Camera, Lighting, and Set Sound department of the Cine Main Unit Film Shoot Team.

Happy Valley – This is what the large ranch property located in Castile Canyon, California was called. It not only housed the RPF for the Int Base, but was also used as a schooling and housing facility for the young children of Int Base staff members. This property was sold to the Soboba Indian Tribe in 2003. Also called HV, the Ranch, Int Ranch or Int RPF.

Hat write up – This is a write up that one is required to do on a post that one is assigned to. In case the staff member leaves and is not there to tell another how to do the post, a hat write up would be used to train a new person on the post.

HCOB – Hubbard Communications Office Bulletin. This is a technical issue written by L. Ron Hubbard that details out technical procedures and is printed in red ink on white paper.

HCO Cope Officer – This is the person that works in the Hubbard Communications Office division in a Scientology organization. This person mostly deals with the flaps that occur daily and is there to do exactly what the post title implies – cope with it.

HCO PL – Hubbard Communications Office Policy Letter. This is an administrative issue written by L. Ron Hubbard that details out administrative procedures and is printed in green ink on white paper.

HES – HCO Executive Secretary. In a Scientology organization, this is the executive position that is over the first four divisions of the organization: Exec, HCO, Dissemination and the Treasury divisions. In Sea Organizations this same post is called the Supercargo.

HFA – Held From Above. This is how any empty posts in a Scientology organization are referred to. If there is a post that is empty and it is below you on the organizing board, you hold it HFA.

HGB – Hollywood Guaranty Building. Located in Hollywood, California. This is the building that houses most of Scientology upper and middle management organization as well as OSA Int.

Horwich House – This is where Jon Horwich and his daughter Roanne live on the Int Base in Gilman Hot Springs, California. Roanne is LRH's granddaughter.

HV – Happy Valley.

IAS – International Association of Scientologists. In order to participate in any major Scientology training or auditing services, one must purchase a yearly or lifetime membership with the IAS. This is separate to any fees paid directly to the organization delivering the services.

IAS 1993 – This signifies the large convention that was held in Los Angeles, California on the 8th of October 1993. At this convention COB RTC, Dave Miscavige, announced that the 50 year war waged with the IRS (United States Internal Revenue Service) had ended with Scientology organizations being granted tax exempt status within the US.

I/C - In Charge.

IG Admin – Inspector General for Administration. In the 1990's, this was a post located in RTC directly under COB RTC. This post was held by Marc Yager until the post was abolished and he was demoted back to his old post of CO CMO Int. The "Inspector General" post titles come from the same used to describe investigators of government and military organizations whose job is to ensure the respective organizations are operating in compliance with general established policies and to discover misconduct, waste, fraud, theft or certain types of criminal activity by staff within these agencies.

IG Ethics - Inspector General for Ethics. In the 1990's, this was a post located in RTC directly under COB RTC.

IG Tech - Inspector General for Technical. In the 1990's, this was a post located in RTC directly under COB RTC. This post was held by Ray Mithoff until the post was abolished and Ray was demoted back to his old post of SNR C/S Int.

IG MAA RTC – Inspector General Master At Arms. This is a post that is located in RTC and its sole purpose is to locate and eliminate distractions to production at the Int Base and make sure that Int Base staff are on post working when they should be.

IHQ – Int Head Quarters. Also called Int or Int Base.

IMPR – International Management Public Relations. This is the unit that is responsible for putting on large conventions for Scientologists to increase the public relations value of International Management and their actions. This unit, along with Golden Era Productions, produces these conventions under the direction and heavy scrutiny of COB RTC, Dave Miscavige.

INCOMM – International Network of Computerized Org Management, The network of Scientology computer based programs and computer systems used by management to send messages to each other and catalog, create and maintain a database of all critics and former members of Scientology.

Int Base – This refers to the large property located in Gilman Hot Springs, California that houses all of the international management organizations of Scientology. RTC, CMO INT, AVC, RTRC, CMO GOLD, WDC, R/COMPS, Translations Unit International, Int Landlord, Exec Strata, SNR C/S INT Office, IMPR, CMU, and Golden Era Productions are all located at this facility. All of the staff that work here are also housed on the property and seldom leave for any reason.

Int – Int Base.

Internal Facing – Any posts with a Scientology organization that deal with activities local to the organization and do not have to do with anything outside of the org.

Int Landlord – The international unit located at the Int Base that buys buildings for Scientology organizations internationally and then renovates them and charges the local organization rents for these properties.

Introspection Rundown – A series of counseling procedures done within scientology that address the subject of introspection. This rundown is regularly used to handle someone who has had a psychotic break or some sort of mental breakdown. As part of this rundown, a person is often isolated and not allowed to talk to others and those who do come in contact with the person are instructed to not answer the person under any circumstance but to only note down what the person has said and send this information to the person's Case supervisor. This rundown was heavily publicized in 1995 after it was administered to Lisa McPherson before her untimely death.

ISO – Isolation. At the Int Base, this building was right next to OGH. This is where you went if you were sick. Isolation. There was a men's section and a women's section. If you had a cold or got sick, you would have to stay here until you recovered. You could not go back home or be with the general crew as then you might get more people sick. The smell that came from this place alone was enough to keep most people from ever getting sick.

KTL – Key To Life. This is a basic course in Scientology that is a glorified course in grammar and communication. The idea is that if you can communicate well then you have the "Key to Life".

KSW #1 – Keeping Scientology Working #1. This is the overriding HCO Policy Letter that exists in Scientology. It appears at the beginning of every single training course in all of Scientology. In this policy letter written by L. Ron Hubbard he writes, "we would rather have you dead than incapable". In essence, KSW#1 says that Scientology is a deadly serious activity upon which the fate of all mankind depends, and that no alteration of Hubbard's technology can ever be allowed under any circumstances.

LA DAY – Los Angeles Day Organization. This is a lower level Scientology organization located within the "Complex" in Los Angeles. The staff of this organization are not Sea Org members, they are on 2 ½ or 5 year staff contracts.

The Lake – At the Int Base, the lake was a huge man-made lake just east of Building 36. It even had fish in it. It was very nasty though, and had dead animals and pretty much several feet of sludgy muck beneath the few feet of water. There was a small island at one end of it that had a stone veneer bridge that allowed access to the island which had a huge cottonwood tree on it.

Learning Book – This was a children's book that covered study technology as laid out by L. Ron Hubbard in an easy to understand format for young children, including extensive illustrations. It was published by Heron Books.

Lecture Mix – This is where all LRH's lectures are restored, mixed and made ready for high speed duplication using Clearsound technology.

LRH – L. Ron Hubbard. Science-fiction writer and founder of Scientology. Commodore of the Sea Organization. Original Executive Director International of Scientology Worldwide.

LRH PPRO – L. Ron Hubbard Personal Public Relations Officer.

LRH Biographer – Danny Sherman. This is the individual who has been writing LRH's biography for nearly 15 years.

LOC – Life Orientation Course. A Scientology course where one finds out what his hat (profession) in life is. The course was found to be faulty in that most people discover that their hat in life is whatever hat they are doing at the time. The course has known faults that have needed to be corrected since shortly after its release over 15 years ago.

Lower Lodges – This is where Pre Production areas of the Cine Division were housed. Logistics, Art Dept, Research & Assembly, Scriptwriting, Casting, and Pre Prod Director offices were all located here before they were moved to the Cine Castle.

Lower RAV – This is the mixing studio that RAV uses to mix special edition products.

MAA – Master at Arms. This is a post in Scientology organizations that is supposed to remove any type of "distractions" from the organization. This person is usually the person that does one on one Scientology based ethics or justice handlings with members or staff of the organization. This person is usually called on to be the "Scientology police officer" – inspect periodically throughout the day to make sure staff haven't blown and are doing what they are supposed to be doing. If a staff member on the Int Base wants to talk to a family member or anyone not at the Int Base, they are required to get approval from the MAA, and this person then listens to the phone call as it is happening on a phone with two headsets, set up specifically for that purpose.

Mad Hatter Studios – A studio originally owned and operated by jazz musician Chick Corea. In 2003, Dave Miscavige instructed that the studio be purchased by the Golden Era Productions and turned into an extension studio that could be used by Golden Era Productions in Los Angeles.

MCI – Massacre Canyon Inn or MCI is the dining facility for the entire Int Base. Originally the inn located in Gilman Hot Springs was where dances and local banquets were held. It has both crew and officer dining halls that service all of the Int Base orgs. It also houses the offices for all of Gold's Domestic Services Division staff.

Medical (Liaison) Officer (also MLO or MO) – This is the Qualifications division staff member that is responsible for giving medical treatment to the crew and bringing them to a hospital if needed.

MEST - Matter, Energy, Space and Time; the physical universe. Any time hard labor is done, it is usually called MEST work. Apparently because one has to confront all of the components of MEST.

MEST work – See MEST above.

MFG – Manufacturing. A division of Golden Era Productions responsible for the mass production of Cassette tapes, CDs, DVDs, films, and audio visual presentation systems for Scientology organizations around the world as well as Scientology broad public promotion and sales items.

MFG SEC – Manufacturing Secretary. The division head over the Manufacturing division of Golden Era Productions located at the Int Base.

Midrats – Midnight rations. The meal served at midnight in Sea Org installations, usually consisting of the prior days leftover meals.

M&M or Maintenance Man's House – This house was originally the house that the maintenance man for the Gilman Hot Springs resort used to live in. It is now used for staff berthing.

Motor Pool – The vehicle maintenance facility located in the Garage at the Int Base.

Music Rehearsal – This is the building at the Int Base where the Gold Musicians rehearse for upcoming concerts and performances.

Narconon – A drug rehabilitation program based on L. Ron Hubbard writings that employs the use of heavy amounts of vitamins, sauna use and Scientology counseling to get a person off drugs. While Narconon itself often boasts high success rates by manipulating statistics, independent studies have shown the success rate to be no higher than other drug rehabilitation programs.

Narconon Chilocco – A Narconon facility located in Oklahoma that was later shut down for failing to get proper authorization and accreditation from local authorities. The facility was later moved to another Indian reservation in Oklahoma.

NY 2000 – Often referred to as NY 2000 or New Years 2000 or Y2K event, this was the Scientology New Year's event that was held at the Los Angeles Sports Arena in late December 1999.

OGH – Old Gilman House is the house that the family that owned and ran the property for most of the early and mid 1900's lived in. This house is used for temporary staff berthing.

119 & 40s House – This is where CMO Gold was located at the Int Base. CMO Gold was the CMO unit directly responsible for making sure that WDC Programs get done in Golden Era Productions. 119 now contains the printshop that produces OT materials.

Org Board – Organizing Board or Organization Board. Every group, business or organization affiliated or run by Scientologists has an Org Board. It is a large chart that has every post or possible position listed with the person's name right below it. This board shows the chain of command and who is responsible for what.

OSA – Office of Special Affairs. Formerly known as the Guardian's Office, OSA is the public relations and legal arm of Scientology.

OT Levels – Operating Thetan Levels. These are listed out on the Bridge to Total Freedom and are considered the highly confidential scriptures by Scientology. To get through all of the currently released OT levels, one could spend up to $300,000 USD. Although over the past decade, Scientology officials have denied reports and accusations about these materials being released on the Internet, in more recent times, they have acknowledged the contents of these materials as accurate and consider discussing them an attack on their beliefs.

OT VIII – The highest Scientology counseling level released as of 2009. The official Scientology printed chart of levels list OT IX to XV (OT 9 to 15) as "Not yet released."

Overt – Something considered bad in Scientology. Also referred to as an Overt Act.

O/Ws - Overts and Withholds. These are acts of commission or omission that are contrary to the survival of Scientology. Members are required to routinely write up any and all O/Ws and submit these for review in order to be upgraded from lower conditions or to become a member of the group again. Also, as a requirement to begin routine counseling sessions, members are required to explain in detail any O/W's that they might have committed since their last counseling session. When, why, how and any other pertinent details are required before the counseling session can be started.

Overt Product or OP – This is any product produced that is not acceptable. Usually referring to something produced within an organization. At Golden Era in 1990, several hundred thousand cassette tapes were deemed OPs by Dave Miscavige. Sea Org members that produce OPs routinely are sent to the RPF or are subject to justice actions or both.

PAC – Pacific Area Command. This consists of most of the organizations located at "The Complex" in Los Angeles, California. Located between Sunset Blvd and Fountain Ave, this area is most often referred to as PAC.

PAC RPF – This is the RPF located in PAC. In 2004, the PAC RPF numbered in the hundreds, and had more staff than any other Scientology organization in the Western United States. In 2007, after a series of offloads, it had just under 100 people in it.

Pancake – A large reel of audio cassette tape specially manufactured for use on high speed mass production reel to reel cassette machines.

PC – Preclear. In the early days of Scientology a Pre-Clear was someone who in Scientology was not yet Clear. Later on it just came to mean any person receiving Scientology counseling.

PC Folder – Preclear Folder or folder. This is a folder where all records relating to all counseling of a person is kept. Each time a person receives counseling, notes are taken of what the person says and what counseling was done. These items are placed in the person's PC folder. Each time a folder is filled, a new one is created. Someone who has been in Scientology for years could have anywhere from 25-100 folders or more, depending on how much counseling they have had.

PDO – Planetary Dissemination Org. This was what Central Marketing Unit was called for a brief time in the 1990's. It is now generally referred to as CMU and is a division within Golden Era Productions.

Perimeter Council – At the Int Base, this is a council at the Int Base that is generally responsible for handlings being done on staff that have either voiced having thoughts of leaving or who have tried to leave and were caught. People who have tried to escape are put on detailed correction or handling programs (often including heavy manual labor for weeks or months and sometimes years and assignment of a buddy until the staff member says they no longer want to leave) and progress on these handling programs is discussed and coordinated at Perimeter Council. A list is made of all of these staff who have tried to leave or had thoughts about leaving and most on the list are restricted to the base at all times (meaning they are watched closely and are not allowed to go home but must sleep on the Base). They are not allowed to go beyond the perimeter of the property, thus the term Perimeter Council. Those that are allowed to go off base for any reason must be escorted and other staff are alerted to keep an eye out for these people. Perimeter Council is made up of the Security Chief Int Base, Port Captain Office, Staff Chaplain, HCO and Qualifications Division posts in Gold as well as the HCO Chiefs of all Int Base Orgs. Conversely, most of the staff that make up the perimeter council are also part of the blow drill called when someone blows from the Int Base.

Pink House – At the Int Base, this house is used for crew berthing. It is called the pink house based on its exterior color – pink. It was located on the south side of the property. (This building was later demolished.)

Port Captain – The Public Relations head in Sea Org orgs. Originally from the maritime post that was responsible for all relations with the local port that Sea Org ships were stationed in.

PTS – Potential Trouble Source – This would be any person that is connected to an SP or any person that is against Scientology. In order for a person to not be PTS, they must either handle the person they are connected to or disconnect. In most cases, this involves families and friends of Scientologists.

QC – Quality Control.

QC Gold – Quality Control Gold. The post at Golden Era Productions that is responsible for spot checking the technical quality of products mass produced.

QM – Quarter Master. Originally the person that was stationed on the gangway of a ship, the QM system was put in place at the Int Base to watch staff during the night to make sure that they did not blow. Two male staff members were stationed at each location where staff berthed and would stand watch during the night to make sure no-one blew.

Qual – Qualifications Division. The division that is responsible for training staff and reviewing and correcting them as necessary. Most RPFs are located under Senior Qual of the local management organization

(CLO).

Qual Sec – The Qualifications Secretary. The divisional head over the Qualifications Division.

Ranch – This is the large ranch property located in Castile Canyon, California. It not only housed the RPF for the Int Base, but was as well used as a schooling and housing facility for the young children of Int Base staff members. This property was sold to the Soboba Indian Tribe in 2003. Also called Happy Valley or Int Ranch or Int RPF.

Ranchos – This is where both the TU or Translations Unit and the RCOMPS (Ron's Compilations) were located on the Int Base. They took approved manuscripts from RTRC and turned these into courses and books for Scientology organizations around the world. They had typesetting, book design and even did glossaries and other book items here.

Routing Form – A form used in Scientology orgs to route a person from one place to another. When one finishes a course or counseling action in Scientology, one is given a routing form that has one see a series of people – end result is that one is signed up for the next course or action. Until you finish the routing form, one is usually not allowed to leave or do anything else.

RPF – Rehabilitation Project Force. A program that is done by Sea Org members only. It is for those who have performed badly or who have upset seniors. Sometimes the RPF program can be assigned as part of a Sea Org justice action. The RPF mainly consists of a person working long hours and doing at least 5 hours of Scientology counseling each day, seven days a week with no days off. The counseling they receive is to find their crimes and evil purposes (FPRD). There are several rules specific only to the RPF, such as a person on the RPF is not allowed to speak unless spoken to. People have been known to spend anywhere from a few years to over a decade on the RPF program. There used to be RPFs at every Sea Org continental installation. Former members who have done the RPF have claimed them to be comparable to prison camps or gulags.

RTC – Religious Technology Center. RTC owns the Scientology trademarks and advanced technology. It licenses these trademarks to CSI for sublicense to subordinate organizations and directly licenses the advanced technology to appropriate Advanced Organizations. RTC is located at the Int Base and Chairman of the Board RTC, Dave Miscavige, micromanages all aspects of anything that occurs at the Int base through this position in RTC.

RTC Rep – RTC Representative. With the advent of the Golden Age of Tech, RTC representatives were assigned to all major continents to oversee the application and adherence to the new standards laid out for training and counseling.

RTRC, LRH Technical Research & Compilations – The unit in CMO Int that compiles and/or issues revisions to existing LRH Bulletins and Policy Letters. They compile all checksheets and courses in Scientology. They did the revisions to all Scientology training materials in 1996 for the "Golden Age of Tech", under the close direction of Dave Miscavige. RTRC became a department in RCOMPS in 2006.

Sandcastle - A hotel located in Clearwater that was converted to being used for auditing rooms for Scientology and rooms for Scientologists to stay in while getting services or counseling at the Flag Land Base.

Sea Org - The Sea Organization, Sea Org or SO is an association of Scientologists established in 1968 by L. Ron Hubbard. Its members are found in the central management organizations of Scientology as well as in individual organizations. While it was initially created around maritime customs and traditions while at sea, those customs and traditions persist today even in the land-based branches of the organization.

Sec Check – Security Check. Security checking has the purpose of "remedying the compulsion or obsession to commit actions which the person then feels must be kept secret." They are given to all Scientologists on the Bridge, every six months to all OTs, according to officials, "to make sure they're using the tech correctly", and to members who are leaving staff. As with traditional auditing or counseling, the subject holds the cans of the E-Meter as a drill of questions are posed.

Shore Story – This is a cover story that is usually made up to explain away some flap that has happened that locals might find out about. Originally the term came from when the Sea Org was ship based and a story was needed to tell people at shore to explain something that had happened aboard one of its vessels. When someone was injured or any accidents happened at the Int Base, a shore story was usually decided upon and all involved were told to make sure that all their stories matched. Also the shore story for what we did at the Int base was always "make movies for Scientology" even though it was the International Headquarters for Scientology and making movies was a tiny portion of what was done there.

SMI – Scientology Missions International. This is the group which collects tithes from missions all over the world and is charged with the creation and establishment of new missions.

SNR C/S Int – Senior Case Supervisor International. This is the most senior technical post in Scientology. Since the inception of the post there have been at least four known incumbents. All but one has been declared a Suppressive Person.

S.O. - Sea Organization.

Soboba – The tribe of Native American Indians that are located near the Int base and eventually bought the Int Ranch property from Scientology.

The Spa – The Spa is now the location of the Qualifications Division of Gold. The Spa used to be the main location on the property where the hot springs would surface and several large steam bath facilities were located here. After the United States Government drilled a large underground tunnel though the back side of the mountain, they hit the underground river that fed the hot springs and the springs dried up. Old Man Gilman, who ran the hot springs resort since 1913, had several boilers set up beneath the Spa, and continued to run the hot springs resort for several years before finally retiring in 1978 and selling the property.

Star Rate – See checkout.

Star of California Clipper Ship – The Star of California is a large "clipper ship" that was built into the property to be used as a local attraction for people from nearby Hemet and San Jacinto. Promoted as a movie set, local residents are given Public tours on Sundays to see how a real movie set looks. The Star of California also has an Olympic size swimming pool, Jacuzzi, sauna and other facilities that can be used for entertaining and local events. Sometimes referred to as the Ship on the Int Base. The *Freewinds* cruise ship is sometimes also referred to as "The Ship."

Station One – The main security booth on the Int Base. This is where the security chief or watch chief usually sits and controls the security of the entire Int base from this location. This is also command central for any drills that are called on the base such as fire or blow drills. Also called the Main Booth.

Studio One – This is the LRH Music Studio Complex. It has a state-of-the-art music studio and is one of the most advanced music studios in the world. Adjacent to the main studio are music scoring, and storage for all of the Golden Era Musician's equipment. Also in this same building are very upscale conference and dining facilities for visiting musicians that are brought up to the Studio for recordings.

Studio Two – This is the Studio where all Film Mix downs are done by the Audio Division of Gold. There is also a PLS (Post Lip Sync) studio located in this same building, as well as the film sound transfer facilities used by Manufacturing.

Study Technology - Study technology, or study tech, is a methodology for learning developed by L. Ron Hubbard, founder of Scientology. Hubbard's "Study Tech" is used by Scientology members as part of their training, and is also promoted outside Scientology by the affiliated corporation known as Applied Scholastics, which presents study tech as a universally applicable method to enhance the comprehension of any student, studying any topic.

Sublet Road – This is the public road that was adjacent to the main property and ran along the golf course. Several houses were located along this road. Some of the houses were purchased and used as staff berthing while others had local residents living in them that had nothing to do with the Int Base or Scientology.

Supercargo – A borrowed term from maritime law, in Sea Org organizations, this is the executive position that is over the first four divisions of the organization: Exec, HCO, Dissemination and Treasury divisions. In Scientology organization this same post is called the HES or HCO Exec Sec.

Super Power - The Super Power Rundowns were described by Scientology's founder, L. Ron Hubbard, as: "A super fantastic, but confidential series of rundowns that can be done on anybody whether Dn [Dianetics] Clear or not that puts the person into fantastic shape, unleashing Super Power of a thetan. This means that it puts Scientologists into a new realm of ability enabling them to create a new world."

Super Power Building - The Super Power Building is an edifice in Clearwater, Florida that will be Scientology's largest property in the city when completed. The huge high-rise complex, which occupies an entire block at 215 S Fort Harrison Ave, will be topped by a 15-story tower surmounted with a bronze Scientology cross that will be visible over a wide area of Clearwater. Construction began in 1998 but was halted in 2003 and has yet to resume.

Tavern – The tavern is a VIP facility where actors brought to the Int Base for Cine or Audio productions can be serviced. It is done up in the motif of the Knights of the Round Table replete with a large sword embedded in a stone as you enter the building.

Team Share Cards – At the Int Base, team share cards are given out to each staff member. There are a series of five cards. Each one of them entitles its holder to privileges only available to those that have the applicable cards. There is a social card that allows one to take part in any social events taking place or liberties (a day off every two weeks if approved). There is a bonus card that would allow one to receive bonuses if they were being handed out. There is a pay card that allows one to pick up his weekly allowance. There is a chow card that allows one to be able to eat. Then the last card is a berthing card that allows one access to a place to sleep. If one's weekly production were to be less than the prior week, a card would be revoked. This would continue week after week until one's stats went back up. Upon having up statistics, one could request that a card be returned. If one upset one's senior or the senior was displeased with the staff member or he broke any one of the hundreds of Sea Org regulations, a card could be revoked at any point. It would not be uncommon for Int Base staff members that were having troubles to have zero Team Share cards in their possession. When you lost your last card, the berthing card, you were to be assigned to "pig's berthing". While the original purpose of the Team Share system devised by LRH was supposedly to increase production, the system was uniformly abused by seniors all the way up the line since its inception, the system was eventually dropped out of use completely in the early 2000s when most all Int Base staff were assigned lower conditions by COB RTC and all privileges were cancelled on a widespread basis.

Thetan - In Scientology, the concept of thetan (pronounced THAY-tan, /ˈθeɪtən/) is similar to the concept of spirit or soul found in other belief systems. The term is derived from the Greek letter theta, which in Scientology represents "the source of life, or life itself."

Tone Scale - In Scientology, the tone scale or emotional tone scale is a characterization of human behavior. It is based on the idea that some people appear to be more lively and alive than other people. Author L. Ron Hubbard spelled the idea out saying, "just draw a horizontal line on the page. Put the people who are less alive on the bottom and the people who are more alive on the top."

Trailers – The trailers are a collection of temporary buildings that were set up to accommodate the addition of CMU (Central Marketing Unit) as well as the Tape Editing and Technician Departments of Audio. They later housed RTRC & SNR C/S Int offices.

Treas Sec – Treasury Secretary. This is the division head over the accounts department of a Scientology organization.

TRs - The Training Routines are introductory services used in Scientology as well as affiliated programs Narconon, Criminon and WISE. They are described as a way of learning to communicate effectively and to control situations. According to investigators and former Scientologists, the training routines have a strong hypnotic effect, and may cause hallucinations and an out-of-body experience known as exteriorization.

The 200's – The 200's are where network heads for several CMO units were housed. SNR C/S (Senior Case Supervisor International), LRH PPRO INT (LRH Public Personal Relations Office International, RTRC (LRH Technical Research Compilations)

12 Mic – This is the recording room located in Lower RAV. It is called the 12 mic as it has a set-up with 12 separate microphones that are used to get the most realistic recording possible.

Ultra Barrier – A brand name of barbed stainless steel spikes that are often installed atop fences and walls at the Int Base to prevent climbing over. Touted by the company that makes it as the *"ultimate physical & psychological barrier for commercial/residential fences."* These exact type of metal spikes are installed on most of the fences at the Int Base. While the shore story is that these are to keep intruders out, most of the spikes are installed with the spikes facing inwards, preventing someone from getting *out*, not into the property.

Uniform K – The Sea Org uniform classification given to normal civilian street clothes or "civvies" as they are sometimes also called.

Upper Lodges – This is where all of Gold's Film Editing department were housed. There was a large 35 mm film theatre in this building where the Cine division watched all their daily footage as well as feature films.

Upper RAV – This is where LRH's **A**udio **V**isual Unit or RAV is located. This is the unit that is responsible for maintaining all of LRH's arsenal of personal audio equipment. They are also responsible for running all of the programs that are being done in the Audio Division of Golden Era Productions. They are the unit that produces any LRH special edition audio releases that Gold is not allowed to produce.

VAX/VMS – A type of computer system made by the Digital Equipment Corporation. The majority of Scientology INCOMM computer systems were VAX/VMS based until more recent years when the VAX/VMS systems were no longer made and use of them dwindled.

Villas – This is where RTC was located. There are three Villa buildings, the Upper, Middle and Lower Villas. Not only was RTC located here, but some top RTC executives also lived here, including Dave Miscavige until recent years. Marc Yager and Guillaume Lesevre lived here as well.

WDC - **W**atch**D**og **C**ommittee. This was the group of Sea Org members located at the Int Base that was responsible for overseeing the strategic progress of various groups of Scientology. WDC Chairman also used to be the CO CMO Int. There were WDC members for the following areas. WDC OSA, WDC RESERVES, WDC FLB, WDC FSSO, WDC CC, WDC SMI, WDC WISE, WDC ABLE, WDC GOLD, WDC I HELP, WDC SCN, WDC SO, WDC PROGRAMS and WDC PUBS. In 2007, there was no one on any of these posts.

White Glove Inspections – an inspection that is done in the Sea Org where a white glove is worn by the person doing the cleaning inspection. If the person inspecting wipes his hand across any surface that produces any sort of blemish on the glove, the area has to be re-cleaned and re-inspected until the glove comes up white every time.

Word Clear(ing) – This is a type of action in Scientology where various methods are used to clear up the definitions of words. Most usually it involves a dictionary or the person having to fully define a word while another person verifies he has it correct.

WQSB – Watch Quarter Station Bill. This is a large chart that is located in Sea Orgs that lists out where each person lives, what their cleaning station is, whether they are on port or starboard watch, and any number of other details about the person.

WUS – Western United States.

Index

G

H

J

Jacobs, Larry 279
Jentzsch, Heber 290
Johnston, Sharon 332

K

Kegel, Veronika 47
KFI AM 640 radio station 302
Kidman, Nicole 111, 277
Kingsbury, Dan 32, 176
Kingsbury, Maxwell J. 337
Knight, Coby 65
Koon, Sue 233
Kugler, Brad 116
Kugler, Tasha 116

L

Lambs Canyon 152
LA Sports Arena
    IAS 1993 event 165
    New Year's 2000 event, and the 204
Lebanon Hall 54
Lesevre, Guillaume 167, 233, 246, 290
Levitsky, Martha and Boris 45
Lewis, Geoffrey 26
Lewis, Juliette 27
Lewis, Stefan 303
Lewis, Tanja 303
Limp Bizkit 255
Lower Grades of Scientology 235
LSD 41
Luigi 106, 135

M

N

O

P

R

S

W

Y

www.blownforgood.com

INTERNATIONAL HEADQUARTERS OF SCIENTOLOGY
GILMAN HOT SPRINGS, CALIFORNIA

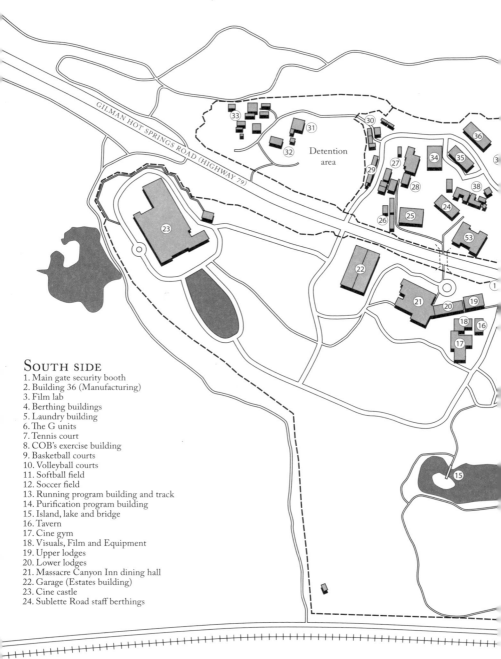

GILMAN HOT SPRINGS ROAD (HIGHWAY 79)

Detention area

SOUTH SIDE
1. Main gate security booth
2. Building 36 (Manufacturing)
3. Film lab
4. Berthing buildings
5. Laundry building
6. The G units
7. Tennis court
8. COB's exercise building
9. Basketball courts
10. Volleyball courts
11. Softball field
12. Soccer field
13. Running program building and track
14. Purification program building
15. Island, lake and bridge
16. Tavern
17. Cine gym
18. Visuals, Film and Equipment
19. Upper lodges
20. Lower lodges
21. Massacre Canyon Inn dining hall
22. Garage (Estates building)
23. Cine castle
24. Sublette Road staff berthings